The Nature of Health

The Nature of Health
How America lost, and can regain, a basic human value

MICHAEL FINE M.D.

and

JAMES W. PETERS

Foreword by

ROBERT S. LAWRENCE M.D.

CRC Press
Taylor & Francis Group
Boca Raton London New York

CRC Press is an imprint of the
Taylor & Francis Group, an **informa** business

Michael Fine dedicates this book to Rosie, Gabriel and Carol,
with love and thanks.

James Peters dedicates this book to Janet.

First published 2007 by Radcliffe Publishing

Published 2016 by CRC Press
Taylor & Francis Group
6000 Broken Sound Parkway NW, Suite 300
Boca Raton, FL 33487-2742

© 2007 Michael Fine and James W. Peters
CRC Press is an imprint of Taylor & Francis Group, an Informa business

First issued in paperback 2019

No claim to original U.S. Government works

ISBN 13: 978-0-367-44619-2 (pbk)
ISBN 13: 978-1-84619-206-7 (hbk)

Visit the Taylor & Francis Web site at
http://www.taylorandfrancis.com

and the CRC Press Web site at
http://www.crcpress.com

British Library Cataloguing in Publication Data

A catalogue record for this book is available from the British Library.

Typeset by Egan Reid, Auckland, New Zealand

contents

Foreword by Robert S. Lawrence vii

Michael Fine's preface xi

Jim Peters' preface xiii

About the authors xvi

Introduction xvii

PART ONE WHAT HEALTH IS NOT 1

Demented and Contracted 3

1 The health we have 9

2 The health we buy 15

3 What we measure is not health 21

4 Medications are not health 29

5 Medicine is not health either 37

6 Science is business, not health 43

Hancock County 48

PART TWO WHAT WENT WRONG AND WHY 53

The Happy Victim 54

7 The human tsunami 59

8 The reductive trap 75

9 The trap is sprung 83

10 How longevity kidnapped health 91

11 Medical services and communities 97

12 The zero-sum game 103

Three People, Three Aortas 117

PART THREE WHAT HEALTH IS 125

      A. Fib   127

13 What Webster thinks   131

14 Old villages, new lives   141

15 Toward a social definition of health   145

16 Health and community together   151

17 Health and fairness   165

      Amish Boy   169

PART FOUR WHAT'S NEXT? 173

18 Who gets what?   175

19 How should it look?   187

20 How should we pay for it?   199

21 Which doctors?   213

References   225

Bibliography   237

foreword

The litany of problems associated with health and healthcare in the United States seems to lengthen each week. We Americans are just under five percent of the global population yet consume almost half of the global health budget. We are approaching $2 trillion per year in expenditures while leaving 15 percent of our fellow citizens without health insurance. As the debate swirls among presidential hopefuls about how to fix and reform the healthcare system and the Congress prepares to appropriate additional funds to expand SCHIP (State Children's Health Insurance Program), President George W. Bush says about those children without health insurance, "I mean, people have access to health care in America. After all, you just go to an emergency room."[1] Despite the clumsiness of his speech and the callousness of his remarks, the President's views are shared by enough Americans to help explain why we remain one of the few OECD (Organization for Economic Cooperation and Development) countries without a health system providing universal access to healthcare. Mexico and Turkey join us in this dubious category among the 30 member countries. All other high and upper income countries of the OECD are in compliance with Article 12 of the International Covenant on Economic, Social and Cultural Rights (ICESCR), which asks that steps be taken to create conditions "which would assure to all medical service and medical attention in the event of sickness."[2] But I forget — the United States is also the only OECD country not to have ratified the ICESCR.

Historians, political scientists, and other scholars debate whether our failure to ratify ICESCR (and a number of other social justice covenants constituting the body of international human rights law) and to embrace the concept of a right to health reflects de Tocqueville's concept of American Exceptionalism or is a manifestation of a deep-rooted commitment to American sovereignty or both. In *Democracy in America* Alexis de Tocqueville identified the values of liberty, egalitarianism, individualism, populism, and laissez-faire as the key elements to our success as a democratic republic.[3] Notably absent from these values is a commitment to community or the value of social cohesion, and therein lies the dilemma and explains how we can be so passionately committed to civil and political rights, indeed be John Winthrop's "City on a hill," while tolerating with almost pathologic indifference enormous inequities in health status, educational opportunity, job security, and livelihood in this, the richest country on earth.

Murray and his colleagues documented the burden of suffering in the United States in a recent study of health inequalities using data aggregated at the county level, by gender, by race/ethnicity, and by income. They noted, "The gap between the highest and lowest life expectancies for race-county combinations in the United States is over 35 years. We divided the race-county combinations of the US population into eight distinct groups, referred to as the 'eight Americas,' to explore the causes of the disparities that can inform specific public health intervention policies and programs."[4] Asian-American women in Bergen County, N.J., had the highest average life expectancy in the nation at 91 years, and Native American men in several South Dakota counties had the lowest life expectancy at 58 years. Seven Colorado counties, two Iowa counties and Montgomery County, MD, were tied for the highest average life expectancy at 81.3 years while six South Dakota counties had the lowest average life expectancy at 66.6 years. At the state level, Hawaii recorded the highest average life expectancy at 80 years, followed by Minnesota at 78.8 years. The District of Columbia — the seat of our national government and often regarded as the power center of the world — had the lowest average life expectancy at 72 years, followed by Mississippi at 73.6 years.

Our neighbors to the north grappled with health disparities decades before we began to pay attention. Pierre Trudeau, elected Prime Minister of Canada in 1968, asked Marc Lalonde, Minister of Health and Welfare from 1972–77, to chair a commission on the causes of health inequalities and disparities among Canadians. *A New Perspective on the Health of Canadians* — commonly referred to as the Lalonde report — was presented to the House of Commons in 1974. The report identified two objectives for improving the health of Canadians and narrowing the gap between the healthiest and the sickest: 1) reforming the healthcare system to improve access to care, and 2) reducing health risk by greater attention to prevention of health problems and promotion of good health. The report also introduced the concept of "health fields" or the domains of influence on health status that deserved attention. The four fields are healthcare services, environment, biology, and behavior. The Lalonde commission concluded that differences in health promoting and health damaging behaviors accounted for about 40 percent of the disparities in health status among Canadians with each of the other three fields contributing about 20 percent. Of course, had the definition of environment been expanded beyond the physical environment ("horse kicks and lightning strikes," as one Canadian wryly observed) to include the economic and social environment, then much of the difference in health promoting and health damaging behavior would be linked to the environment as well. Lalonde believed that good health was the foundation on which social programs were built and that the healthcare system was only one of the necessary methods to maintain and improve health. Reducing poverty, preventing violence, protecting the environment, expanding educational opportunity, and assuring equity became as important to increasing the health of Canadians as improvements in the healthcare system.

In 1986, WHO convened the first International Conference on Health Promotion in Ottawa and adopted the *Ottawa Charter for Health Promotion*, defining health promotion as a "process of enabling people to increase control over the determinants of health, to improve their health."[5] The United States was one of the participating countries in the conference but the lessons brought home from Ottawa had no discernible impact on health policy during the Reagan era.

So here we find ourselves mired in a system that consumes an ever-increasing share of our national income without diminishing health disparities among our people or improving our standing in the world ranking of healthy societies. How did we get to this place and what can we do about it? In this book Michael Fine and James Peters present a provocative analysis of the meaning of health and the way in which clinical medicine is practiced in the United States in the early years of this new century. They bring their analysis to life with clinical stories about real patients suffering the real indignities imposed by our dysfunctional system of clinical care and the failures of jury-rigged safety nets. These stories illustrate the historic and philosophic discussion of the meaning of health, the illness experience, the role of social capital in health, and the challenges to medical professionalism posed by the commodification of medicine. We Americans remain ambivalent about whether healthcare is a right or a privilege, and this ambivalence is reflected in our tolerance of living with 45 million of our fellow citizens uninsured while simultaneously expecting and demanding the maximum application of life-saving and life-extending treatments for ourselves and our families. When the authors say that "health is the ability to have relationships, not the demand of living forever . . . health is the love of others," they correctly focus on the very essence of being human. Their definition of health as "the biological, social, and psychological ability that affords an equal opportunity for each individual to function in the relationships appropriate to his or her cultural context at any point in the life cycle" moves us beyond the WHO definition of health as "a state of complete physical, mental and social well-being and not merely the absence of disease or infirmity" to capture our true nature as social beings functioning within the context of family, friendships, and other social networks. This expanded concept of health provides a framework for addressing Rudolf Virchow's "barriers that obstruct the normal completion of the life cycle," and honors the stirring sentiments expressed in Articles 1, 3, and 23 of the Universal Declaration of Human Rights:

1. All human beings are born free and equal in dignity and rights. They are endowed with reason and conscience and should act towards one another in a spirit of brotherhood.
3. Everyone has the right to life, liberty and security of person.
23. Everyone, as a member of society, has the right to social security and is entitled to realization, through national effort and international cooperation and in accordance with the organization and resources of each state, of the economic, social and cultural rights indispensable for his dignity and the free development of his personality.[6]

The authors have given us much to think about, and the healthy debate this book will engender promises to move us forward in the quest for decency, fairness, and justice in health and healthcare for all Americans.

Robert S. Lawrence, M.D.
Professor of Environmental Health Sciences,
Health Policy, and International Health
Johns Hopkins Bloomberg School of Public Health
Professor of Medicine, Johns Hopkins School of Medicine

Michael Fine's preface

The idea in this book that is most likely to prompt controversy – that we should not spend public money on medical services after an individual reaches the average expected life span – is not the book's most important idea. The most important idea – that health is the equal ability of individuals to function in the relationships important to them at any point in their life cycle, in the context of their culture – is barely new or controversial at all. Understanding that longevity is not health, and is, after a certain age, a consumer commodity; that we only wish to live as long as others in our culture; that we look at longevity as fairness, not health; and that the United States does not have a healthcare system but rather the medical services sector of the national economy – these ideas are neither new nor revolutionary. But we hope they are liberating to people who are trying to make sense of the healthcare mess in the United States.

What is new, here, is the construction of a healthcare system from the ground up, using an understanding of what health is. The healthcare system we present is a healthcare system after all; that is, it is an integrated system of moving parts, each of which has a role to play in producing a product, and that product is health, as we have defined it.

We rely on a few central assumptions: that justice is fairness, that we cannot have a sustainable society unless everyone has equal opportunities (because inequality creates social instability), that it is possible to build and sustain local communities in 21st-century America, and that we all want a healthcare system that is personal, rational, affordable, efficient, and just.

A word on who we are, and on the experiences that produced this book. One of us is a healthcare administrator and writer, with 25 years' experience working in and thinking about healthcare systems from the perspective of explaining those systems to the people who will use them. The other is a community organizer and primary-care physician, who has worked in

America's poorest communities, both urban and rural, as well as worked with government, with healthcare institutions, and with middle-income communities. He has listened to what people want, what people need, what works and what does not, and watched, with amazement, as what started as a noble profession dissolved into an industrial behemoth that exists to extract wealth from the communities it purports to serve.

Many thanks are in order: to my family, Carol Levitt Fine, Gabriel and Rosie Fine, who put up with my disappearances from dinner and appearances at wee hours of the morning to search the internet, dining room tables covered with paper, and dinner table conversations about the meaning of health, a topic no 13 year old should ever be forced to bear. To my patients, who I can't name, but who have shared their lives and stories, answered patiently when I asked them what *they* thought health was, and who ultimately take care of me. To many friends, who listened patiently and provided counsel: Paul Stekler, Roberta and Jerry Ehrlich, Ellen and Uri Bar-Zemer, Richard Godfrey, Nancy Evans, Tom Sorger and Miriam Weizenbaum, Sam Frank, Chris Koller, Greg Carter, Sam Mirmirami, Christine Heenan, Rick Reamer, Rabbi Wayne Franklin, Eric Hirsch, Paul Housberg, Sheila Haggerty, Joshua Gutman, Anne Nolan, Elizabeth Roberts, Ken Thompson, Bob Lawrence and David Rothman. To my colleagues at the Institute for Medicine as a Profession, who inspire me when we meet, and bear with my many wild and unorthodox ideas. To my professional partners and co-workers, who dealt with my being sequestered many mornings and helped provide exquisite patient care in my absence: Drs Carol Levitt, Barbara Jablow, Christine Kennedy, Chris Campanile, Ken Sperber, Cristina Mitchell, and Michael Klein, and everyone who now works or has ever worked at Hillside Avenue Family & Community Medicine. To my co-workers and colleagues on the Scituate Health Plan, who make health – real health – happen. To my brother and sister-in-law, Paul and Amy Fine, the source of wisdom and lots of experience with the publishing process. To my parents, Adell and Seymour Fine, the source of endless succor and support, as well as the name of this book. To Emmy Liscord and Rachelle Noorpavar, research assistants extraordinaire, who did all the actual grunt work of making this book real. And finally, to James Peters, whose discipline, intellectual curiosity and patience made this book happen.

James Peters' preface

Our book goes back several years, to a conversation in Michael's medical office. You see, along with being Michael's co-author I'm his patient as well. For that matter, so is my son, Geoff, and before his recent death, so was my father.

Before I became Michael's patient, I knew him slightly through our mutual attendance at a few meetings held for some forgotten business-planning purpose within the heath system where I directed communications, public affairs and marketing activities and Michael was a Young Turk among the primary-care physicians. Then my internist at the time was nailed for some hanky-panky with one of his lady patients and lost his practice. I needed to find a new doctor, so I asked the person who does physician referral for the system to recommend someone. "Oh, Michael Fine would be great," she said without hesitation, "but he's not taking any new patients, so here are some others to consider . . ." Never lacking gall, I sent Michael an e-mail anyway, asking if he would take me on. With his characteristic kindness and humility he mailed back that he would be "honored" to have me as a patient – not typical physician language, at least in my experience.

Some months later, during my first visit to his office, I mentioned that I had recently left Lifespan, the system where I had worked, and was intending to make a living as a writer. After almost 30 years of corporate work I was overdue for a change. I had written all my life and knew enough about management, medical issues and technology to be able to make a reasonable living as a freelancer. Michael said that he had been toying for several years with some ideas for a book about the meaning of health, but hadn't taken the time to follow through. He had written a sort of first chapter several years back, he said. We agreed that maybe we should consider working together on the book and a few days later he sent me the chapter to see if I had any interest.

I liked the ideas in the essay very much. It outlined the social and cultural context of health and broadly criticized the status quo. I had long ago concluded that the United States had a wasteful, disorganized and unjust medical process that desperately needed fundamental reform. The notion of a book that would consider health in a philosophical and sociological light intrigued me. We soon met to discuss how to organize what turned out to be a long-term project.

We began with a set of 55 questions, everything from: "What is the name of this book?" to "What do we mean by health?" to "Are people in other countries healthier than we are?" to "Every reform has bombed out – is real reform possible?"

From there we blocked an initial outline and assigned ourselves either the writer or editor role for the first draft of each chapter. As we developed and added to the manuscript we continued to swap writing and editing roles – a practice that we continued through the final manuscript. We also began weekly Thursday-morning sessions at local coffee shops, during which we'd puzzle over our text, recent medical and policy news and whatever ideas about the book either of us had hatched since our previous meeting. Now that we're finished, I miss those skull sessions very much. Perhaps they weren't the most efficient route to a completed book but they were closer to those heady and exhilarating late-night college discussions with good friends than anything I can recall in many years.

Along the way, I suggested that we should mine some recollections from Michael's clinical career and create a series of stories or vignettes to explain how he had adopted certain ideas and points of view and to punctuate the book's expository text with these more personal experiences. These vignettes are naturally in Michael's first-person voice, while in the rest of the book "we" expresses our shared opinions.

As in any substantial project, a good many other people have helped us along the way. Michael has mentioned some of them in his preface. I should add several others here.

My wife Janet has listened to me talk about this project far more than any patient and supportive friend deserves. I thank her for her support and confidence in this and countless other things.

Our daughter, Alicia, a doctoral candidate in medical anthropology, has offered helpful insight and expert guidance on several topics within the book.

Craig Schuler, John Schibler, Sue Mellen and Luisa Deprez have also taken the time to read various iterations of the manuscript and to offer valuable comments. I sincerely thank them all.

Finally Michael and I must tip our hats to the patient and hospitable folks at the Kountry Kitchen in Greenville, Rhode Island, were we met every Thursday morning for nearly three years, nursing countless cups of tea and coffee and talking, talking, talking.

about the authors

Michael Fine M.D. is a family physician who is also trained as a community organizer, and divides his time between practices in urban Pawtucket, Rhode Island, and rural Scituate, Rhode Island. He is the Physician Operating Officer of Hillside Avenue Family and Community Medicine, the largest family practice in Rhode Island, and Physician-in-Chief of the Rhode Island and Miriam Hospitals Departments of Family and Community Medicine.

Fine's professional life has revolved around using healthcare as a focus for community organizing, practicing family medicine, and advocacy and organizing in communities across the United States.

Dr. Fine lives in Scituate, Rhode Island with his wife Carol Levitt M.D. (also a family physician), and their two children, Gabriel, 17, and Rosie, 15.

James W. Peters is a Rhode Island-based writer and consultant in strategic communications. During his 35-year career he has managed communications, government relations, marketing and other administrative functions for large integrated healthcare systems in Maine, California and Rhode Island.

Peters is a 1969 graduate of Fordham University, where he studied communications and philosophy and spent a year of independent study under the late Marshall McLuhan. He has won many national and international awards for a wide variety of projects, films, scripts, and publications and has consulted on numerous communications projects for governmental, political, corporate and non-profit clients.

introduction

Healthcare consumes over 16 percent of our gross national product, but many people are left out and very few Americans are truly secure in our access to medical services. At the same time, our communities – our villages – have largely succumbed to an impersonal, fragmented environment in which families and relationships are often unable to withstand the assaults of long commutes, isolation, anxiety and materialism. Compared with other industrialized nations, we spend through the nose on medical services and have little health to show for our spending.

When Americans complain about the medical services industry, our criticisms usually concern cost, quality, fairness, and access. Among our common characterizations are these:

- Healthcare costs too much (now absorbing about one of every six dollars in the national economy).
- The medical services system is cumbersome, impersonal and bureaucratic.
- There are huge disparities in who gets what service or what resource, inequities arising from race and class, and age. These inequities often determine who gets to live, how we get to live, and for how long.
- Our spending on medical services has exploded, while our spending on other social services, particularly housing and education, has collapsed.
- The medical industry spews out information that seems to change every week, so that last week's gospel is this week's threat.
- The industry appears more interested in selling than in fashioning a system that is caring, rational, personal, and just.
- The "providers" (medical institutions and professionals) have designed the system for their own convenience rather than that of patients.

Amid all these criticisms, we live in a culture that likes to finger a culprit when things are not as we would like them. If the medical services system does not suit us, culprits abound:

▶ Doctors are too greedy.
▶ Patients have unrealistic expectations.
▶ Specialists use their market power to enrich themselves at the expense of the system.
▶ Primary-care doctors want to go home early, and so are not accessible to real people with real people's schedules and problems.
▶ Hospital boards want only to run high-tech, high-visibility glamour programs, which they support at the expense of healthcare to the community.
▶ Communities do not want to pay for public health.
▶ Insurance companies are only interested in dollars, and not in people or communities.
▶ Government is either too involved, creating vast bureaucracies that perpetuate themselves without really doing much to improve health, or too little engaged, refusing to create a one-payer, universal-access system, thus making us the only country in the industrialized world without universal access to healthcare.

All of these observations, critiques and complaints have some justification, but they also all ignore the two central problems about health. The first is that being healthy in the United States today is very difficult, because we have largely wiped out community, which, as we will soon discuss, is a necessary condition of health. The second problem is that the medical services we are buying and selling are really not what we want when we define health. There is a huge disconnect between the vast enterprise we call "healthcare" and the reality of health. That is the fundamental argument of this book.

We lost sight of the meaning of health gradually and by accident. Life span – the expected period for which a person is expected to live – is easy to measure, while health is both hard to define *and* hard to measure, so we began to substitute longevity – a long life – as a stand-in for health, and pretty soon began to believe that longevity *is* health. In fact, measurement can and in this context does function as a trap. We measure a thing because it can be measured, and then we find our system trying to supply what we measure, not because it is what we want, but because it is what we can measure, and thus disseminate. Because we can easily measure life span, and people desire a long life span, our system is almost totally devoted to supplying longevity. If you are a hammer, said Mark Twain, you think the world is a nail.

But the health we want is not really longevity at all, but rather the equal opportunity to function in the relationships appropriate to our culture and our place in the life cycle, which is a much more robust sense of health than mere longevity. This book argues that health is the ability to be part of a family and community that is supportive and secure. Our society's disappointment with its medical services industry arises from numerous inefficiencies, true, but even more it stems from the fact that the *health* we are paying for is very different from what we actually *want*. We seek the ability to be with our families and our friends, and to see our children grow up. Instead, it often seems that healthcare gives us harangues about risk reduction, aimed at providing us an unending life, the manipulation of body image, so we can all aspire to look like an image crafted on Madison Avenue, and the relief of any discomfort or deviation from an externally defined ideal. We are all playing – and losing – a high stakes game of Three Card Monte; we put our money down where the card was but, all of a sudden – no money and no card.

Health, both in individuals and communities, describes our ability to function as people in relationships. Thus, health is not possible unless the context of those relationships – families, communities, even states and nations – is intact and functioning as well. Still, it is the *village*, the community, where people *experience* health. Urban or rural, rich or poor, the character of the community affects the subjective experience of well-being. The objective conditions of the community may influence both longevity and happiness, but that does not change the fundamental requisite, namely, that individuals cannot be healthy without functioning families and communities for individuals to be healthy *in*.

Our widespread confusion about the meaning of health largely explains why the medical services system in the United States in an expensive failure. But even if we can revive a robust definition of health, and steer toward it, health will not happen. Our culture, which might best be called postmodern consumer capitalism, eats social infrastructure for breakfast. Postmodern consumer capitalism is successful to the extent it can atomize individuals, families, and communities into the smallest unit of analysis that can trigger the purchase of a product. This perverse market system has triumphed by deconstructing the families and communities that are necessary for health security.[1]

The death of community in America is the roadblock the healthcare system must get around if it is to be about health for all, and not just profit for a few. How we understand health necessarily determines what the healthcare system looks like. If we want to fix the many problems of the current system, we must first understand, and agree on, what health is. In recognizing the function of community in the well-being of individuals, we have arrived at this definition:

Health is the biological, social, and psychological ability that affords an equal opportunity for each individual to function in the relationships appropriate to his or her cultural context at any point in the life cycle.

If health is as much about community as it is about longevity, our healthcare system will need to refocus on helping people enter into and maintain relationships. It will need to focus on building, supporting, or regenerating community itself, in the hope that with the regeneration of community will come the capacity to help people lengthen their lives, relieve pain and feel secure in the world as it is. Is so much change possible? If we did not think so, we would not have written this book.

PART ONE

what health is not

"Should medicine ever fulfill its great ends, it must enter into the larger political and social life of our time; it must indicate the barriers that obstruct the normal completion of the life cycle and remove them. Should this ever come to pass, Medicine, what ever it may then be, will become the common good of all."

— Die Einheitsbestrebungen in der wissenschaftlichen Medizin

"The physicians are the natural attorneys of the poor and the social problems should largely be solved by them."

— Rudolf Virchow

"Places have the power to transform – people, nations, even ideas."

— Bruce Feiler

"Analysis belongs to science, and gives us knowledge; philosophy must provide a synthesis for wisdom."

— Will Durant, *The Story of Philosophy* (1926)

"Any game becomes important when you know and love the players."

— W. P. Kinsella

A senior professor of medicine was making rounds at the hospital with his usual retinue of medical students, interns, residents, and fellows. They stopped at the bed of a strong-looking 28 year old. An intern presented the case: this was a well 28 year old who had suffered eight hours of vomiting and diarrhea the previous day. His symptoms had completely resolved. All his x-rays, blood and urine testing had been normal. He was, said the intern, a completely healthy man.

"A healthy person?" queried the professor. He paused and surveyed the assembled trainees, all on edge in anticipation of the next difficult question, letting the weight of the moment sink in. "A healthy person . . . Can anyone give me a definition of a healthy person?"

There was a long, uncomfortable silence, as the group of young doctors eyed their professor and each other, each terrified of making a mistake.

"I think I know," said one of the fellows, the one with a answer always ready. "It's simple. A healthy person is a person who has not yet been adequately examined."

— An old medical school joke

DEMENTED AND CONTRACTED

One early spring Saturday in 1984, when I was an intern on call at an urban community hospital, the emergency room doctor beeped me. "2191, 2191," the beeper said, a number that still makes all my muscles tense, my heart pound, my breath quicken, and the hair on the back of my neck stand up. Interns then would typically be called to the emergency room five to ten times a day, and asked to assume the care of people who had just come in. Their situations were not well known yet. They were people who could crash and die, people who could scream and yell, people who could complain and threaten. Sometimes they were people whose medical care we would, inadvertently, screw up, leading to their worsening incapacity or death and to a lifetime of finger pointing and recrimination for us, the interns. The common thing any of us knew about those people was that someone with the power to decide had determined that they should be admitted to the hospital, and that the intern was responsible for admitting them, then finding the problem and fixing it, whatever the problem happened to be.

An admission is a frightening time for an intern, because all that is known about the patient is what the emergency room doctor, who washes his or her hands of responsibility for the admitted person's life and health by calling "2191" and talking to the intern, knows and can tell. And sometimes the emergency room doctor, in a hurry to be absolved of responsibility, does not know or tell the intern very much at all.

What I heard that snowy, early spring, was "demented and contracted". "An old woman (70? 80? 90?), lives in a nursing home, demented and contracted. No history obtainable. A GI bleeder. She had thrown up blood."

Sometimes, what you hear is what you get. What I found when I went to the emergency room to meet the old woman and begin her treatment was nothing more, and nothing less than what I had heard: demented and contracted. She lay on her side in a bed, her arms and knees bent in a fetal position. She could not talk. Could not walk. She lay in a bed and was fed. Bed sores. No family. A scribbled record from the nursing home; a barely legible few words from the warehouse where they had 50 of them all the same. Vomiting blood. No history, no sense of what she was like before her admission to a nursing home, or when that happened, no sense of who she was or what she felt. She had thrown up blood in the nursing home twice, but her blood count was still normal. No bleeding from the rectum. No sense of the human being, the person in the body, the self. No sense of self or dignity. A body in a bed who had thrown up blood. But in the next 28 hours, that poor old demented and contracted woman would help me understand something new about the meaning of life, and help me begin to understand the meaning of health.

The treatment was straightforward – so automatic I can still write the orders for it today without thinking. Two large bore IVs, one in each arm. Six units of blood, typed and crossed and on the floor. NG tube for iced saline lavage to constant wall suction. IV cimetidine and Q2h Maalox alternating with Mylanta. GI consult for EGD.

If someone who has bled from the stomach once starts to bleed again, they can bleed to death within minutes, so you have to be ready to give them a lot of blood quickly. You monitor whether they are actively bleeding from the stomach by putting a large plastic tube in the stomach and sucking the stomach secretions – acid blood and saliva – out, looking for evidence of blood. (This story is from before we figured out that our large plastic tubes actually cause the ulcers they were thought to treat.) You then use medicines to stop the stomach's production of acid, and get a gastroenterologist to look into the stomach by performing a procedure called esophago-gastric-duodenoscopy, and look for the source of the bleeding, which can usually be stopped with an electric current.

The problem was, much of what I was about to do hurts. Inserting the IVs hurt. The large plastic tube inserted through the nose into the stomach hurts as it is passed ("passed" – a euphemism if there ever was one. Can you imagine someone putting a large plastic tube into your nose? Imagine what it must feel like as it hits the bone and the top of your nostril, and bends around a corner by pressing against the immovable hardness of the bones of the skull. Then imagine feeling the tube in the back of your throat, and forcing yourself to swallow so that it goes into your stomach and not your trachea. Imagine gagging as it goes into you trachea on the first and second try, and the shortness of breath that you experience before it is pulled backward, out of your lungs. Then imagine the tube just sitting in the back of your throat, making you feel like there is something there for you to swallow at the same time as it makes you want to gag) and keeps hurting for at least a day. The gastroscope hurts too, but at least you are sedated when it is "passed".

All this pain is one thing for a conscious person, who can understand what it is and why we are doing it. But pain is another thing again for people who are not aware. For them, pain is just pain, a searing discomfort to run away from. For the lady in the bed, demented and contracted, I was not going to be Florence Nightingale or Marcus Welby, hurting her a little but bringing succor. I was just going to make her hurt.

As if the pain was not enough, I wondered about the ethics of treating a person who is demented and unconscious. "Quality of life" is a high-falutin' phrase, used by Ph.D. philosophers in panels on medical ethics. "Should they pull the tube?" is an expression used by tabloids about people in Florida and New Jersey whose relatives are struggling with grief and loss.

But "demented and contracted" means only one thing to an intern. It means a body in a bed, long passed caring about tubes or quality of life, just existing, breathing, and maintaining a heart beat, a body who is in a bed only because there is someone to feed it and change it. "Demented and contracted" means that there is no one to help guide the end of suffering at the inevitable end of life, no one who loved her enough to say with kindness and mercy that life has ended —, "No hospital and no drugs please, let her body die in peace."

For me, the intern, who did not know her, the body in the bed might have been a person once. For me, the human being, she was a human being still. In her shoes, what would I have wanted? Someone to hold my hand and let me go to sleep.

But there was no one to hold her hand. There was no one to tell me, "No NG tubes please, thank you very much. No IVs. Make her as comfortable as you can. We love her very much and we want to be with her, so she feels safe and loved as her life ends."

What was I supposed to do, inflict pain on a person who did not understand the pain? Perpetuate the life of a person who should have been allowed to die?

Suddenly, I got it . . . For me, the intern, and for the healthcare system, and for society, her life was a body in a bed, breathing with a heartbeat. For her, life was over. For us, life is not either breathing or a heartbeat. Life should have been defined by the love of the people around her, and was defined, right then, by their absence. There was not anyone to defend her. There was not anyone to protect her from pain. There was not anyone to simply let her sleep. She had become just a body in a bed, because life is defined by a person's relationships; by the people around you who love you. But there was no one to love and protect her.

That is when I first understood that what we call the healthcare system is off its tracks. Representing the healthcare system, I was trying to protect a life that was already gone. The role of the healthcare system is not to extend life that has no meaning. Its rightful role is to help build and strengthen relationships, and to protect people from being old, abandoned, and alone.

So I had my doubts as I began treatment.

The first step, and the first roadblock, was the IVs. I tried five times, and could not place an IV. Not in the crease in front of the elbow – her arms were contracted, the elbows bent and stuck bent. Not in a hand vein. Not in a forearm vein. Not in her foot. It was the springtime of my intern year, and I was already about the best person in the hospital at placing IVs, but I had to call a resident in to help. He tried. After four or five more sticks, now a total of eight or ten needles in the flesh of someone who did not understand what we were doing or why, we had to quit. There was no large IV. There was no small IV. She needed a cutdown.

A cutdown is a surgical procedure. The surgeon comes to the bedside, prepares an arm or a leg for surgery by clearing the area with a brown disinfectant solution, covers the area with surgical drapes. He or she then uses a scalpel to cut through the skin, and searches the flesh for a vein, using a process called blunt dissection, in which metal instruments carefully and systematically pull apart flesh.

In order to get a cutdown done, I needed the permission of her attending physician, the mature, fully trained physician who was ultimately responsible for her care. So I paged her attending physician.

I called the answering service to have the regular attending physician paged, and then waited 45 minutes for a return call. That night the patient's attending physician was off; the covering physician was a very nice woman who knew nothing about the demented and contracted woman lying in front of me, and was only trying to tread water until the attending physician reappeared the following day.

What was I to do? The covering-attending physician's instructions were tentative, but clear: Unless I could find family to tell me not to proceed, I was to do everything required to preserve her life. If everything required included a cutdown, then we were to do a cut down. If she needed a blood transfusion, we were to give her a blood transfusion. If she needed surgery, she should have surgery.

The covering doctor gave me the name of a surgeon to call for the cutdown. I called. The surgeon was off and his coverage was paged. Another 45 minutes later, I spoke to the surgeon. He said that he would send a resident surgeon.

All this time I was worried sick. On the one hand, there was a woman who should have been allowed to die and who we were keeping alive because there was no one who loved her to stop us. On the other hand, the entropy of hospital life was getting in the way of me keeping her alive. She was becoming dehydrated and dying slowly, and painfully, in front of my eyes, despite my doing everything I could think of to keep her alive, though in my heart I knew that was the wrong thing to do.

An hour later, now five or six hours into the process, the resident surgeon arrived. "I need a cutdown tray," she said, a sterile tray that contained the sterile instruments needed to perform the cutdown. Another hour.

It was evening when the tray arrived, and after I had her paged to tell her that the tray had arrived, the resident surgeon returned. She painted the woman's arm with Betadine (a disinfectant) and draped her arm with a sterile cloth. The resident injected the area she was going to cut with local anesthetic. Then she picked up the scalpel and cut.

The patient's arm was so dry there was very little blood.

BEEEEPBEEEEPBEEEEP. It was the surgical resident's beeper. In those days the telephone operators could talk over people's beepers. "Traumerrr code in the Er aRrrrr, Traumerrrr code in the Er ARrrrr," hissed the beeper.

The surgical resident did not even look up. The scalpel that had been in her hand clanged onto the surgical tray where she had found it, and she was gone.

Now I had a demented, contracted patient, who we probably should never have started to treat, who could not understand what we were doing or why, who was dying of dehydration, who could start throwing up blood any second, who was dying despite my best and worst efforts to save her inappropriately, lying covered in green surgical drape, her wound open to the world.

That was the moment I discovered that life has no intrinsic meaning. There is no sacred, inviolate value to one person's life. If life was holy, the whole hospital would have stopped to help this poor demented and contracted soul who lay in a bed, covered with green drape, her open wound exposed to the world. If life was holy, no one would have ever asked me to do things to her that hurt. If life was holy and someone, for whatever reason, asked me to do things that hurt, they would not have let me wait five or six hours before doing them, and they would not have let the surgical resident run off to the emergency department without thinking twice.

If life was holy they would have called the hospital president, called in eight more surgeons, transferred the poor lady to another hospital, called the Department of Health, called the governor, demanded an inquiry, even fired me for letting things get so out of hand, though I swear I was doing everything I could to prevent this craziness. If life was holy, someone would have told me to sit by that woman's side, and stroke her dry, now brown, withered hand, and never put needles in it again.

But life is about relationship, about love, not holiness. And health is the ability to have relationships, not the demand of living forever.

You will want to know what happened next. My feelings of revulsion, which had been mounting, began to crystallize. I looked at the nurse who was with us, and the nurse looked at me. "You have to do something," she said. "I am not a Nazi," I replied, by which I meant that they could not make me torture people, even people who were demented and contracted.

So I called the attending back, and told her what had happened, hoping she would tell me to stop. She told me to call another surgeon. So I called another surgeon. I knew what they were going to say. And so I called yet another surgeon, and then another after that, and when they called me back, they each told me the same thing: call the resident. "The resident is in the ER," I replied. Their galling, yet obvious response: "A cutdown is not a surgical emergency. A trauma code gets attention first."

And then I decided. It took too long. I should have decided five hours earlier, but I was still too young to realize that I had the moral responsibility to judge the meaning of the orders they were asking me to follow, the rules they were asking me to obey. I am not a Nazi. I am not a torturer. I could not continue to hurt a defenseless person to protect my own skin, to save my own career.

I took off the surgical drapes, and stitched the poor woman's wound. There was no cutdown, and I knew there was not going to be a cutdown. I covered her with a blanket. I did not type and cross six units of blood. I did not call the gastroenterologist. I did not place the nasogastric tube that hurts so much. I sat and held that poor demented and contracted, abandoned woman's hand for a few minutes, until she and I fell asleep. Eventually I pulled the drapes around her bed, told the nurse to keep her comfortable and to call me if anything went wrong, and then I went to my call room for two hours of sleep.

She was not there in the morning. The nurse had found her cold and dead. They did not call a code, thank goodness, because she had been dead too long. She died peacefully, in her sleep. She did not have the luxury of dying with the people she loved surrounding her and making her feel safe, but at least she did not have the horror of being tortured as she was leaving this earth. We are not Nazis. We defeated the Nazis because they were the incarnation of evil.

Life is relationship. Health is the love of others.

the health we have

Despite some spectacular achievements and capabilities, the American medical services market system frustrates patients, caregivers and consumers alike. It is wasteful, patchwork, inconvenient, and incomplete. It sometimes achieves wonderful, seemingly miraculous results, but it also ignores obvious solutions and efficiencies. It provides some Americans with the best that modern science and technology can muster, but compared to the healthcare systems of other countries, it has done a poor job of addressing the medical needs of, much less maintaining the health of, the population as a whole. We are seventh in the world for infant mortality, sixteenth in maternal mortality, twenty-second for healthy life expectancy. Yet we spend about 50 percent more on medical services than the next highest spending country, nearly three times the international average, and more than twice the spending by industrialized countries, who, together, have an average life expectancy at birth that is exactly what ours is.[1] Our healthcare "system" leaves at least a third of us under-insured and a sixth of us with no real access to reliable medical services at all. What's more, people of different races, social classes, cultures, and language groups experience massive disparities in the availability of medical services and in their overall health status.

For all our healthcare spending, we still have many active social problems, which keep us from being the best people we could be, and keep us from being the country we long to be. Twenty percent of American women and 10 percent of American men are depressed at any given time in our lives, five to eight percent being depressed or having another mental or behavioral disorder at a at any one time.[2,3] At least six percent of us – 19.5 million Americans— use illicit drugs currently.[4] Eighteen percent still smoke cigarettes daily.[5] We have the highest divorce rate of any country in the developed world, the second highest gun murder rate and the third highest overall murder rate in the world. We have the largest number of people, per capita, in jail, and the highest percentage of single-person households in the world. About 3.5 million people are homeless in the United States during any single year – some 800,000 at any given time. Our educational attainment is just average, and we have a greater than average, and growing, split in educational achievement between rich and poor.

With all its faults, the American medical services industry is gargantuan, providing employment to over seven percent of the population and costing about $1.5 trillion per year. The directions and priorities of this behemoth have consequences not only for health-related matters but also for the entire economy and society. The cost of medical services has become so great that it exerts a major influence on the economic competitiveness of the United States in the world market, and is a major contributor to the speed with which industrial production has left the country, fundamentally changing the political landscape of the nation, perhaps forever. Our health spending has cannibalized our ability to build new housing and invest in education, fundamentally altering the social fabric of the nation. Our national future thus depends on the choices we make about health, medical services, and medical services spending, which influence our national situation at least as intensively as what our foreign policy looks like, or which political party is in power.

Despite major investments that are reshaping our economic and political landscape, we have neither enviable population health nor a sense of widespread well-being. We do not live longer. By various specific measures, such as pediatric immunization rates, we trail many countries. By various medical/social measures, we are worse off than many others. The only category in which we overwhelmingly excel is spending the most on medical services.

An international survey by the World Health Organization, conducted in 2000, ranked the United States thirty-seventh in overall health system performance, sandwiched between Costa Rica and Slovenia. This dismal showing occurred despite the fact that the United States spends more on healthcare than any other of the 191 WHO nations.[6]

The WHO study, using a slightly different methodology from a very different source, evaluated nations using three broad criteria. It measured health by life expectancy adjusted for the likelihood of a range of disabilities. As this book will consistently argue, this definition of health as mere longevity is deeply flawed.

Nevertheless, the study found the five longest-lived nations to be:

1. Japan: 74.5 years
2. Australia: 73.2 years
3. France: 73.1 years

4. Sweden: 73.0 years
5. Spain: 72.8 years

The United States trailed in twenty-fourth place at 70.0 years.

More recent data from the Organisation for Economic Co-operation and Development (OECD) also show the United States trailing other developed nations in terms of life expectancy (and leading them in infant mortality).

FIGURE 1.1 U.S. spending versus health status indicators (2003 data)

Country	Rank			
	Health spending as % of GDP	Female life expectancy (at birth), years	Male life expectancy (at birth), years	Infant mortality (deaths per 1,000 live births)
United States	1 (15.2%)	7 (80.1 yrs.)	7 (74.8 yrs.)	7 (6.9)
Germany	2 (10.8%)	5 (81.4)	6 (75.7)	3= (4.2)
France	3 (10.4%)	2 (82.9)	4 (76.7)	2 (4.0)
Canada	4 (9.9%)	4 (82.4)	2 (77.4)	4= (5.3)
Italy	5 (8.4%)	3 (82.5)	3 (76.8)	3= (4.2)
Japan	6 (8.0%)	1 (85.3)	1 (78.4)	1 (3.0)
UK	7 (7.8%)	6 (80.7)	5 (76.2)	4= (5.3)

Source: OECD heath data set.

The WHO's second criterion was *responsiveness*, as judged by a nation's respect for the dignity of individuals, the confidentiality of health records, prompt attention in emergencies and choice of provider. Here, the United States, which places great value on the ability of those who can afford to do so to freely choose their medical providers and approaches to care, garnered first place, trailed by Switzerland, Luxembourg, Denmark and Germany. This strong showing, however, was more than counterweighted by the third criterion, *financial fairness*, which measured the equitable distribution of the health cost faced by each household. In this category, the top five nations were Columbia, Luxembourg, Belgium, Djibouti and Denmark, with the United States far behind in fifty-fourth place.

Beyond financial fairness, the United States also fares badly when we look at the effect of race on health status and equal access to services. Here, there is no easy cross-national comparison, because the racial makeup and social context of the United States is unique. But it is possible to compare health status and access to treatment among races in the United States, a comparison that is at best painful and at worst devastating to those of us who think of ourselves as living in a just community.

African American men have an average life expectancy that is eight years less than white men and some American Indian men have a life expectancy that is almost 20 years less than white men, a gap that has increased over the last 40 years despite the civil rights movement, and the expansion of national medical services spending.[7] In some U.S. cities, the life expectancy of African American men in 1990 was less than that of men in Bangladesh.[8] Infant mortality rates are 2.5 times higher for African Americans and 1.5 times higher for American Indians than whites.[9] African Americans have more heart disease, more strokes, more cancer, more asthma, more kidney failure and more diabetes than whites, and are less likely to have health insurance than whites.[10] The causes of racial disparities in health status are complex, and probably include access to care and discrimination, cultural factors in the organization and distribution of medical services, geographically variable availability of medical services, and the impact of social class and educational attainment (both heavily influenced by the impact of past discrimination). However, little if any of the disparity in health status can be attributed to genetic differences, since the genetic meaning of race in the United States is unclear.[11]

But disparities in health status are not the sole issue; we must also consider disparities in *treatment*. Racial minorities in the United States get totally different treatment than do middle class whites, and it appears that widespread discrimination in treatment based on race persists nationwide, despite years of cultural change. Hundreds of studies, looking at almost any treatment you can imagine, find this huge and persisting difference. African Americans get fewer heart bypass operations, fewer balloon angioplasties, fewer heart vessel stints, far fewer kidney transplants (though have much more kidney disease), fewer limb-saving peripheral vascular surgeries (and thus more amputations), fewer prostate surgeries for prostate cancer, and less antiretroviral treatment for HIV when they are found to have the disease.[12] All these studies control for the severity of disease, and almost all find a disturbing and consistent pattern: the U.S. healthcare system discriminates in the treatment it offers people, at least by race, and probably by educational attainment and social class as well.

In terms of the expense of medical services among nations the United States stands stunningly in the forefront of every international comparative assessment. In a 1998 study, the Commonwealth Fund compared medical services expenditures for several developed nations. The United States topped the list by a substantial margin (nearly 43 percent more costly than the closest runner-up, Germany).[13] More recent figures continue to demonstrate the trend.

Our health status is not as good as that of other countries. Medical services here are expensive and unfairly distributed. Socio-medical problems such as depression, drug use, and homelessness are rife, yet all our health spending does not seem to be able to fix these problems. And we are spending through the nose – spending so much that our health spending may be impacting our ability to compete successfully in the world economy.

Does health spending yield health? We do not have long life expectancy. We do not have happy, well-adjusted people. We do not have a benign presence in the world, or the ability to help prevent genocide, or help the poorer nations of the world develop that we would like to have. We do not even have equal treatment in the United States. No, our health spending does not buy health.

Why do we spend so much more than other nations that have better outcomes? Let's think about possible explanations. We might spend more because we have set the prices for medical services higher than other countries do, if, for example, because hospitals and physicians have effective lobbies and have been able to convince government that they should be paid well in publicly funded medical insurance programs like Medicare and Medicaid. We might spend more on medical services than other nations that have better outcomes because we use more services but they have little or no extra benefit despite being used more. We might spend more because we include spending on services which other nations do not count as health services in our health services accounting, and, thus, comparisons with other nations are unfair. We might spend more because we provide services to population groups that other nations do not care for, like the aged, who we treat aggressively even after the point at which they have become infirm. Perhaps we spend more on medical services than other nations that have better outcomes because we are misdirecting our spending on services that do not create health and not spending on the services that produce the necessary conditions for health.

The truth is that all of these factors in some part explain and contribute to our unparalleled medical spending and concomitant poor performance. Doctors and hospitals have negotiated a pretty good deal for themselves, using their political muscle. We include the cost of nursing home care in our Medicaid spending, which increases the apparent medical services spending when we compare ourselves to other nations. We also include spending on consumer goods, like cosmetic surgery, medications that improve sexual function, and over-the-counter medications for headache and runny noses, when we measure our spending. As a consumer society with discretionary income, we are much more likely to buy such products than countries with different cultures. We devote a huge part of our medical spending to hospitals and specialists and little to primary care, though only primary care is associated with improvements in measured health status. Our legal process – which treats life as a property right and is governed by the laws of a marketplace that protects business entities, instead of protecting advocates of the common good – requires we "leave no stone unturned" (for paying customers, at least). As a result, we allocate some of our spending to care for people who cannot achieve any benefit (from the perspective of social utility) from that care: the aged infirm, and others who cannot protect themselves but have little hope of functionality. We also devote resources to their day-to-day care after we have preserved their lives, something else not all countries do.

On the other hand, all countries have experienced pressure on their health spending, and almost all have found themselves in the uncomfortable illogic of spending more and getting less. The pressure from consumer capitalism, combined with new technological developments, have produced medical means to treat or change more areas of human endeavor, have expanded life spans all over the globe, and have hiked medical services spending in all countries. The United States started this trend, but our culture is very powerful and is infecting cultures everywhere with it.

Of all the factors that contribute to our ineffective spending, however, we will argue that the most significant comes out of a fundamental misunderstanding about the meaning of health and the necessary conditions for health. It is a misunderstanding that has its roots in the *ménage à trois* of science, medicine, and consumer capitalism. Little by little we have confused longevity with health because the pursuit of longevity spawns innumerable products. Contrariwise, family and community, the necessary conditions for health, are being progressively undermined by the urbanization of the planet, and the centralization of capital (which perversely allows the resources needed to support the economic survival of small communities to be diverted into profit for large multinational corporations). Misunderstanding health, we spend money on medications, hospitals and specialists, instead of building a community-based healthcare system or investing in education and housing. Because we misunderstand health, we place the highest priority on material goods instead of relationships; we tolerate societal inequalities that make some people richer but all of us poorer, from the perspective of the possibilities of human relationships and life chances. Community is pulled apart by the split between rich and poor, and community is necessary for health.

the health we buy

The late Illinois Senator, Everett McKinley Dirksen, famous for his sten-
torian voice, shock of snow-white hair and Grammy-winning, Vietnam
War-era recording of "Gallant Men," once quipped of federal spending:
"A billion here, a billion there – pretty soon, you're talking about some
serious money!" By that measure, medical services have grown very serious
indeed, now accounting for over 16 percent of our national economic
activity – currently topping out at a staggering $1.7 trillion annually and
growing steadily. Medical services have become the single largest market
component in America. The sector employs over seven percent of the
workforce and lies in the crosshairs of immense political power and significance. Whole industries, vast fortunes and millions of jobs rise or fall on
the tides of healthcare policies and decisions, and the money they control.
That $1.7 trillion amounts to over $200 per person per year for every
human being on the planet today; it amounts, in fact, to about $15 for every
person who has ever lived: four million years worth of humankind.[1] Now
that's real money!

One of the paradoxes of the healthcare financing debates of the last 40
years is our failure to grasp what health actually means; we keep trying to
figure out how to pay for health and healthcare, but we show little sign of
acting to achieve what health or healthcare truly *is*. In this chapter, we drill
down on medical services spending, using that spending as a window on
what the United States *thinks* or *acts as if* health is.

Figure 2.3 indicates the various sectors of the healthcare/medical services economy and their respective economic shares. Expenses represented
by hospitals and by the care obtained from physicians and other health
professionals remain the largest component of healthcare/medical services
spending, as they have been for decades.

FIGURE 2.1 National health expenditures

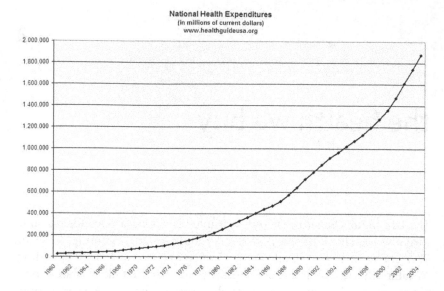

Source: Centers for Medicare & Medicaid Services, used by permission of HealthguideUSA.

FIGURE 2.2 Projected national health expenditures

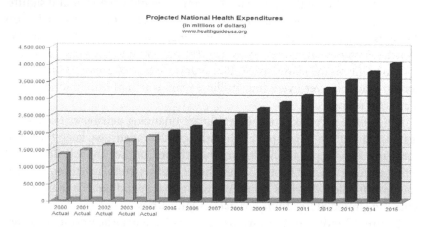

Source: Centers for Medicare & Medicaid Services, used by permission of HealthguideUSA.

FIGURE 2.3 Breakdown of national health expenditures (2004)

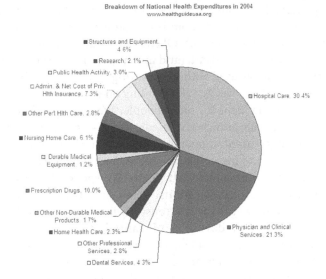

Source: Centers for Medicare & Medicaid Services, used by permission of HealthguideUSA.

WHAT ARE WE SPENDING ON?

What are we spending our "health" dollars on? Hospital care, physician services, prescription drugs, and nursing home care. Hospital care, physician services, and to some extent, prescription drugs do three things: they delay death (treating the kind of serious illness that is likely to cause death), they treat pain or discomfort, and they facilitate the return to function or correct disability, which also permits return to function. It is not possible to tell from information about spending how those three functions are weighted. But, clearly, the delay of death and the relief of pain figure prominently in what American society regards as health, at least as prominently as does returning people to functioning in the context of their family and culture.

Nursing home care neither delays death nor corrects disability, although sometimes it aids in the treatment of pain or discomfort. Nursing homes have a social, not a health, function – they transfer the work and responsibility of caring for infirm elders from one part of a community to a segregated space, and industrialize that work. For the purposes of this discussion, spending on nursing homes has little bearing on the meaning of health, and we join the chorus of others who do not believe nursing home care should be considered a healthcare or medical services expense.[2]

As we will argue later, a considerable amount of spending stems from research that seeks to lengthen life and delay death. Here are two often-quoted but confusing statistics: 20 to 30 percent of all Medicare spending is devoted to people in the last year of life; and about 36 percent of all healthcare spending is devoted to people over 65, with 22 percent of that spending devoted to people over 75, and eight percent (or about $89 billion in 1999), devoted to people over 85.[3,4] Of course, not all spending on people over 65 is devoted to delaying death (and much spending in the last year of life is for services that are used without knowing if the year of their use is the last year of life). Moreover, not all spending on goods and services that are intended to prolong life is for older people. We now spend about $20 billion a year, for example, on a class of medications – cholesterol-lowering drugs – that are largely used in people younger than 65, and that are not used not to treat current illness. Instead, these medications, called *statins*, aim to prevent heart disease and early death. We spend almost as much on blood pressure-lowering medications, which aim to prevent stroke and death from stroke, and we use them extensively in people under 65.

Still, it is clear that we devote a substantial effort and expense to prolong life and delay death, and considerable expense is devoted to the care of people who have already achieved considerable longevity. Viewed from the perspective of spending, we might think health is at least in part longevity.

But is this true? Is health longevity? As we will argue later, many older Americans, tied down to wheelchairs and closeted in nursing homes, unable to recognize themselves, are far from healthy. On the other hand, many people, who will die young accidentally or from sudden illness, are strikingly and vibrantly healthy at the time of their death, so their early death does not make us think they were unhealthy just because their lives were short – they were profoundly unlucky, but not unhealthy. Our point is that longevity is a value, fundamentally different from health, and probably most closely akin to a consumer good. We all want to have, or attain, long *healthy* lives and we sometimes measure some of the quality of a life by its length, but we do not need longevity to achieve health. Health, however, helps us to achieve longevity, which is the source of part of the confusion between health and longevity. Viewed from the perspective of fairness, what most people want is an equal shot at longevity as everybody else in their society. We want a fair shake at living as long as others and do not want to be *unfairly* deprived of longevity because of race, religion, or economic status. For most of us, living longer is desirable, *as long as we are healthy*. But clearly health and longevity are not the same, despite the resources we devote to longevity, under the guise of health.

Let's next consider the effort to relieve pain and prevent discomfort – certainly a major medical focus. Some relief of pain is clearly an attempt to restore health, because some pain interferes with function, and being in pain itself is an experience most of us would describe as part of the definition of ill-health. So some of our spending on pain control is directed at the restoration of health, and some of our beliefs about pain relief as revealed by spending are intimately tied to our beliefs about the meaning of health. But how about all the money we spend to relieve minor discomfort? Perhaps 30 percent of all visits to primary-care physicians, for example, are for minor back pain that will go away by itself. We now spend several billion dollars a year on treatments to stop rhinorrhea, or a runny nose, a condition that some people cannot tolerate, while others are barely bothered by. How about erectile dysfunction? Is Viagra necessary for health? If so, how much and how often? The relief of pain and discomfort is one part healthcare, and one part consumerism. The marketing arm of the medical services industry uses health as a cover to sell consumer goods that vary greatly in their ability to mitigate discomfort but have no bearing on health, *per se.*

How much spending is devoted to helping people who are sick or injured return to function? By contrast, how much is simply unnecessary health plan-administration expense, spending to correct the errors of the healthcare system, spending for tests and procedures that are ordered and obtained to prevent malpractice lawsuits, or spending to support the profit needs of corporations and investors, who lobby congress and the marketplace to buy products that help no one? It is impossible to quantify these factors precisely, because we track only what we bought, and seldom what we got. But an analysis of our spending does reveal that our culture thinks health is about longevity, pain relief, and return to function, as well as profit, administrative expense and malpractice expense.

So much money. Is it not amazing that we do not know much about the health we bought with it – if any? One thing is certain, though: health is not money, because if it were, we would surely have the best health in the world.

Some years back, the comedian Marshall Ephron did a very funny television skit. Dressed in a chef's smock and toque and standing at a lab bench replete with test-tubes and complicated glassware, Ephron mixed the ingredients listed on a well-known brand of frozen lemon cream pie to create his own version. When he had finished he held a bowl of gruesome-looking froth up to the camera and chortled, "There you have it – no lemon, no cream . . . just pie!" We contend that the same thing has happened to healthcare, which is now increasingly appearing in a particularly loathsome form: no health, no care . . . just healthcare.[5] As we review the current elements and directions of the healthcare industry, we believe it is possible to follow Ephron's example and conclude, "Here we have it – no health, no care . . . just healthcare."

3

what we measure is not health

One useful activity to arrive at health's current prevailing definition is to review how we measure health. Measurement is a powerful process. Apt measurement can expand our accurate assessment of health and thereby identify ways to enhance it. Misapplied, measurement can narrow the significance of health, focusing on relatively inconsequential factors and ignoring important ones. It all depends on what and how we measure. If those who perform health measurement take the wrong track, they can easily become more concerned with ways to improve the process of measurement itself than with ways to improve health.

We use two kinds of measures when we talk about health: we measure the health of populations, finding ways of comparing people living in a place to see which group appears to be doing better; and we measure the health of individuals, to see how one person compares with another. The first, "proxy measures" of public or population health, are, as their name implies, very rough ways of gauging the health of groups of people living in a defined locale and comparing them with similar groups elsewhere. Some proxy measures, such as *infant and neonatal mortality* rates, provide information about how well local, state or national societies and governments care for pregnant women or infants. These measures also prompt questions about environmental exposures or social conditions that affect pregnant women and infants who live in a particular place. Other proxy measures, such as *childhood mortality rates* or *adolescent suicide rates*, provide comparative information about the care and safety of children and teenagers. Still other proxy measures, such as the *cancer mortality rate* or *heart disease mortality rate*, supply information about the number of people in adult populations who die from specific diseases. The *total mortality rate* simply tabulates all deaths within a given population. Proxy measures can also supply data about environmental exposures or social conditions that affect selected populations.

21

Most of these proxy measures are actually measures of life span – of how long people in a specific place are likely to live, or how likely they are to die comparatively young. While we have measures of specific diseases or conditions, called *population-based incidence or prevalence of disease states*, these measures are rarely very accurate in the United States, because we lack an organized healthcare system or disease-registry system able to track the health of the population or the diseases or conditions present in the population. We really know very little about which diseases or conditions are present in each portion of the population. Our "healthcare system" is unable to keep track of either the population in a given place or the diseases within that population, in an organized and consistent manner.

What we do not generally measure about health is the degree to which the population of a place is able to develop relationships with one another. Measures of that kind, called *social capital measures*, are beginning to emerge, but they are very new, not generally agreed upon or accepted, and only rarely applied to discussions of health. Instead, social theorists use these measures as gauges of civic participation; only recently have they even been discussed as population health status indicators.[1]

The second kind of health measures currently in widespread use assess the health of selected individuals in a population to detect or treat specific diseases. We can use these measures to evaluate the current condition of individuals, as well as their risk of contracting diseases or conditions that might impair functionality or reduce longevity. We call the simplest measures, not surprisingly, *vital signs*: pulse, blood pressure, temperature, breathing or respiratory rate, weight, and pulse oximetry – a measure of the degree to which the heart and lungs are supplying oxygen to the body. We can obtain these measures quickly and easily, yet they go far to tell us a person's likelihood to survive for the next few minutes, hours, or days.

Analyzing and evaluating the tissues, fluids, wastes and other substances produced by the body is the next sort of commonplace individual measurement. For example, we measure levels of sodium, potassium, chlorine and other elements in the blood to evaluate the short term and long term function of vital organs. Concentrations of blood sugar, or glucose, indicate circulating energy stores. Breakdown products of metabolism in the blood tell us about stomach, intestine, liver and kidney function on a moment-to-moment, day-to-day, and month-to-month level. The presence of enzymes associated with a specific organ can help to gauge injury or level of function. Cellular components of the blood can indicate how quickly it will clot, the status of the immune system, the presence or absence of infection or bleeding somewhere in the body, and how well the bone marrow is functioning. We also measure various fats or enzymes that predict genetic and nutritional long-term risk of various dysfunctions, including heart disease, stroke and kidney disease, any of which might eventually impair the body's functionality or limit longevity if the risk factor is not modified.

A particular measure of the somatic status of individuals is the presence and projected consequence of disease itself, using the techniques of *diagnosis and prognosis* – concepts that help to reveal what we mean by health, at least reflexively. Diagnosis is the process of lumping together a number of complaints and "findings" into a single description of an individual's condition, meant to be predictive of life expectancy and future functionality. Findings typically include the results of a physical examination, evaluation of the individual's mental state and functionality in relationship, laboratory, x-ray or imaging studies. Prognosis, usually based on diagnosis, is the prediction of life span and functionality.[2]

Diagnosis also provides information that allows us to consider disease prevalence of segments of the population and the population as a whole. Diagnosis and prognosis both support the notion that the individual can only be understood in a broader context, because they are necessarily differential processes that contrast functions of an individual with normative values. Diagnosis and prognosis only have meaning insofar as they combine the experience of the individual with the experience of the population.

Diagnosis, and to a much lesser extent, prognosis, enable measurement of the health of individuals, and can also focus our thinking about illness in different ways. It is interesting to note how diagnosis has been used in the last 50 years to expand the boundaries of what we categorize as *medical* problems, because what we consider *medical* rubs up against what we consider *health*. Fifty years ago a runny nose was an inconvenience, ameliorated by a box of tissues. Impotence among aging males was a predictable occurrence in the normal life cycle, but, owing largely to cigarette smoking, the condition was a relative rarity because many men died too young for its onset. A nervous breakdown was a statement about a person's social condition, not about their health or medical situation. And men often beat their wives, a situation which more than occasionally caused those wives to suffer nervous breakdowns. Now, of course, we have four diagnoses: allergic rhinitis, erectile dysfunction, depression, and domestic violence. All, of course, are amenable to treatments that require medical services and pharmaceuticals and that generate bills and charges, cash flow and profits. The *medicalization* of the social world is a complex process and has been studied extensively by Illich, McKnight, and Callahan,[3] among others; it reflects the extent to which the boundaries of the medical and the social dimensions overlap in our understanding of health itself.

Along with individual assessment and treatment, diagnosis and prognosis are commonly used to track our ability to detect or treat specific disease states within populations. These measures are most commonly used in medical studies of drugs or procedures. They range from the occurrence of new diseases or conditions in individuals being studied, such as the new *cardiac event rate*, to the death rate from a specific disease in a study population, such as *cardiac mortality*. Studies of this kind may include measures of the life expectancy of people with a disease or condition under treatment, such as *disease-free survival* or *average life span after treatment*. Graphic representations, called *Kaplan-Meier survival curves*, can display survival of people after treatment, comparing the survival of two or more groups who have received different treatments for the same disease or condition. Occasionally, we measure the ability of people with specific disease states to function in their daily lives, assessing that function using an instrument called *Karnovsky status*. However, we rarely rely on this kind of functional measurement and use it mostly to estimate the effect of treatments for cancer in people thought to be dying. Again, we do not measure the ability of individuals to function in relationships, and we do not even have a commonly used tool to assess the condition of a person's relationships as we think about their health.

Clearly, prevailing measurement practices implicitly characterize health as the absence of disease, or as a physical status that permits longevity, irrespective of the quality of life. From the perspective of customary measurement interests and priorities, relationship and function are trivial considerations.

IS HEALTH LONG LIFE?

There is a powerful tendency in our culture and in the efforts of bioscience to define health as longevity. Our society devotes enormous resources to prolong life, regardless of its quality. Nevertheless, is longevity *per se* a token of health? Let's pose the question as it applies to the health of animals. We do not say that a Great Dane, which normally lives eight or nine years, is less healthy than a mutt, which might live 16 years, even though the life span of a Great Dane is considerably less. Instead, we accept this typical life span as a given. We would like to have a longer-lived Great Dane, but we do not consider its relatively short life span reflective of its health. In much the same way, we think of those who live long healthy lives as lucky, and people who live short but healthy lives as less lucky, and people who live short lives consumed by illness as terribly unlucky.

Lucky or unlucky, yes – but not healthy or unhealthy. Following Daniel Callahan, we contend that longevity beyond the average expected life span is a consumer good as well as an overvalued goal of bioscience, but not a necessary condition for health.[4] Indeed, the converse is closer to the truth: health is an almost necessary condition for longevity: bioscience has targeted life extension as an achievable goal, but, as we noted above, medication, medicine, and science are not health, and neither is longevity. Longevity does relate to health in the following way, however: we are likely to characterize a society that predisposes or allows unequal life spans based on some arbitrary characteristic, like race or religion or location or language, as an unhealthy society, because such a society does not allow its individuals equal life chances. That inequality is likely to lead to social unrest, and social unrest often leads to violence, which can affect people's health and their longevity. But, for the individual, longevity is a combination of luck, property rights (because, in general, wealthy people live longer), and a number of practices (like diet and exercise) that make both health (as well-being) and longevity more likely.

IS HEALTH FREEDOM FROM PAIN?

Pain and suffering or their absence are sometimes contributing factors, but are neither necessary nor sufficient to define health. The presence or absence of pain is often more reflective of luck than of health. First, let's draw out the distinction between *pain*, the physiological process by which noxious stimuli are communicated from a disrupted body part to the brain, and *suffering*, which is the subjective experience of pain. We measure suffering, the subjective assessment of pain, as a window on pain, but it affords an imprecise view. Suffering is easily generalized from discomfort, another subjective experience, particularly by marketers who attempt to isolate an experience to generate a want, need, or desire, directed toward a product. (Remember "the heartbreak of psoriasis"?) Being in pain is unlucky, and, to the extent it limits freedom to function or have relationships with others, is a source of ill-health. Being free from pain, in the case, for example, of someone with cancer, is lucky.

Pain does, of course, have some bearing on health, because we would tend to say people with many serious kinds of cancer, or someone whose body is wracked by pain, is not in good health. But we would not say that someone with occasional headaches, psoriasis, or an occasional runny nose is in poor health. So pain and suffering affects our thinking about health, but the presence of pain or discomfort alone does not make someone unhealthy, and not all unhealthy people have pain or are suffering.

Why is someone with cancer-related pain not in good health? How do we differentiate ill health from bad luck? People in pain from cancer are in poor health for three reasons. First, their cancer and its attendant pain is likely to keep them from being able to function in general, and, in particular, their pain keeps them from functioning in relationship with the people and communities that are important to them. Second, we have a perception that younger people with cancer will fall short of their allotted years of life. Third, the presence of suffering – the subjective experience of pain over time – all other things being equal, represents both bad luck and ill health. Suffering may not define ill health, but may contribute to it. Pain is part of health only to the extent that its presence limits function. The lines between suffering and discomfort are easily blurred, and suffering, which is the way we measure pain, is also used as a marketing tool in a possessive individualist society that treats life as a property right and any discomfort as an infringement on that property right. Yet suffering or its absence, the subjective experience of well-being, is also part of our understanding of health. The absence of suffering alone is not health, but is a contributing factor to health: health has an existential dimension; health is a measure of how it feels to be alive.

In this way, a person with pain from cancer is in worse health than the person with cancer but without pain, given equal projected life spans, because of the considerations of impaired function, the existential dimension, and fairness issues, but not because of the presence of pain itself. Someone who breaks an arm and is in pain for two weeks is in pain but not in poor health, because of the expectation of return to function. A person with a compound fracture of the arm, which requires many surgeries, is in worse health because of the loss of function, the incapacity, and the persistence of incapacity and suffering over time. We are sympathetic that the injury has caused so much pain, and efforts to control the pain are certainly appropriate, although it is not pain itself that makes the person unhealthy, but the fact that the pain and the medication to treat it have undermined the person's normal level of function and relationships, and because of their suffering over time. If the presence of pain does not itself necessarily signal the loss of function, then freedom from pain, like long life, is essentially a consumer good and not a precondition or defining element of health, at least up to the point that pain impairs function or causes protracted suffering.

But what separates the suffering that contributes to ill health from the pain and discomfort (the runny nose, the pain from a broken arm) that is more like a property right, a consumer good? The suffering that contributes to ill health is sustained, interferes with the ability to function in relationships that are important over time, or undermines the value of life itself to the individual. (Consider, for example, the 82 year old who has a sound body and a sound mind, but suffers the loss of a spouse, an event that, taken with other losses of family and friends, is so devastating that she or he does not want to live anymore. Or consider the 30-year-old intellectual who analyzes the condition of the world, and sees nothing but pain and failure – both are unhealthy states of mind for people who are not ill.) Thus, not all pain and suffering causes ill health, and health does not require freedom from pain and suffering, but pain and suffering alone can make health impossible, if it is sufficiently severe and long-lasting. Health is not freedom from pain and suffering, but pain and suffering can impair health.

IS HEALTH FAIRNESS?

The issue of fairness also appears to be at play in the assessment of health. In considering ourselves healthy we not only expect a reasonable level of function, but also the same function as everyone else. Long life is not a defining aspect of health, but a shot at life with a length in years equal to others is a hope of healthy people. Fairness appears to have some role in how we think about health: we measure the health of individuals so that we can compare individuals. We have an understanding of inequalities in health, and widely perceive that longevity and freedom from suffering should not be distributed on the basis or race or class or even on the basis of income (although longevity, at least, is very clearly associated with income).

But fairness is not health. One might imagine (not a very difficult thing to do, given the condition of the world) a country in the middle of a famine, in which everyone is staving to death together. It's fair, but people are dying, and the question of health is barely on the table. Conversely, one might imagine (also not a very difficult thing to do, given the condition of the world) an oligarchy, in which the mass of people live miserable lives in virtual slavery, where elites live long and healthy lives, with lots of exercise, good nutrition, and warm and happy relationships with family and friends. One might argue that the oligarchs are perpetuating an unhealthy society, which is likely to give rise to social instability and violence, but, while it appears that the society is dys*functional*, the oligarchs themselves are healthy, as we understand the word and concept. There may be some kind of association, some relationship, between health and fairness, but clearly health and fairness are very different.

We conclude that health metrics are mostly measures of longevity and discomfort control, both consumer products of the medical industrial complex. But we rarely measure health directly. Could our measurement have altered our perception of health itself? Could the process of measurement have changed the direction of the medical services sector of the service economy, tilting it toward selling products and away from the preservation and augmentation of health? And if health is not longevity or discomfort control, what is health, after all?

4

medications are not health

Think for a moment of the popular press and the frequent articles about older people, who, before 2006, had no prescription drug insurance benefit, and who it was claimed, would go hungry or eat dog food so they could afford to buy their life-saving medicines. The normal reaction to such a story is shock and guilt. How could we allow poor elderly people to go hungry? What kind of society allows its elders to eat dog food? Who are we? The government has failed! We need a new government program!

What is most amazing about such stories is how many assumptions they are built on, how frequently they are written, how predictably we react, and how little substance underlies the stories themselves. Among the assumptions are:

- that drugs really are life-saving for many people;
- that people using medications have no choice between starvation and death;
- that there are many older people who really cannot tell the difference between the need to eat and the need for medicine;
- that these stories appear because of sincere concern for the well-being of older people, and not to leverage public payment for medications for older people, notwithstanding the huge financial benefit for drug companies.

We simply do not know how many people must actually choose between food and life-preserving medicine, but it is abundantly clear that many people have been fooled about the importance and effectiveness of many medications. Indeed, few medicines have much impact on either longevity or function, and even fewer of those are commonly used. In fact, only kidney dialysis and, sometimes, insulin and other diabetes medicines, some chemotherapeutic agents, and some medicines that slow the heart rate or improve the pumping ability of people whose hearts have been damaged, are likely to have as much ability to prolong life as does food. These medicines only matter, in terms of life and death, for a very few people. Indeed, much of the need for diabetes medicine exists because people overeat, and many diabetes medicines and heart rate-slowing medicines are inexpensive. Some medications for multiple sclerosis and rheumatoid arthritis, and some cancer therapies, are very effective and very expensive – so expensive that the cost of food pales in comparison. Even if you skipped eating, you could not pay for them. For many medicines, there are effective, inexpensive substitutes, and for many more, a change in eating habits or exercise habits or emotional stress would make them unnecessary.

When we speak about efficacy of medicine, let's remember what, at best, medicine can do. It can help individuals to function. It can relieve pain or discomfort. It can help protect or improve one's physical or mental condition. It can sometimes help us live longer. It cannot – at least by our definition – make us healthy. And it cannot make *anyone* live forever. In fact, were we a healthy society, medicine's influence and prevalence would be far more limited that they are.

But we do not often think about the social costs of medicine, which is to say, how our spending on medicine may actually undermine our health by depleting the amount of money we have to spend on food, on housing, and on education; and by increasing income inequality by concentrating wealth in the hands of the few.

MOST FREQUENTLY USED AND MOST COSTLY MEDICATIONS

Let's look at medications we use commonly, and see how much of our medicine use has to do with health, how much is to compensate for a culture that has taken health away from us, and how much of our spending is to benefit drug companies first, and individuals, families, and communities second.

The most frequently prescribed medications in 2000:
Lipitor
Premarin
Synthroid
Hydrocodone
Prilosec
Norvasc
Glucophage
Albuterol

Claritin
Zoloft

The 10 most costly (to the nation as a whole) medications:
Prilosec
Lipitor
Previcid
Zocor
Prozac
Celebrex
Epogen
Zoloft
Zyprexa
Procrit[1]

The most frequently used and most costly medications can be broken down into eight classes:
1. stomach acid-reducing drugs (Prilosec, Previcid);
2. cholesterol-reducing drugs (Lipitor and Zocor);
3. antidepressants (Prozac, Zyprexa and Zoloft);
4. pain and arthritis drugs (Celebrex and Vioxx);
5. narcotic pain medicine (Hydrocodone);
6. medications that increase the number of red blood cells for people with kidney failure or cancer (Epogen and Procrit);
7. medications to control chronic diseases: hypothyroidism (Synthroid), high blood pressure (Norvasc), diabetes (Glucophage), asthma (albuterol);
8. medication to control allergies (Claritin).

Let's look at each class from the perspective of function, longevity, and value.

Stomach acid-reducing drugs
In a few people with intractable heartburn, acid-reducing drugs are the only path to function and, in a very few, these drugs reduce the risk of a precancerous condition called Barrett's esophagus and reduce the risk of esophageal cancer. For most people, however, acid-reducing drugs compensate for extra stomach acid caused by the effects of stress, overeating (also often stress-related), nicotine, alcohol, and caffeine. Most overproduction of stomach acid can be traced to the stresses of modern life, or to a side effect of one of our ways of dealing with that stress. In other words, acid-producing drugs promote comfort, but do so in a way that compensates for the ill effects of our society.

Cholesterol-reducing drugs

Cholesterol-lowering drugs, on the other hand, have no immediate effects on comfort, and, in fact, can rarely even be said to change an individual's likelihood of specific disease events or life span. As we will describe later, we use cholesterol-lowering drugs to lessen the incidence of heart disease, and perhaps stroke, in the population as a whole. That is, we know that if we reduce the cholesterol of everyone in the population with high cholesterol, we can reduce the occurrence of heart disease and stroke in that population. But here's the rub: although we can use medication to reduce the occurrence of heart disease in the population, we do not know who in the population will benefit. So there is no certainty that any individual who takes the medication will benefit from it (at least in terms of longevity or function) and it is much harder to assign this choice to spending on function versus spending on longevity, although the imperative to lower cholesterol is clearly a product of our ability to measure and impact longevity.

But consider the risk factors for heart disease and stroke: smoking, diabetes, insufficient exercise, and obesity. These risk factors for heart disease and stroke, which we are trying to counteract with lipid-lowering drugs to counteract, are, at least to some degree, byproducts of our *culture*. That is, smoking is most often effective self-treatment for anxiety, and anxiety is often caused by social isolation, mixed cultural messages, and occupational or financial pressure. Diabetes, obesity, and insufficient exercise are the byproducts of a passive, profit-focused consumer culture, in which we develop calorie-rich foods to maximize profit for their producers, and develop "labor-savings" technologies to produce more leisure time, and then develop methods of entertainment to consume that leisure time, methods which are passive and socially isolating. Although we cannot assign spending on cholesterol-lowering drugs to either function or longevity, we can reflect on the way in which we use drugs to try to compensate for the breakdown of community and its replacement by the culture of consumerism, issues we'll discuss at length in Chapters 10, 11, and 12.

Antidepressants

Antidepressants usually address function, although for people who are seriously depressed, they may promote longevity by preventing suicide. (They also have been recently associated with increasing the risk of suicide in both adolescents and adults.) The interesting thing about antidepressants is the increasing frequency of their use. The well-documented increasing incidence of depression in industrial and post-industrial democracy, and its association with social isolation, should give us pause.[2] Our spending on antidepressants helps compensate for the social effects of consumer capitalism. By pulling money and resources out of communities and concentrating capital in pharmaceutical companies and their stockholders, we helped create a death spiral for community, in turn making depression vastly more common. So, although antidepressants may have an almost immediate effect on function and longevity, that effect only compensates for the detrimental effects of consumer capitalist culture on health. Are antidepressants about health? Or would we be better off if we could change the culture, improve the function of communities, suffer less depression, and reduce the need for antidepressants in the first place?

Pain and arthritis/narcotic pain/red blood cell-increasing drugs

Pain and arthritis drugs, as well as Hydrocodone, help compensate for the effects of aging. They are only about function. Hydrocodone is sometimes a drug of abuse, and is used by people looking to escape the loneliness and isolation of a consumer society.

Medications that increase the number of red blood cells for people with kidney failure or cancer are only about function and comfort for those who are seriously ill. They are used by comparatively few people and are very expensive. That they appear on these lists is evidence of their expense, as well as that we are keeping more people with life-threatening illnesses alive. As in so many spending policy decisions, one must reflect on the social cost of this choice. How high should be our priority in helping to extend the lives of those who are seriously ill, and improving the quality of life for those whose health is most compromised? We do so at tremendous cost. Do we give the same consideration to our young people, and our young families, and our communities, as we do to those who may be older and sicker? What is the appropriate balance?

Medications to control chronic diseases

Medications to control chronic disease seek both to preserve function and increase longevity. But look at the chronic diseases: hypertension, diabetes, and asthma, again frequently artifacts of consumer society and its stresses, poor nutrition, and environmental effects. In a more community-oriented society, would these expenses be as intense? Does our extensive spending on them contribute to the death spiral of community?

Allergy medications

This rapidly growing segment of pharmaceutical spending appears to be only about function: someone with a runny nose and allergic headache is miserable indeed. But think for a moment about how allergies were treated 30 years ago: with a box of tissues, which cost 49 cents. Now, the same problem consumes multiple physician visits and often a sinus CT scan, and then daily medications costing a dollar or two per day or more. What used to cost a few dollars a month now consumes hundreds if not thousands of dollars a year. Are allergies a medical problem? Certainly we have medications which can be used to control them, but by medicalizing allergic rhinitis (runny noses) and moving the cost of control from the personal to the public sector, we have added billions to our national medical services spending. Should this be a public or private process? What if we could move this spending back into the private sphere, so it was not covered by health insurance at all? If we did, people could choose to buy these medications and pay for them themselves, and pay for the doctor visits and CT scans themselves. Would the public health be threatened? How? How would communities be affected? How would the cost of medications be affected?

THE RELATIONSHIP BETWEEN TREATMENTS AND HEALTH

For any medication or medical treatment, these questions are worth asking:

- "If I do not take this drug what will happen?"
- "If I do not get this treatment what will happen?"

Let's consider the impact of *not* having various treatments.

I will die right away:
- Insulin (for people with severe diabetes)
- Treatment for anaphylactic shock
- Major trauma care
  - —Dialysis
  - —Heart attack care
  - —Embolism surgery

I will die fairly soon:
- Bypass surgery
- Pacemaker
- Treatment for asthma attack
- Appendectomy

I will be much less functional or feel much worse:
- Joint replacement surgery
- Antidepressants
- Anti-psychotics

▶ Treatment for chronic back pain
▶ Ulcer medications

I will have a higher statistical risk of dying or being incapacitated at some point:
▶ Cholesterol lowering medications
▶ Immunizations
▶ Osteoporosis medications
▶ Hypertension medications
▶ Diabetes medications

I will be inconvenienced or uncomfortable:
▶ Allergy medications
▶ Heartburn medications

I will be less attractive:
▶ Botox treatments
▶ Liposuction
▶ Acne medication

Nothing of much consequence will happen:
▶ Most over-the-counter medications
▶ Most alternative therapies (chiropractic, acupuncture, therapeutic touch, reiki)

The treatment might kill me:
▶ Estrogen-replacement therapy
▶ Cox 2 Inhibitors (Vioxx and Celebrex)

The first demonstration, as noted above, that medications are not an inherent requirement of health is their limited immediate effect on either function or longevity. Beyond this, the great prevalence and expense of medications not only fail to achieve health but actually interfere with it. Spending on medications reduces the economic resources of communities. This works through a principle of Keynesian economics called the multiplier effect.[3] This calculation looks at government spending and considers the extent to which the impact of that spending increases as it bubbles through a nation's economy. The notion of a multiplier effect has been expanded by post-Keynesian economists and others to consider the effect of a specific business or industry on the economic status of communities and nations. Viewed from this perspective, the multiplier effect tries to measure how spending is recycled inside a community, arguing that spending that recycles and multiplies builds wealth in a community, because it is distributed inside the community and stays there.[4] Spending that is not recycled, and which does not multiply, comes out of the community as profit for another place or entity. Certain types of spending, like road work, education, and housing, have a larger multiplier effect and can be used by governments as economic stimuli in times of recession, sometimes yielding both positive economic and positive social effects. Other types of spending (spending on arms and armaments is the classic example) have a more limited multiplier effect, because output is either stockpiled against a time of national defense emergency, or used in war, and once used, of no further economic value.

Spending on medications produces a very limited multiplier effect; because medications cost very little to manufacture and because their production is centralized most of the spending goes for marketing, distribution and profit – all functions that occur largely outside local communities. For the most part, spending leaves the community and carries a negative long-term economic impact. To the extent health is a matter of relationships, and communities are the places where those relationships occur, spending on medications weakens the community's economy and, thus, increases the difficulty of attaining and maintaining health.

Billions of dollars worth of drug advertisements aside, medications are not health, nor do they produce health. Just as the treatment for malnutrition turns out to be food, and the treatment for homelessness is housing, much of the treatment for illness may well be not drugs, but family and community.

medicine is not health either

Medicine as a profession is essentially irrelevant to the health of the population, although the services of individual physicians can be important to the life, function, and comfort of individuals. Let's look at the process of medical care, and see if we can learn more about the distinction between population health and individual health, and how both help us understand what health actually is.

MEDICINE AS A PROFESSION

The ancient profession of medicine is defined by a social contract, an implicit and explicit relationship between society as a whole and physicians as a class. The contract places obligations on the relationship between individual patients and individual physicians, as well as on the relationship between all physicians, taken as a class, and society as a whole. In theory, individual physicians provide individual patients with *un-self-interested advocacy* – advocacy for the patient's health, provided by the physician without interference from any self-interest. In turn, physicians are supposed to be shielded from the marketplace, provided an adequate living and afforded sufficient protections so that there is no need for self-interest. Physicians individually, medicine as a profession, and physicians as a class have some obligation to advocate for the health of society as a whole, but that obligation, though present, is not nearly as strong as the obligation to provide unselfish advocacy for the health of individuals.[1,2]

Of course, there are all sorts of stresses and strains on the social contract that defines medicine as a profession. Physicians often allow self-interest to filter into their patient care and are not good at policing themselves to forbid that self-interest. Society often allows the marketplace shield to break down, particularly at times when mores and values are changing, when there is societal uncertainty about how much marketplace protection is appropriate. (For example, should physicians' incomes be the same as teachers', or more like CEOs', in order for the marketplace shield to be considered effective?)

WHO IS GETTING ALL THIS "CARE"?

The incipient field of medical ecology studies the utilization of medical resources within a population. As Figure 5.1 shows, and as anyone would expect, most people's medical requirements are neither acute nor especially demanding in any given month. Only about 20 percent see a physician for any reason, fewer than 10 percent experience a hospital stay and only about one percent wind up in an academic medical institution. The expense associated with each of these levels of care, however, is very nearly the inverse of its utilization. That is to say, the least used levels of care tend to consume the greatest percentage of resources – the greatest good for the smallest number.

FIGURE 5.1 A typical month of healthcare in the United States

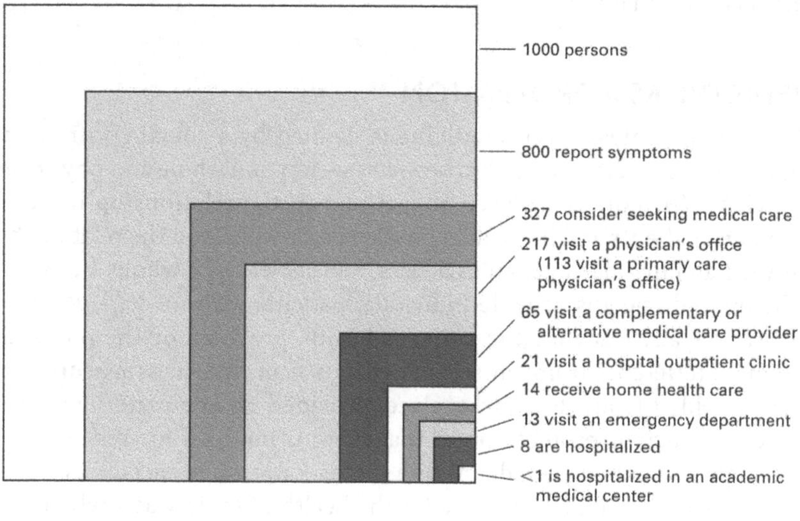

— 1000 persons

— 800 report symptoms

327 consider seeking medical care

217 visit a physician's office
(113 visit a primary care
physician's office)

65 visit a complementary or
alternative medical care provider

21 visit a hospital outpatient clinic

14 receive home health care

13 visit an emergency department

8 are hospitalized

<1 is hospitalized in an academic
medical center

Source: http://www.graham-center.org/x244.xml

INDIVIDUAL HEALTH AND POPULATION HEALTH

The role of the physician and physicians as a class in un-self-interested advocacy for patients and for the health of society points to a disjunction between the health of individuals, of populations, and of society as a whole. Individuals define their own self-interest, sorting out for themselves the contribution of function, pain control, and longevity to their own health, and expressing that self-definition to any physicians they employ in a dynamic interchange. Think of the conversation between patient and physician about a bad back, for example: the patient wants pain medicine, the doctor explains how too much pain medicine might get in the way of a return to function, or might even create a risk of dying (for someone with severe lung disease). Perhaps they compromise on short-term pain medicine and physical therapy to promote rapid return to function, minimizing any risk to longevity. This kind of negotiation characterizes the practice of medicine, as patient and physician discover the dynamic tension between three elements of health: pain relief, function in relationship, and longevity.

Population health is a different concept entirely, namely, the aggregate well-being of a population living in a specific geographic area. Population health refers to collective comfort, function, and length of life. Unlike individual health, which is self-defined, we understand population health only when we measure some aspect of the comfort, function, or life span of a defined population and compare the result with a population living in another place. As we will discuss below, the act of measurement has a major impact of our understanding of population health, and the population characteristics we are able to measure easily have had a major impact on our understanding of the health of populations and individuals. What we have chosen to measure distorts our perception of health, in what we will call the reductive trap. But leaving the act of measurement and the distortions it produces aside for a moment let us now consider the relation of medicine as a profession to individual and population health.

As we discussed earlier, there is no measure of the effect of medicine as a profession on individual health, because individual health is self-defined. Some people use physicians often to improve their health, but most, as shown by studies in medical ecology, use physicians only occasionally. From the perspective of individual health then, medicine is on the whole irrelevant to health, which people define and secure for themselves.

The effect of medicine as a profession on population health is also problematic. Our measures of population health are distorted by measurement artifacts. Our ability to envision what we really mean by the health of populations is imprecise, and we tend to skew population health data toward inflating the positive impact of medicine on health.

Over a hundred years of studies, by the most skilled analysts in medicine and social science, have failed to show that medicine as a profession has a significant positive impact on population health. From John Snow to

Rudolf Virchow to Rene Dubos to Thomas McKeown to Daniel Callahan to Barbara Starfield, Lisa Berkman, Ichiro Kawachi, Bruce Kennedy, and Leilu Shi, the practitioners and theorists who have examined the social determinants of health are continually rediscovering the same phenomenon: social organization, *not medical care*, determines population health.[3] There is ample reason to believe the converse – that medical care worsens population health, but the balance between some medical care being somewhat protective and too much medical care being dangerous to population health has not been well worked out.

What are the major predictors of population health or ill health in the United States? They are smoking and environmental exposures, income inequality, and the enduring effects of racism on racial minorities – all measures of our ability or inability to function as a just community. Only one measure of the impact of medicine as a profession, the number of primary-care physicians per 10,000 population, measured state by state in the United States, appears to correlate with the variables we use to measure population health, such as infant mortality and total mortality. That correlation is not as strong as the correlation with smoking, income inequality, and race as a marker for racism.[4] A number of measures of the impact of medicine as a profession, number of specialty physicians per 10,000 people, and number of hospital beds per 10,000 people, appear to have a *negative* impact on population health. Not only is medicine (except, perhaps, primary care) not population health, medicine may be *injurious* to population health.[5]

Of course, understanding the determinants of population health begs a central question: what, exactly, is population health? The determinants of population health all actually reference population life span (which is what we actually measure), and not population health *per se*. What is it that medicine as a profession is supposed to advocate for when it advocates for public health? There is no clear answer to this, but consider the kinds of things that medical professional organizations advocate for (other than their own pocketbook issues). These organizations tend to speak out for broader and more equal access to healthcare. They work on issues like immunization policy, environment and sanitation that seek to reduce the risks to individuals and the community from the infectious disease, toxic byproducts of social organization, from overcrowding and industrial organization. They have advocated banning smoking, for research spending by government, and for government policies to improve nutrition and safety. Sometimes they have advocated for rational drug-enforcement policies that keep government from blocking access to good pain-control options for individuals. Broadly considered, these initiatives are predicated on the notion that public or population health is essentially a means of removing the roadblocks to individual health thrown up by our sometimes pathologic social organization. Or, conversely, we appear to think that population health is the creation of coherent social organizations that improve comfort, allow relationships, and do not unfairly restrict the life span of individuals inside them on the basis of arbitrary criteria. A healthy population is one that is robustly engaged in the process of living, one whose members spend their days relating to one another and their environment, one that does not struggle with an inappropriate burden of illness (compared to another population) or premature mortality of some of its members on the basis of preventable social pathologies. Medicine as a profession can *advocate* for social change to improve population health, but it is very clear that the existence of medicine as a profession does not *represent* population health.

Could a just community be a necessary condition for population health, or is a just community simply a necessary condition for population longevity? Although our measures of population health are primitive, it appears that community *is* important to population health. Just how important is not clear from the measures we have available to us in 2007. Certainly other, somewhat related factors, such as population density, the local environment, the culture and behavioral choices of people living in a place, and perhaps, the genetic makeup of the population in a place, have a role to play as well.[6]

But the distinction between individual health (pain control, function, and longevity) and population health (social justice, population density, local environment and culture, and genetics) is important when we consider the impact of medicine. The profession may affect individual health but its work is not a necessary condition for health; primary care is a weak predictor of population health as we measure it today, but other aspects of medical care may influence population health adversely.

On the other hand, one might argue, look at the increases in life span that our medical technologies have brought to people in the industrialized world in less than 100 years. Does not that increased longevity show that medicine and medical technologies have a huge impact? But the question itself contains the answer. Medical technologies improved the *life span* of the population, and not necessarily its health. And – one other small detail – while the life spans of populations in the industrialized world have increased, the total world population has doubled, with most of the increase in the developing world, in populations that have not experienced any increased length of life. So the average life span around the world has stayed about the same, despite medicine and medical technologies, with the bulk of the world's population still living short lives. Viewed from this high-altitude perspective, medicine as a profession may have spread misery because it has become an agent of a world economic system that extracts longevity and wealth together from the many, and concentrates wealth and longevity into the hands of the few. That is not what medicine as a profession ever *intended* to do, but clearly it is possible to argue that a worldwide increase in suffering may be the end product of medicine as we know it today.

As we proceed with this analysis, let's remember how easily individual health and population health can be confused, especially when a profession (medicine) or an industry (pharmaceuticals) has a product or service to sell, and marketing conflates the two.

science is business, not health

Many doctors like to think of themselves as scientists – it's good for the ego and good for business. From their earliest student days, aspiring physicians are swaddled in white lab coats, accoutered with stethoscopes and made to speak in the clipped, Latinate argot of "medspeak". But this is largely a disguise. For the most part, good physicians are capable and empathetic technicians, not scientists. The vast majority work in applied clinical areas and have little interest in or need to apply rigorous scientific methodology to be effective in their work. Medicine is largely the application of accepted, tried and true methods developed by scientists for physicians, tempered, one hopes, by a genuine concern for people and a reasonably insightful understanding of their behavior. The clarification that physicians are typically not scientists is significant because by deluding themselves about their scientific prowess, physicians collectively confuse both themselves and the public about the efficacy and importance of many medical issues.

SILLY SCIENCE

The misguided medical pseudoscience, mumbo jumbo, and superstition of past ages amuse us all. Unfortunately, medical foibles, missteps and incompetence are by no means entirely a matter of history. *Silly science*, as we have decided to term it – we might also think of it as "Scientific Method Lite," or "McResearch" – has become an increasingly embarrassing trend within biomedicine in recent years. The most notable behavior of silly science is to allow fragmentary research findings to steer the efforts of clinical practice, willy-nilly, with too little reliance on prudent judgment or common sense. Just as the medical services industry has either fallen or jumped into the trap of replacing health with longevity, silly science stems from confusion between data and knowledge. The premise is that by piling facts high enough they will yield understanding (possibly in a process somewhat akin to spontaneous combustion). The belief among many physicians that, as scientists, they should evaluate and promptly apply these data to modify approaches to care is among the most potent enablers of science gone awry. In fact, silly science has added enormously to the cost of healthcare while subjecting thousands of patients to needless and painful interventions, to the use of toxic or ineffective pharmaceuticals, and to reliance on ultimately failed technologies.

Consider the tortured course of medical practice related to the use of mammography to diagnose breast cancer, and various surgical methods to treat it. From year to year – sometimes from month to month – new research findings drive clinical practice first in one direction and then lurch abruptly in the other. Today, mammography is an annual must for every woman over 40. Next month, the efficacy of mammography is of questionable value for any woman at all. Now, mammography appears to lower breast cancer mortality, but not all cause mortality, making the value of screening with mammography uncertain.[1] For the unfortunate women diagnosed with breast cancer, first radical mastectomy, with or perhaps without lymph-node dissection, is the only reliable surgery. But, it turns out after all, lumpectomy is equally effective. Wait! Lumpectomy is, once again, highly suspect. A blaring parade of discoveries and therapies *du jour* marches past the increasingly wary eyes of a concerned, confused public, rightfully appalled that medicine has become a process of short-lived fads. The media, another pillar of silly science, enthusiastically dish up (and print up, and talk up) this spectacle, clutching their early-release copies of the latest medical journals, wrapping themselves in the mantle of protection of public interest and the right to know everything – useful or not. Physicians do not often resist: they are largely unable to judge the reliability or significance of research. Yet they fear falling behind the pack for lack of clinical currency, or undermining patient confidence that they are up to date, or risking legal liability for not using the latest and greatest.

FEAR OF MALPRACTICE: ADDING EXTRA COST

Indeed, there is pathos in the often correct perception of liability, because the fear of malpractice lawsuits often fuels the practice of defensive medicine, which costs the nation billions of dollars a year, and contributes to both profit for the medical industrial complex, and impoverishment of communities. Every wasted dollar poured into profit for unneeded medication and testing is a dollar not available to cycle inside communities, not available for making communities stronger. Here's how *this* absurd reductive trap works. Medical "science" discovers a test or cure, and loudly proclaims it to be the latest and greatest. The news media, anxious for a story, spread the word. Regardless of the specifics, their coverage carries implicit messages: that medical science can fix all humanity's ills; that everyone can live forever; that life is a property right and not a gift that flows from the individual's families and communities in partnership with one another; and that if someone dies it is because someone else made a mistake. Over time people instill these messages, which feed into two core sentiments of consumer capitalism, one healthy and one dangerous. The healthy sentiment is that everybody ought to have equal rights in a free society. The dangerous sentiment is that if your property right is infringed on, you have a moral obligation to defend it in the courts. You get sick: should you sue? Mom or Dad dies: should you sue? Who? Someone must be guilty. Someone must be available to pay.

The large, aggressive personal injury bar reaps personal profit from the defense of the property rights of others, and juries swim in the same cultural milieu as people who get sick *and* the personal injury bar. All hear the same message: "Medical science has made it possible to live for ever, and when someone dies or is injured, it is because the property right to life has been infringed upon." Though relatively few malpractice suits are successful, there are enough successful suits, most of which come out of the impression created by the media (fanning the flames of often silly medical science) to frighten the medical community into believing they have a moral and legal responsibility to put silly science into practice. They order more drugs and tests. The health profiteers bank more profits. Communities have less money to spend on their own interconnectedness. People experience less of what a rich vibrant community life is like, and become persuaded by the steady drumbeat of the medical industrial culture that life is a property right. People become more likely to sue, and the whirlpool of bad science, community, culture, cost, money and greed spins faster. We spend more, get less, and lose the possibility of health as we devote more resources to medical services and watch communities wither.

The best recent example of this is the PSA test for prostate cancer. The PSA test is a poor test at its best, because there are probably at least two populations who get prostate cancer. One population is men who get an aggressive form of prostate cancer, which kills men within two or three years of diagnosis. The other population contracts a very slow growing cancer, which sits quietly in the prostate for 20 years or so, and lets the men who have it age naturally and die in their 80s and 90s of something else. The problem is both cancers produce a chemical called prostatic-specific antigen, and both look the same under the microscope; we cannot tell them apart, except retrospectively, so it is hard to tell if any of our prevention and treatment for prostate cancer actually works.

Enter the PSA test. A few intelligent scientists thought they could predict who is at risk of dying of prostate cancer by measuring the amount of prostatic-specific antigen in the blood. These scientists published scientific papers in very good journals, and these papers were seized upon by both the media and urologists, who have both an ethical and personal financial interest in helping reduce the incidence of death from prostate cancer. Before long, the lay press was filled with proclamations about PSA, and how PSA was making prostate cancer a preventable disease. Soon, many primary-care doctors were offering the PSA test to their patients, both because of the media and because they had heard of other primary-care physicians who had been successfully sued for not ordering the PSA test. (They had heard correctly.)

The problem is that the evidence about PSA itself is contradictory. On the one hand, we have never been able to show that the widespread use of PSA prevents death from prostate cancer. Indeed, as we study PSA, the epidemiologic evidence supporting PSA as a good test becomes weaker and weaker, with no one quite clear what counts as an abnormal PSA. On the other hand, the death rate from prostate cancer has fallen since PSA came into wide use, suggesting that *perhaps* all this attention to prostate may reduce the incidence of death from prostate cancer. (A dispassionate observer might suggest that PSA is probably useless but routine prostate biopsy at 60 and 70 *might* prove to be the most useful strategy in identifying all prostate cancers, and in reducing the incidence of death from prostate cancer, to the extent, at least, that early identification and treatment make a difference in reducing prostate-cancer mortality, something we do not know.)

Malpractice attorneys now believe that yearly PSA is the standard of care, and will sue and recover should that test not be offered and ordered; PSA is now widespread despite a growing body of evidence that it is useless as a test. So, we are spending millions, and perhaps billions, of dollars generating profit for sellers of medical services, money once again unavailable to local people improving schools, building local low-income housing, improving the local environment, creating bike paths, or doing one of myriad things in local communities that would keep that money in the community from which it comes.

THE ADHERENTS OF SILLY SCIENCE

Anyway, back to the physician as scientist. It is certainly true that some physicians have high scientific aptitude and have made appreciable contributions to the science of medical services. For the most part, however, physicians are very practical and concrete empiricists with little aptitude for or interest in science and research. While it proves nothing, anecdotally it is notable that of the 21 people awarded the Nobel Prize for Medicine and Physiology during the last decade, only three possessed a medical degree. All the rest were Ph.D. bench scientists. From this extremely limited but rarefied population it is perhaps possible to infer, at least, that the cutting edge of medical science is honed not by physicians but by a cadre of actual scientists, working in laboratories far removed from patient care. Or perhaps one might conclude that the Nobel Committee and our culture at large most highly values discoveries that are based in quantifiable research on physiologic processes because they can be easily measured, but does not or is unable to reward the much more difficult to measure emotional calculus involved in medical practice.

The other adherents of silly science are legion and all feed on the new directions that emerge from research developments, no matter how fragmentary or fleeting. They include:

- the drug and medical equipment industries, whose viability relies on pumping out this year's models;
- hospitals, eager to market new and improved gizmos to help pay for an immense horde of old and outmoded ones;
- advocates of "evidence-based medicine," who try to persuade themselves that the best medicine is based on rigorous scientific studies, but who forget that science is always skewed by people with money who will pay for research into that which can make a profit, but who will never pay for research into what is simple, practical and inexpensive;
- the politically attuned folks within the federal and state health bureaucracies and associations for whom politics dictates medical policy;
- the seemingly infinite assortment of disease interest groups, for whom any new twist in treatment is worth a shot – cost not an issue.

There is an old barb about opera that whatever is too silly to be said can always be sung. A similar notion might apply to medical science: whatever is too silly to practice for long can always be proven – for now.

Science has been hijacked by the media, by healthcare profiteers, and by liability lawyers, and because science has sidetracked into a silly attempt to create an infinite life, the relationship between science and health is essentially non-existent. Science *might* someday let us understand what health is and how to improve health, but only if *we* understand health and develop ways to measure and improve it. As we shall see in the next few chapters, our attempt to measure health has been co-opted by people who had something to sell. Science itself has been similarly co-opted, so medical science is hard at work making money, promoting the idea of an infinite life, and creating a culture that is at war with the possibility of health itself.

HANCOCK COUNTY

Hancock County Tennessee was, in 1986, the fifth-poorest county in America, and the poorest county that was not an Indian reservation. I spent three years working there as a National Health Service Corps doctor, working as a family doctor at the Hancock County Health Department. The department is responsible to all the people of the county, its duties ranging from maintaining birth and death records, to checking the purity of water in wells (there was a small city waterworks, but most of the county lived off wells, and many people did not have running water), to running immunization clinics, to dental care (which was mostly extractions, because that was about all the county and state could afford), to running a visiting nurse service, to primary care, which was what I did.

The federal government had paid for the bulk of my medical education, in return for which I had agreed to spend three years serving the underserved, wherever the need was greatest. Because I was trained as a community organizer in the South Bronx, and was an experienced rabble-rouser, I had hoped to serve in the inner city, where I thought my experience could be put to the best use. But just before I finished my medical training, the government had become convinced that family doctors, who can deliver babies and care for children, adults, and elders, were most needed in rural areas. I chose Hancock County both because of the need and because my placement was in a County Health Department, which combined primary care with public health in a way I thought, and still think, makes sense.

Still, nothing prepared me for Hancock County, and nothing prepared Hancock County for me.

I was used to believing that poverty was the result of exploitation or oppression of one group of people by another. Social justice happened when the oppressed group learned to understand the system that was used to keep them down, came together to change the system, and to create justice for themselves as they learned to focus and to function as a community.

Hancock County was different. The people of Hancock County were mostly of Scots-Irish descent. Their ancestors had come in the 1700s and marched up the Cumberland Trail with Daniel Boone, settling in hilly high country with steep mountains and narrow creek and fertile river bottoms. They had eked out a living as farmers and hunters. There was almost no coal in Hancock County and the roads switched back and forth over a succession of mountain passes, so there was no easy way to get goods in or out and no reason to manufacture anything there. The Clinch River flows through the county, but it is not navigable. You have to want to go to Hancock County pretty badly in order to get there, and it's far easier to leave than it is to get there in the first place, not that leaving itself is easy.

And leave is what most people did. It was hard to make a living farming in Hancock County, but when farming was all that practically everybody in America did, people stayed to farm. For 200 years there was a rich community life supported by agriculture. People grew corn in the bottomlands, tobacco on the hillsides, and raised cattle and fowl. Every year, in the fall, there was a huge turkey drive, when all the turkeys that had been raised on the smallholds were driven over the mountain roads to market at the railhead 30 miles away.

But as soon as industrialization happened, there were other options, and the people who could compete in an industrial economy streamed away. The county's population was some 14,000 in the 1920s and 1930s. By 1986, it was a little over 6000.

The people who were left were split between retirees, who had grown up in the county, moved away, but came back to retire, and people who had trouble leaving at all, often because of physical or psychological disabilities. Concentrated in one place, the disabilities multiplied, and produced a setting where the legal system did not work, the educational system did not work, and the medical system, as I will explain, was a sham at best. Few people could read or write. Fewer still had expectations of a community in which people could care for each other.

This was not a poverty of exploitation. It was a poverty of illiteracy, evaporation, concentration and abandonment, and from the perspective of most of America, Hancock County was out of sight, out of mind.

Added to Hancock County's troubles was its healthcare system, which made a bad situation worse. In those years, the county had a 20-bed hospital, owned by the county but leased to the county's two doctors for a dollar a year. It was a hospital in name only. It had no laboratory. (I started the first lab in the county at the Health Department when I got the director to buy a culture incubator, and started running throat, blood and urine cultures by myself in a little room with a microscope, which I suspect was the only one in the county as well.) The hospital had no operating room. Its entire staff smoked, and the hospital was usually smoke-filled. Its emergency room was staffed at night by a licensed practical nurse, and everyone who came there got the same injection – lincomycin, an antibiotic that had gone out of use 20 years before, diphenhydramine, an antihistamine, and triamcinolone, a steroid. If a woman in labor got into trouble, all they could do was call Knoxville for a helicopter, wheel her out into the parking lot, and hope the weather would allow a landing. The helicopter was the treatment of choice for anyone with a serious illness, or at least, with an illness that the hospital's doctors could recognize and could figure out they needed help.

But mostly, people with serious illnesses died. There was no one in Hancock County who had a serious chronic illness that required occasional hospitalization – things like heart failure, bad lung disease, or kidney failure. People with those diseases quickly died, and they just were not there any more for any one to worry about.

As you might imagine, I had mixed feelings about using the county hospital, and the doctors in the county hospital had pretty mixed feelings about this government doctor from the East. We danced around each other for a few weeks, and finally it was decided I could admit patients there, although I also arranged to use a much more modern hospital, 30 miles over the mountains to the south.

When I started admitting patients to Hancock County Hospital, I learned how the U.S. healthcare system worked. As we took each other's measure, the hospital's doctors must have decided to try to treat me as a peer, I guess because they had no other choice, so they knuckled under, and hoped for the best.

One day in the fall of 1986, old Dr. Pierce, who hailed from Mountain City, Tennessee and who had done a one-year internship 40 years before, sat me down to educate me about how to practice. I was not without the arrogance of the young and energetic, but I really did want to learn, and I really did want to work with the town's medical community and see what we could accomplish together. But I was not prepared for what I was about to hear.

"Here's how we work it," Dr. Pierce said, drawing on a cigarette. "You tell some people you see, those that look pretty bad, that they are sick and likely to die, and have to come into the hospital. We put 'em in for a week or two, and give 'em antibiotics and vitamins. If they get better, folks will think you're a great doctor. And if they die, folks will think you're a great diagnostician. We do not have much here, just an old x-ray machine, so we have to make do with what we got."

I learned later what Dr. Pierce did not tell me, and why he wanted me to follow that advice.

What Dr. Pierce did not tell me was what happened to the people who got admitted to their hospital and did not know how the world worked. For people with Medicare, the government paid their bill. For people with "combine" insurance, they got a check for every day in the hospital, which was usually much more than they could ever hope to earn in the County, and the hospital got paid as well. But people without insurance (few people in town had commercial insurance, because there were no jobs and no employers to supply it) were expected to pay the bill themselves. People who could not pay were taken to court, even though they had stayed in a county-owned hospital. Because first Dr. Pierce, and then Dr. Bell (his partner), chaired the County Commission (they were elected because people respected their education and profession), the county court always found for the doctors; they would put people into bankruptcy and take their homes and land away. Pierce and Bell were the wealthiest men in the county, each owning thousands of acres of the best grazing land, on which they ran herds of purebred cattle.

And the county sank deeper and deeper into poverty.

My time in Hancock County stirred plenty of controversy. The local doctors leaned on their Congressman, and I was forced to stop delivering babies, because I could not imagine doing deliveries in Hancock County and arranged to do them at the more modern hospital over the mountain. I tried to put a stop to the practice of admitting people with combine insurance so they could collect, and that did not add to my popularity. I was not willing to give people open-ended prescriptions for narcotics (prescription drug abuse was one of the county's many social problems), and that did not make me popular either. I ended up feuding with the aging, diabetic nurse practitioner, who feuded with everyone who came on her turf. But I was able to get a lab started, get more patients seen, start a case conference with the county's visiting nurse service and social workers, and we started one of the first HIV prevention programs in the country. I learned a lot about being a doctor there, and Hancock County put up with me for three years, because a number of jobs depended on my being there in the Health Department, and good federal jobs are hard to come by.

In Hancock County, the relationship between medicine, health, community, and economy was laid out most starkly. It was clear there that health is a concept that can be exploited, twisted and used as a cover for profit and as cover for one person to get economic advantage over another or one class to get economic and political advantage over everyone else. Medicine can be the equal application of science and experience. It can be put to use as un-self-interested advocacy in the service of individuals and communities by promoting the relationships that make the whole greater than the sum of the parts and make life chances equal for everyone. However, medicine usually is an instrument of exploitation, the piano on which the tune of health as a cover for profit is played. A viable community depends on balance, on a level playing field, where all the players are willing to contribute equally, and everyone recognizes the need to make the whole greater than the sum of the parts. For health and medicine, that means focusing on the health of the community, on the ways in which medicine can improve the ability of people to function in the relationships needed to make the whole greater than the sum of the parts, instead of turning shared resources into personal profit. And if someone in a community takes advantage, be it doctors or lawyers or police or judges or teachers or used car salesmen, and no one stops them, the economy of a place will slide into collapse, and carry the culture of a place into collapse with it.

There are relationships among community, income, health, and healthcare. These linkages are complex, but they must be addressed if we are to evolve a healthcare system that is rational, personal, affordable, and just, and if we are to have a society in which we are to be able to lead lives with value and meaning.

PART TWO

what went wrong and why

THE HAPPY VICTIM

It is pretty unusual for me to see someone wearing sunglasses in the examining room, but that is the first thing I remember about Betty Devon. Betty, a nurse, was 60 when I met her, and I could not see her eyes. She was angry at me, though she and I had just met. She was angry at me, angry at doctors and angry at the world. It was an anger that would pass, and an anger that I would come to understand, but still it should have never been allowed to grow in the way it grew, or damage others, and Betty herself, in the way it did.

Betty was referred to me by a very wise, very kind gastroenterologist who I barely knew. She had chronic stomach pain, had every test in the book, and Dr. G. hadn't been able to help her – what did he know? She smoked two packs a day and assured me she was never going to quit even if it killed her, drank a little, and was taking every expensive stomach medicine known to man. She had come to me when Dr. G. had given up on her.

Her sunglasses and anger told me that she was a woman who was going to have a hard time tolerating any pain, no matter how slight. A very smart gastroenterologist hadn't helped reduce her pain, so I decided we were going to look other places and at other options. First, we were going to try antidepressants. Then we were going to look for other causes of her pain, such as her back and chest, both of which sometimes cause abdominal pain.

It took some doing before I got Betty to try antidepressants, and no trial was ever a bigger failure. Each drug we tried sometimes caused side effects, and Betty had all of them. Not only did the medicine not work, it made her sicker, angrier and more depressed. The evaluation of her back, by x-rays and physical therapy, yielded nothing. Finally, we got a chest x-ray. That showed a shadow, which led us to a fancy CT scan. On the CT scan was Betty's large lung tumor.

No one likes to give another person bad news and having learned to live with Betty's anger, I was not looking forward to telling her about the lung cancer, but I called her and asked her to come right over. Usually, when I make a call like that, the person I call gets incredibly anxious. So I was prepared for that anxiety, in addition to the anger, and I was probably feeling a little guilty for not having started with the chest x-ray. Knowing Betty, I prepared myself for an angry lecture, an accusation, and probably a lawsuit.

When I walked into the room, Betty's sunglasses were off, and she was smiling at me. "I know about the tumor, doctor," she said. "The tech told me. I hope you aren't angry at me."

I then witnessed the most amazing transformation I have ever seen in a patient. Betty suddenly became a person of sweetness and light. She understood the meaning of her lung cancer, and she was committed to fighting and winning, though she knew few people survive lung cancer for more than about a year. She was marshalling her forces. She was realistic enough to start getting her affairs in order and she was going to be spending every waking moment with her family and friends, the people who were closest to her. She was going to manage her pain with natural remedies, diet and exercise and perhaps a little help from me. She even worried about how I was feeling, because she knew that telling someone about a cancer must be a very hard thing to do.

I was really surprised by what was happening and how it had happened. It was almost as if Betty's cancer was a sort of gift – a challenge that had awakened her hidden goodness. I arranged for her to see an oncologist and started her on pain medicine to use at night, so she could sleep.

The next few months brought more of the same. Betty remained the happy, motivated person she had suddenly become. She started chemotherapy and radiation therapy with some success; her tumor shrank and for a time was undetectable. Her pain slowly progressed but we were able to control it with a mix of various, mostly narcotic, medications, which I am only comfortable using chronically when cancer causes intractable, and finally terminal, pain. It's the only compassionate thing to do. When the cancer recurred, as I knew it would, Betty cried. We talked about what she wanted, and I told her that all the choices were hers, that she was in charge of what happened. We talked about very hard choices. Did she want heroic measures? Did she want to be at home? Who would make decisions for her? Her choices were much the same as I think I would make for myself. She wanted hospice, she wanted to be at home, she wanted medications to keep her comfortable. She could not decide on a decision maker but she wanted no heroic measures. She did not want to go on a ventilator because it was unlikely she could come off it, and she treasured her independence and autonomy. There is no such thing as a good death, but she wanted to die with dignity and at peace.

Then one day I got a call from the emergency room. Betty had been brought to the hospital by ambulance because she was completely disoriented. She had overdosed on medications. As I drove to the hospital, I downplayed the significance of what I had heard. With the amount of narcotics she needed to control her pain, Betty might easily slip and take too much. We would watch her in the hospital for a day or two to make sure she was safe, and review how to take the medications more appropriately, and get her home quickly.

I was not prepared for Betty's two sons. They were both younger than me and were both extremely concerned, but not about the cancer. They were concerned about her drug abuse.

And so the truth unfolded.

Betty had been a prescription drug addict all her life. Her parents, who were addicts themselves, had addicted their little girl to prescription drugs when she was only a child. She had lived her life skirting the law and inventing one ailment after another to get drugs. She was always angry at doctors because she was afraid they wouldn't give her drugs, and her anger seemed to work as a way to get drugs for her because doctors would often prescribe something just to get rid of her. She had become a nurse to get drugs; she used to steal them from patients and lost her nursing license when she finally got caught.

Now her transformation made sense to me. For Betty, whose life was made hard by her inability to get drugs, cancer was a gift, an open door to what she wanted – a treatment, if you will, for her underlying anxiety. She had a way to get drugs. She did not need to lie, cheat or steal. The pressure was off.

The only problem was, once she had access to drugs, she could not control herself. Her sons told me she had been drinking bottles of morphine, which we administer by the dropper, or at most, by the teaspoon. She drank morphine until she was unconscious. Then she would sleep away the day.

Betty's sons did not believe she had cancer. We spent a very tough half hour together as I told them that her cancer was very real and that she was dying.

The next few months were difficult. On the one hand, Betty did better than expected and functioned for two and a half years. On the other hand, managing her medications, and balancing compassion against drug pushing, was a tight wire act. She overdosed a few times. We talked. She got anxious again. The cancer stopped working as an automatic way to get drugs.

As I came to know Betty and her sons, I began to understand that hers was a life and these were relationships that had been put on hold. Her focus on drugs had made Betty defer all the rest of life's pleasures. She rose in the morning and went to sleep at night thinking about drugs and putting off for tomorrow all the other useful, important, and pleasurable things about which people dream. Because there was still a kernel of goodness in her, she had lots of hopes and dreams about helping people and being with people, but those were never realized. They were, from her perspective, only postponed, including her relationships with her children. Both her sons were worried about her, felt responsible for her and yearned for her attention and approval, which they never even once received – because all her attention was directed elsewhere. It was not an unfinished life. It was a life that had never really stared.

Finally, the cancer recurred and was everywhere. Betty's body was failing. There was cancer in her trachea, which began to close. She came to the hospital, and I worked out a medication plan that would keep her comfortable as her breathing stopped. I rechecked the plan with her. That was what she wanted.

Soon the hospital called. Betty was being moved to the ICU. Her sons had come to say goodbye, and suddenly insisted that she be put on a ventilator just as her breathing was stopping. The hospital staff did what they were supposed to do. They work to preserve life if there is any question. Betty was on the ventilator.

In the ICU, and in the weeks thereafter, we discussed again what Betty wanted. There was no hope of ever coming off the ventilator. Betty would spend the rest of her life on a ventilator, in the hospital (because none of her children were willing to take care of her – her daughters hated her and refused to come to see her), unless she chose to stop the ventilator. But she did not make that choice. Hustling herself to the end, pushed hard by the sons who could not let go of a mother they never really had, Betty convinced herself that maybe she would have a chance to finish the life she never even really started.

Eventually, she moved to a special hospital that cares for ventilator patients. She lived for about 15 months, always on the ventilator, weakening into coma, and never even able to talk.

Here's the problem: Betty's choices are hard to second-guess. Her life was all she had, and she chose to not value it, which broke my heart, thinking about her and the good life that she abandoned. Perhaps if Betty had lived her life fully and had been able to see and spend time with the people she loved, she might have refused the ventilator and died peacefully, but who can say?

The cost of her care, at the end of her life, was a million dollars or more. Because of Medicare and Medicaid, it was a cost she or her family did not have to bear.

Every day, I see or hear about people who cannot make ends meet, who strive to make something of their lives but hit roadblocks every way they turn. No education. No good way to make a living. Elderly parents or disabled kids to care for. No good place to live. Disability or disease. I hear about these people, and I think about the million dollars we spent keeping Betty alive to try to finish a life she had postponed. By our current policy choices, we are saying we will support Betty's "heroic" care instead of investing in a kid from the inner city who does not have a decent school, or an immigrant from West Africa or Mexico who does not have a decent place to live, or a tobacco farmer from Tennessee or a Navaho from New Mexico who do not have access to decent medical services.

Betty never started her life, and never took responsibility for repairing it. Many people made a lot of money during Betty's last days, providing expensive, very high tech care because we, as a culture, have confused longevity with health and access to all technology with justice – and because Betty had a diagnosis that justified spending the money, a diagnosis none of those people in need have.

Is this what we want? Is it fair? Is it just? Is it right? Should we all wish for a diagnosis as a way to get our fair share?

We are all asked to pay the cost of Betty's inability to make a life for herself and her family. It is hard to say no to someone who is dying. How, then, are we able to say no to education, jobs, and decent housing, for the millions of people who are only trying to live?

the human tsunami

As we pointed out in Part One, what passes for our healthcare system is a mess. There are at least two explanations for that mess. Perhaps, we have misunderstood the meaning of health, and have not focused on making health. But perhaps we have changed! Perhaps the human project is moving in a different direction, and relationship is not so important to who we are as it once was. Let's look at these two possible underlying explanations of the failure of the healthcare system in the United States. Let's look at the direction of the human project, and at the stresses and strains on our ability to have relationships with one another. In this part, we will look at the culture's understanding of the meaning of health, and the stresses, strains, pulls and pushes on health as a concept itself.

THE NUMBERS GAME

About 50,000 years ago, physical evolutionary improvements, tools, and the development of agriculture removed some of the rigor of life that had limited humankind to a tiny few. Over the past 20,000 years, the human population has grown exponentially, altering the nature of humans and the place of relationship forever. Let us see how evolutionary success has changed the meaning of relationship and community and how the shift relates to the meaning of health in modern times.

For two million years, emerging human life changed little. We made very gradual physical adaptations to our environments, which supported our ability to talk, think, form social groupings, and work together in order to survive. We developed primitive tools that improved our efficiency – stone axes, grinding tools and the like. One hundred square miles of fertile land could support 50 people.[1] Then, suddenly, about 20,000 years ago, we hit an evolutionary tipping point. During the next 500 human generations we evolved the tools and thinking needed to create early agricultural societies. At this time 100 square miles of fertile land can support perhaps 10,000 people – a twenty-fold increase in density from earlier times.[2]

The next great technological jump did not begin until the Renaissance and with it the invention of the printing press, magnetic compass and gunpowder, the liberalizing effect of the Protestant Reformation, along with many other inventions and new ideas. As the scholar Ramus enthused, "In one century we have seen a greater progress in man and works of learning than our ancestors had seen in the whole course of the previous fourteen centuries."[3] By the 18th century, these new concepts and technologies brought on the beginning of the Industrial Revolution. Since then, our tools quickly became so efficient that we could ignore the fertility of the land, creating our own environments in which to produce food, and 100 square miles of settled land now supports as many as 10 to 20 million people.[4]

During two million years, the population grew from a scattered few people to two or three million, thought to be concentrated entirely in Africa until about 100,000 years ago and growing only very slightly from year to year, century to century. The actual change in the percentage rate of population growth was relatively small, but the rate belies the explosion

FIGURE 7.1 Human population growth since 10,000 BC

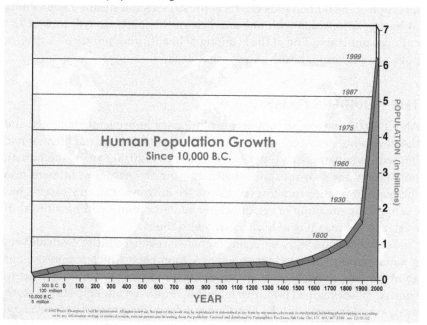

Source: © 2002 Bruce Thompson / Pangraphics LLC. Used by permission.

of absolute numbers crowding into limited space. From 20,000 years ago to 1900, the world population increased by an approximate factor of 750, and, thus, grew by a rate of about 3.75 percent per year. From 1900 to 2000, the population approximately quadrupled, raising the growth rate to about four percent annually. From 20,000 years ago to 1900, the population grew from perhaps two million to approximately 1.5 billion. Over the last century, human population grew from 1.5 billion to over six billion.[5] The full ramifications of our population explosion are very difficult to grasp, but the most obvious fact is that we live in an era of unprecedented human concentration: one-twentieth of all the human beings who have ever lived are alive today.

This one-quarter of one percent increase in the rate of growth produced profound effects during the last century, not only in the sheer magnitude of population growth but also in the widespread social and cultural changes in society brought on by the lives and needs of so many more people. We have gone from a few bands of hunter-gatherers, ranging over open land, to a packed, squirming mass with little usable open space, all within an evolutionary instant: a demographic tidal wave of our own making has washed over us and has carried away thousands of years of culture and values.

THREE CULTURES

The ages-long evolutionary cycle of mutually affecting biological, technological, and social factors has produced a shifting series of intellectual frameworks, which have changed our view of ourselves and our understanding of the human project, and with those changes, have changed the meaning of health. We will call those cultures that take a portion of their sustenance from hunting or gathering, and for whom the greatest value is the support and survival of the group, *primitive* culture. We will term cultures that draw sustenance from farming or manufacturing and that are characterized by a focus on the importance of the individual *modern* cultures. *Postmodern* culture is the culture of abundance, in which the activities of daily living have a weak or unperceivable link to sustenance. Postmodernism is a culture that emphasizes the importance of parts or aspects of individuals, as distinct from the whole person – the ultimate embodiment (actually, *dis*embodiment) of the reductionist, analytic thinking that Burke and Ornstein term "cut-measure-and-control".[6]

These three cultures (or "mindsets" or "intellectual and social orientations"), primitive, modern and postmodern, are not mutually exclusive. They exist simultaneously and affect individuals who experience and are shaped by them in different ways. Primitive cultures persist in parts of the Third World, and, closer to home, in rural America and even within our largest cities. Modern culture, while beginning to give way to postmodernism, still exerts enormous influence in industrialized societies and in the upper, middle and mercantile classes of the Developing World. The influence of postmodern culture is just beginning to make itself felt here and around the world. Its ramifications remain uncertain and incompletely understood, even though information technology and recent developments in communications, bioscience, nanotechnology and other fields are permeating society with disarming rapidity.

The primitive world

In primitive cultures, wandering bands lived in close relationship to their environment, and worked together to survive within it. The band had primacy, and the role of the individual was to support the survival of the band. Though the bands were able to affect their environment, wiping out herds of large slow-moving animals or burning forests to drive animals over cliffs or into lakes, the spiritual life of the bands suggested they did not see themselves as anything but a part of the environment, responding to it. They made no conscious attempt to change the environment in any permanent way and lacked capacity to do so. If we can retroactively assign a political *zeitgeist* to primitive times, we would term it mutual aid; commune-ism or collectivism, noting that it is unlikely individuals even had personal names or a clearly defined concept of selfhood until 20,000 years ago.[7] The primitive self, if not empty, was directed outward toward the interests and survival of the community. Primitive art was integral art; that is, the cave drawings were sacramentals of shamanism and ritual that sought to calm spirits and forces that primitive people did not understand and sought to mollify. Health, in primitive culture, is the ability to function as part of the band, supporting the survival of all.

Two forces supplanted the primitive period, which ended for different cultures at different times and persists in some isolated places even now. First, the development and use of tools increased human efficiency. Tools freed humans from total daily dependence on nature and each other for survival, unlike the situation of the primitive hunter-gatherers. Tools also made the essential connection of people to the natural world and each other less important, seeding the existential doubts and intra-psychic conflicts that have become increasingly pervasive, apparent and destructive, as we have moved further away from the primitive state. Second, tools and the efficiencies they brought allowed population growth, leading to specialization and fixed concentrations of people in villages, towns, and cities.[8] Population growth and the emergence of distinct occupations, classes, religions, castes, and languages separated and concentrated parts of the population into groups, inside which individuals retained relationships, but outside of which people came to be perceived as increasingly alien and apart. This *concentration effect* fostered both group identity and conflict between groups, and changed forever the character of the relationships among people.[9]

Modernism

Modern culture began when technologies arose that allowed individuals to function independently of the group or tribe. Although some elements of modernism emerged as early as classical Greece, the development of the printing press in 1439 can serve as a convenient threshold to the modern era.

The watchword of modernism is the individual's desire and capacity to control context and environment. Modernism values the individual's autonomy, rights, and happiness. In its focus on the individual, modernism deconstructs family and community. The modernistic self has shifted inward to become "full of oneself", "self-absorbed", and "self-directed". For extreme apostles of individualism, like Ayn Rand, selfishness is the greatest virtue and the only authentic behavior; responsibility to others is misguided. This is the hard world of the intellectual cowboy, a grizzled, take-no-prisoners frontier where love gives way to narcissism and kindness is cant. Health in modern culture is a mixture of strength (the ability to function in the marketplace, advocating for oneself), awareness (the ability to be alert to opportunities), interpersonal openness (the ability to welcome relationships, which exist as consumer goods) and longevity (the ability to be around long enough to consume as much as possible).

The negative aspects of modernism are accelerating in 21st-century America, even as the rising swells of postmodernism are breaking on the social shore. Robert Putnam, whose ideas we will discuss at greater length later, has richly documented the declining levels of social interaction, community and political involvement, and deteriorating sense of social responsibility and mutual respect in contemporary America. All manner of social behaviours, from voting to sewing circles to stopping at stop signs, are vanishing, as self-assertiveness, enabled by the mobility of the automobile and the autoerotic passivity of television, overwhelms the (primitive) bonds of community.

Modernism's intellectual attitude is *perspective*, whereby a person sees him or herself as separate from his or her world. That perspective allows the person to analyze the world as an object, as an outside, and to divide it into parts by drawing distinctions between like and dislike characteristics. One can then measure those parts, use them to predict their behavior and then to change the environment in which they exist. As the tools of perspective, mathematics and science are "modern" phenomena. Modernism's political lifeblood is possessive individualism, wherein society's motive force is the need of one person to acquire whatever is needed to establish and maintain autonomy.[10] The role of the state becomes that of a broker, insuring that contending individuals can compete fairly and safely in a rational marketplace. The fully evolved modern economic system is consumer capitalism.

Modernism opened the floodgate to the idea of progress, which emerged with Cartesian mechanics, a sense of the superiority of the present over the past and a robust role for the individual as the champion of change. The ideas of humanity's steady advancement, increasing technological competence and of mastery over the environment were not viable until the approach of the Age of Enlightenment. Before then, the stultifying dominance of the Church and its subordination of earthly aspirations to heavenly ones, the expectation that the world would end, if not imminently, then too soon to bother doing much new, and a cowed inferiority before the intellectual titans of Greece and Rome, all had denied the concept of progress a toehold.

Once in place, progress might apply to the gradual perfection of the intellect, the comity of society, or moral development. We have most often associated progress with the human capacity to control the physical environment, with increasing skill. However, just as with the compass of the self, the machine of scientific progress has gradually turned inward. From a "cut-measure-and-control" attention aimed at the external, phenomenal world, we have refocused the lens to examine human biology as well as human motivations, actions, beliefs, and behaviors. Ready to hand are the millimeter-thick slices of the Visible Human Project and the million connections of the human genome. The psychology of the twenties and thirties, which broke the human psyche and the human community into its constituent parts, has spawned the marketing stratification of 21st-century America.[11] Psycho-demographic mappings of every American market can now be had – for a price. The next step, the deconstruction of the individual as the building block of community and civil society, appears a logical, if unfortunate, forgone conclusion.

Emergence of the postmodern

Postmodernism is our newest intellectual and cultural framework, which began to emerge only as we neared the edges of modernism's reductionist mechanism. In classical art, a picture's point of view allows it to create representational accuracy, but constrains the artist to capture only one momentary glance of an infinitely diverse space-time continuum. Similarly, classical science enabled us to reduce matter to particles and to work as chemists, engineers, and taxonomists, but could not allow us to move beyond matter and into energy.

Late 19th-century and early 20th-century art provides a window on the transition from modernism to postmodernism. Escaping from the hard-edged, rigidly representational and concrete, the Impressionists strove to capture the indefinite and ambiguous – to broaden reality by suggesting its subtlety and ineffability. Seurat and his pointillist colleagues attempted to atomize the material world into artfully deployed dots. Pointillist and Impressionist art straddle the fracture line between the modern and the postmodern, yet both retained a single perspective and so were trapped between two worlds.

It was Picasso who first crossed over, atomizing not only content but also perspective, making it multidimensional and situational. We could experience multiple places and times at once, and gain a fuller view of the world. As the century proceeded, art would seek to escape depiction altogether and to denote itself. Magritte's pipe is not a pipe (*Ceçi n'est pas une pipe*, 1926). Warhol's can is a brand and is the whole of consumer capitalism, turned in on itself.

Niels Bohr, Werner Heisenberg, Albert Einstein and their understanding of quantum mechanics and relativity also peeled away the constraints of earlier material constructs, allowing us to manipulate energy and to imagine a nonlinear universe far more complex than had been conceived before. The hard, knowable edges of the Cartesian device gave way to a soft-edged, fluid and multidimensional universe of approximate locations, uncertainty, complexity, and conditional states. The intellectual solution to the problem of control over the environment was to develop a theory of randomness; our ability to limit and contain, to cut-measure-and-control chaos and complexity provided us a stepping-stone to the next levels of reality, crossing from materiality to energy and time. Randomness also implied the deconstruction of the observer. Our acceptance of randomness allows us to abandon the fixed perspective. The intellectual posture that includes the ability to predict the occurrence of random events also permits us to cut and measure, predict, and control phenomena from multiple theoretical perspectives, from which multiple measurements can be extrapolated. And so more of the environment, which now includes our intra-psychic state and the brain chemistry associated with our emotions, thoughts, and perceptions, can be controlled.

With postmodernism, moral and ethical considerations of progress become detached from the scientific ones. The spirit of the times changed from a belief in progress, to *vicissitude*: a sense of being overwhelmed, or lost, in a world that is progressively complex but in which material goods are abundant. All events, concepts, ideas, and values are equal and appear to occur at once, randomly. There is no need to do anything but consume; there is only the expression, or acting out, of individual, momentary desires, fantasies, wants and needs, so there appears to be no need for family or authentic community. In the postmodern world, there is no human project, so there is no concept of health. Health becomes an old idea, a predicate of an antique culture, like chivalry or animal sacrifice. Looking backward from the "perspective" of postmodern culture, we see that health *was* the ability of people to be in relationship. Looking forward, into the vortex of a post-postmodern future, we see that health is about to become simply instrumentality, just the ability of body parts to function in achieving a goal, like winning a race, or permitting unending life. Unless, of course, we think, act together, and change that future, pulling it back toward the fundamental human project of relationship and meaning.

Postmodernism now seeks to exploit the cut-measure-and-control process to analyze and manage each part of ourselves – each whim and quirk, each tendency and inclination. Our self-directed analysis has enabled us to measure consumer behavior with precision and to sell everything from goods and services to ideas and social issues with considerable success. However, this capability has created a new existential dilemma: we understand our parts, but we have lost our whole. Postmodern culture does not – and very likely cannot – understand or value the unique identity of the individual to whom those parts belong, nor can the postmodern consumerist culture even make sense of the families and communities that made us who we are, and heretofore have given human life meaning and value. Our prowess atomizes us. Our lives are boxed sets. Jobs and professions go here; personal lives go there. Here an interest in skiing and its attendant technologies. There our interest in pinebox derbies, and their attendant technologies. Here gardening, there wood-splitting. Here music or movies on Saturday night, there family time, though it is a family time perceived only as a commodity. But where is the ineffable value of family and community as the source and succor of a larger self, a self that is wise and resilient and reaches back into the beginning of time, and forward, as hope, into the unimaginable future?

Postmodern culture does to individuals what modernism has done to the band and the family – it deconstructs them. The political theory of post-modernism is oligarchy, because the technology of governing interests is unrelated to the needs, rights, and balance between individuals. However, this culture is only dawning and the new day may yet take a different turn. Consumer capitalism persists as the economic spirit of postmodernism, but perhaps a new economic theory will emerge, once the dominant culture successfully undermines the meaning of individuals – or unless we become dismayed by our trajectory and develop the resources to change its course.

Culturally and philosophically, postmodernism signals our arrival at the outer limits of modernism's struggle to control the material world. We have solved the technical if not the moral problems of food and shelter. We live in abundance, if not in comity. Our conquest presents a challenge: now, what are we to do and where is meaning to come from? The world is subjugated, the striving together after food and shelter resolved, and defining a satisfying concept of human function and significance becomes a particularly thorny and frightening task. For perhaps 200,000 human generations, our striving together defined us. Our social nature produced intellect, language, ideas, culture, and meaning that made us who we were. Who are we now? Who do we wish to become?

New technologies (the Industrial Revolution followed by the electronic and biological ones) accompanied by rapidly increasing population have remade us twice in 200 years: first evolving modern culture out of primitive culture; and then postmodern culture out of the modern one. As in some unimaginably vast tectonic upwelling, the inexorable pressure of these huge intellectual and cultural shifts has wrenched and reshaped human self-image, and undermined every dogma, social structure and harbor of emotional refuge. Insofar as these shifts have caused us to remake the totality of our feelings and ideas, they have also changed our concept of health. Massive cultural upheaval within the lifetime and memory of individuals assaults their identity and makes a coherent self-concept, and a coherent notion of individual health, challenging at best, and perhaps, at the end of the day, absurd.

AMERICA'S LONELY CROWD

Time, evolution, language, thought, and technology had repeatedly made and remade humankind over the last three million years. At a far faster pace, over just a few centuries, we have remade the human project yet again in North America. Colonists brought a European culture skimmed off the top of a slowly emerging belief in progress into a continent brimming with rich resources. They combined this with a wanton disregard for what, and who, was already there, and then fired the pot to a rolling boil, making and remaking the human project and our self-conception over and over again.[12]

The United States is a powerful place, energetic and teeming with ideas, rich, profligate and proud. The nation wields more influence than any empire before it, and has changed the physical condition of the world far more profoundly than any previous power. At the pinnacle of the modern world, the United States both enjoys the greatest benefits of human creativity and suffers its greatest consequences. The natural abundance of the land, the dumb luck of historic coincidence, our rich scrappy diversity, our good-natured, damn-the-torpedoes faith in a limitless frontier, our unique national genius – all have had a hand in the crafting of America. However, several overarching forces characterize American life: our social commitment to the idea of progress; progressive, unrelenting urbanization, which that social commitment produced; and the social, political, and environmental change that urbanization unleashed.

FIGURE 7.2 Population of the 24 American urban places, 1790

Rank	Place	Population
1	New York city, NY	33,131
2	Philadelphia city, PA	28,522
3	Boston town, MA	18,320
4	Charleston city, SC	16,359
5	Baltimore town, MD	13,503
6	Northern Liberties township, PA	9,913
7	Salem town, MA	7,921
8	Newport town, RI	6,716
9	Providence town, RI	6,380
10	Marblehead town, MA	5,661
10	Southwark district, PA	5,661
12	Gloucester town, MA	5,317
13	Newburyport town, MA	4,837
14	Portsmouth town, NH	4,720
15	Sherburne town (Nantucket), MA	4,620
16	Middleborough town, MA	4,526
17	New Haven city, CT	4,487
18	Richmond city, VA	3,761
19	Albany city, NY	3,498
20	Norfolk borough, VA	2,959
21	Petersburg town, VA	2,828
22	Alexandria town, VA	2,748
23	Hartford city, CT	2,683
24	Hudson city, NY	2,584

Source: U.S. Bureau of the Census.

Although there is disagreement about when early Americans arrived on the continent, the first humans probably crossed the land bridge from Asia to Alaska twenty to thirty thousand years ago. From a few hunter-gatherer migrants, the continental population slowly grew over a span of between six and fifteen thousand years and probably numbered between 900,000 and 12 million, speaking over a thousand languages and living as hundreds of tribes, by the time of Columbus' arrival.[13] By five thousand years ago, when the Babylonian, Assyrian, and Egyptian civilizations arose in the East, the North American native peoples had developed agricultural societies, and some lived in cities with populations as large as 10,000. Infectious diseases that spread at about the time of the arrival of Europeans decimated these populations. The numbers of European settlers also grew slowly at first, and though that growth quickened as the native population died off or was killed by the European invaders, North America remained sparsely populated and rural well into the 19th century.

At the time of the American Revolution, the United States was a country of frontier people, citizen farmers who lived in isolated farms and villages, slaves who comprised about 20 percent of the non-native population, and native people who lived in tribal cultures.[14] In 1790, the time of the first census, the population of the United States was just under four million people, 95 percent of whom lived in rural places. That year, only 24 towns had populations greater than 2,500; New York, the largest city in the country, had 33,000 residents. The nation's total "urban" population was about 200,000.

Over the next four decades, New York grew some six-fold, to over 200,000, and eight cities had grown to over 20,000 inhabitants. Just as in England and Europe, the Industrial Revolution and the factories and mills it created concentrated population, drawing people away from farms and villages and into rapidly enlarging cities characterized by unhealthful and squalid conditions for much of the working poor.

By 1900, as the United States industrialized, the total population reached 76 million, of whom 40 percent dwelt in urban and 60 percent in rural areas. It was not until about 1915, when the population reached 100 million, that Americans evenly split between urban and rural dwellers.

Since then, we have increasingly become an urban country. Seventy-nine percent of Americans now live in urban areas (defined as places with populations of greater than 2,500) and only 21 percent remain in rural areas.[15] Although urban population figures include both city dwellers and suburbanites (people living in suburbs now comprise about two-thirds of those counted as urban, and about 50 percent of the total U.S. population), we have experienced a fundamental demographic shift from a rural agrarian populace to an urban and suburban one.[16] Indeed, by 2000, only about two million people, or 0.7 percent of the total U.S. population, worked on a farm.[17]

FIGURE 7.3 American cities over 10,000 in 1830

New York	202,589
Baltimore	80,620
Philadelphia	80,462 (155,000 including suburbs)
Boston	61,392
New Orleans	46,082
Charleston	30,289
N. Liberties	28,872
Cincinnati	24,831
Albany	24,209
Southwark*	20,581
Washington, DC	18,826
Providence	16,833
Richmond	16,060
Salem, MA	13,895
Kensington*	13,394
Portland, ME	12,598
Pittsburgh	12,568
Brooklyn, NY	12,406
Troy, NY	11,556
Spring Garden*	11,140

* *Philadelphia suburb*

Source: U.S. Bureau of the Census.

American urbanization has not merely altered demography but the whole of society. In the post-Civil War era, we lived on farms, in rural villages and mill-towns, and a few "walkable" cities. The mill-towns, where much of the urban population resided, were small communities of workers, many of them immigrants, brought together to supply labor to a single factory. Working conditions in mills were arduous and dangerous, and the mill-workers often inhumanly exploited in abysmal conditions sometimes referred to as "northern slavery" by the system's critics.[18] The mill villages supplied workers and their families with housing. Some mills provided medical care and education for the mill worker's children (who were often pressed into child labor, because their small fingers and bodies were invaluable in the tight spaces of mechanized looms and overcrowded mills). The mill owners sold the workers their food and clothing, often at inflated prices, and using inflated interest calculations, which kept the workers in virtual indentured servitude. Despite the blatant exploitation of workers by the mill-owners, each mill village comprised a single, tightly knit, geographically compact community centered on the workplace. In their focus of shared experience and place, these mill villages resembled rural communities. Like the decline of small towns and villages throughout America, the breakup of the mill village system began in the early 1900s and was complete by the 1970s. Occupational and social mobility, especially after World War II, and the enormous popularity of the automobile sealed the fate of many small communities and dissolved some of the social integrity that had previously characterized urban places.

Merely citing America's ongoing trend toward urbanization and noting the social deconstruction that accompanied it fails to capture the full implications of Urban America. Urban environments concentrate not only people but also challenges, opportunities and differences and thus distinguish urban life from that in rural environments in a fundamental social sense.

City life alters the access to and likelihood of relationships and, among many other consequences, undermines, for many urban dwellers, the social context necessary to support health. The *concentration effect* in urban places changes the rules of the relations between people. Because of their size and complexity, cities house many discrete, diverse worlds. Urban places, taken as a whole, may sometimes only vary slightly from rural places in terms of race, class, income, access to healthcare, and environmental exposures. However, urban places magnify differences between people. They concentrate those of one race or ethnicity, those who share a language different from those around them, people who are poor, people with chronic mental illness, and people who are exposed to environmental and occupational hazards in one neighborhood, area, or community.[19]

The benefit of urban diversity is that it is stimulating and intellectually challenging; its serious shortcoming is the degree and intensity of its extremes, and the lack of social contact, much less cohesion and feeling of mutual community, between them. In many rural places, people see themselves as one community. There is a natural opportunity for people to know and care for each other. In urban places, because of the segregation of rich and poor, black and white and Hispanic, and the scale of the urban environment, people are less able to see themselves as a single community and their opportunities to care for each other are lessened as well. Among other results, this intensifies the deprivation experienced by the disadvantaged. Cities have become places in which there is starvation in the midst of plenty, sickness in the midst of the best healthcare technology in the world, and homelessness in the midst of bounty and comfort.

Urban life is not only fractionated but also *complex*, in the sense described by Fitzpatrick and LaGory.[20] The continuous density, stress, and stimulus of concentrated population multiply the concentration effect. Some people have always found the crush and excitement of city life a tonic, but for the very poor and alienated, an urban environment can be a fearful and lonely place. The term "inner city," defined as census tracts within Metropolitan Statistical Areas, in which the household incomes of 40 percent of the residents are below the poverty line, fails to capture the social challenges people must face in some of these urban places. The harsh, vitiating environment of many urban places produces what health theorist Dennis Andrulis calls the *urban health penalty*, in which the intensity, complexity of circumstances, and concentration effect combine to make the health of inner-city residents worse than any other place in the United States. As one pointed example, the life expectancy of African American men in New York City is lower than the life expectancy of men in Bangladesh.[21]

Note that the negative consequences of the concentration effect and urban complexity are neither new nor limited to the United States. Harsh, squalid, unhealthy environments and rigid divisions by race, class, nationality, and income characterize numerous cities worldwide. However, it is arguably among America's saddest distinctions that so wealthy and robust a society has sustained such dismal and extreme conditions in a nation of unprecedented plenty.

WHAT DOES THIS ABBREVIATED CULTURAL HISTORY TELL US ABOUT HEALTH?

Until very recent times, relationship and community have comprised the essential precondition for understanding ourselves. Human beings are social beings; our interaction with each other defines the historical core of humanness. Interaction enabled our gradual development of technology and this role as *Homo fabricans* prompted increased brain capacity, the development of language, thought and consciousness. The modern and postmodern narrowing of focus, first to the individual and then to the individual's components, runs counter to the concepts of relationship, family and community that are innate aspects of the human character and continue to be critical to our comfort and happiness. To the extent that modern and postmodern societies undermine these values, it is the structure of society itself that has created the depersonalization, alienation, loss, stress, and anxiety that lie at the core of America's social derailment. Our social structure appears to be at war with our health.

If, as we believe, humanness is a function of relationship and health is a social attribute, how is health possible in the absence of family and community relationships? Surely, our current situation demonstrates widespread social pathology. Thirty to 50 percent of Americans will be clinically depressed at least one time in their lifetimes, with six to eight percent suffering clinical depression at any given moment. Ten to fifteen percent have or think they have attention deficit disorder. Nearly two percent are in jail. Close to a third smoke, self-treating their anxiety. Twenty-five percent of adults are hypertensive, often a stress-related condition. Nearly a third either have substance abuse problems or are in recovery.

To what extent are what we term "health problems" really problems that result from the disappearance of self, family and community? To what extent are a sense of self, family and community essential to healthy human function, regardless of changes in technology and culture? Is it possible to construct a concept of health or well-being that ignores relationship, family and community, however much the dominant culture tries to discount their significance in the postmodern world?

Indeed, it appears that a concept of health *must* reference the ability to function in community if it is to be logically consistent with what we have learned about the human project from this brief exploration of human history. While we can imagine a future that defines health as the longevity of individuals, what if these future long-lived individuals must exchange living for time and spend their days – like people with chronic kidney failure hooked to dialysis machines – serving the technology that prolongs life? Such a condition is alien to what we have always understood to be the human project. Even if the technology required to achieve long life were not time consuming, to imagine a culture of people focused on living long, instead of in the care of one another, is to imagine a race that we do not recognize as ourselves.

It is the human project, then, that defines the health of human beings.

To the extent that our participation in family and community forms the inevitable grounding of the human project, health is tied to family and community as well. However, we recognize that although we believe that the human condition and the notion of health derive their entire meaning from our social nature, that may not always be the case. It may be possible to split health from family and community, as the human species takes an unanticipated turn. Modernism and postmodernism exert powerful, nearly irresistible entropy. Perhaps it is irreversible as well.

Our understanding of health can take one of two paths. If relationship is no longer essential to human life, then the concept of health shrinks in meaning and denotes the functional efficiency of our body parts. This understanding of health is unarguably gaining ground. We increasingly address the health of the knee to ski, the health of the brain to concentrate for school and job success, the health of the emotions to preserve mood in the face of a world that seems to exist to provoke anxiety.

But if relationship is indeed essential to the human life we want to lead, then we will have to change the culture, resuscitate the conditions under which relationship is possible and redirect our energies toward relationship and community. In this light, our Cook's tour of human social history may prove useful, if it succeeds in reminding us that a healthcare system can only be effective if it arises from relationship and subordinates the function of the parts for the health of the whole. To do this, the medical services sector of the service economy must halt, shift direction, and devote its entire attention to improving people's ability to build, sustain and maintain relationships throughout their lives. Such a redirection will aim it toward becoming a healthcare system after all.

The 30,000-foot view of what went wrong is that human culture changed, and turned from the context in which health is meaningful. Let's look at how health and healthcare changed, and how the meaning of health has been distorted, and see what it will take to put our culture – and our health – back on track.

8

the reductive trap

THE RISE OF THE DOCTOR-SCIENTIST

By the mid 1800s, a very small number of doctor-scientists began to apply advances in optics and cell biology to understand the makeup of the organs and tissues. The new doctor-scientist then began to apply developments in physics to understand the movement of fluids through the body, and used the new science of chemistry to understand the effect of trace-invisible substances on *homeostasis* (the metabolic activity required to maintain the *functional*, as opposed to normal, physicochemical environment that is needed to support the cells which make up the metabolically active and moving parts of the body).

Medicine came to depend on science to make it effective, and science relied on measurement. This was seen from Rudolf Virchow, the great German pathologist and social theorist, to Ignaz Semmelweis, the Austrian discoverer of the bacterial cause of puerperal fever (who was persecuted for his observations, in part by Virchow) to Louis Pasteur, who discovered and explicated the role of infectious agents in causing disease. This dependence was seen with Abraham Flexner, not a doctor and not a scientist but a social critic who railed against the role of commercialism in American medical training, and advocated the importance of scientific training and research in bringing the new European medical *science* to the education of American physicians.

What happened next was an unintended, unpredictable slippery slope. Medicine and science began to overlap. Science relied on measurement, and so medicine began to rely on measurement as well. What did medicine measure? In the late 19th and early 20th centuries, most significant illness in Europe and America (like most illness in the Third World today) arose from epidemic infection. The spread of disease in newly crowded mill villages and cities was itself an artifact of the ever increasing population density of the industrializing world. When people crowded together, when the sanitary conditions were poor, disease passed quickly from person to person.[1]

The new medical science focused first on epidemic diseases like typhus and cholera, yellow fever and tuberculosis. The doctor-scientists, amazingly prescient, studied who died and who became sick and how sickness spread from person to person, mushrooming in crowded conditions. They quickly understood how social conditions caused the transmission of disease, and, working with progressive governments, convinced whole societies to re-arrange themselves, improving living conditions, providing safe water, safe milk, clean food and good sanitation. Before long, epidemic disease became much less common as the cause of early death in industrialized countries generally and in the United States in particular.

MEDICINE BECOMES DEATH PREVENTION

Once the doctor scientists reduced the impact of epidemic diseases, they began to look at the other causes of ill health. But what was ill health? Its traditional measures were the infectious diseases which caused people to die in large numbers. How did we measure ill health? We looked at registries of the numbers of deaths, maintained by state and federal governments, which recorded the causes of deaths of individuals, so that we could decide which infectious disease to try to conquer first.

But here is where a category mistake occurred. Our attempt to make medicine scientific, and measure health by measuring diseases that cause death, led us to assume that all health could be measured by measuring causes of death. A next easy step on the slippery slope led us into a reductive trap. If measuring causes of death measured health, it was reasonable to assume that health was the outcome of removing causes of death, which could be easily – though not necessarily accurately – measured. And so our science became a matter of studying and removing causes of death and medicine began to follow science, instead of the other way around. Science gave us tools to study causes of death and attempt to reduce or remove them; medicine has become the art of preventing death.

Let's see how this played out in the United States of 1910.

Abraham Flexner was the brother of a respected physician, an educator, essentially an interested layperson when he was hired by Henry S. Pritchett, president of the Carnegie Foundation for the Advancement of Teaching, to study and report on American and Canadian medical schools. Flexner traveled the country, personally inspected 155 medical schools in 98 cities, and found most of them wanting. There were no laboratories and no teaching hospitals. There were often no teachers. The courses described in the schools' catalogues often had no relationship to what students actually studied. Often, the physician owners of the schools – many were proprietary diploma mills – used tuition to supplement their incomes, and gave little instruction in return. The quality of medical school graduates varied enormously, from highly skilled, well-trained professionals and medical scientists like those produced by Johns Hopkins School of Medicine, to undisciplined quacks whose diplomas were worth nothing more than the paper they were printed on.

Flexner's 1910 report, "Medical Education in the United States and Canada", would change the course of U.S. medical schools, and profoundly influence the direction, character and composition of the U.S. healthcare system.[2]

THE FLEXNER REPORT

The Flexner report argued that schools of medicine could restore their integrity by building and emphasizing the importance of both real laboratories in which students could actually learn medical *science*, and by requiring research by medical schools' professors. Flexner believed research would force professors to remain in contact with peers and keep them up to date with the most recent developments of medical science.

Laboratories and research gave medicine an objective base – an intellectual foundation that focused on measurability and proof by experiment. The medical schools and the medical profession could begin to show that they served the general good, with objectively measured training and treatment. No longer could medical schools profit from slipshod training nor physicians prosper by recommending useless but profitable treatments whose efficacy lacked independent proof.

The Flexner report and Flexner's later work with the Rockefeller-funded U.S. Education Board (which spent $80 million improving medical schools that together had an annual, pre-Flexner budget of $12 million) changed the course of American education. By 1915, only 95 medical schools remained, and most of the worst diploma mills had closed. Flexner's work with the General Education Fund brought most medical schools into affiliation with hospitals, and improved their funding, so that their professors could focus on teaching and research. The newly combined medical school/hospital institutions turned from a focus on minting diplomas or, in the case of hospitals, from an exclusive role of treating the sick. Instead, a new enterprise developed, the teaching hospital, which we now call an academic medical center, with one foot in teaching and the other in hospital services for the sick. These organizations strode into the world of research and development, using their university affiliations to provide the credibility to obtain government grants to fund research, and their hospital affiliations to supply human subjects on whom to test new products and techniques.

MEASUREMENT AND SPECIALIZATION

The focus on laboratories and research allowed tremendous progress in medical science, because focused research produced real results. Within a few years, by the end of the 1940s, we began to see real technological progress in medicine. Diseases were catalogued and understood. Effective treatments – antibiotics, treatments for heart disease and the rudiments of its prevention, blood thinners to prevent stroke, hormones which seemed to counteract aging, insulin to treat diabetes – were all discovered, tested, and put into use. As Flexner would have predicted, investment in science produced results we could see and measure.

It was this "see and measure" emphasis (remember cut-measure and control?) that caused the first, and most profound, shift in the orientation of America's healthcare system.

Other major trends in American medicine were contemporaneous with Flexner. Research and science in medicine gave way, in very short order, to specialization. Perhaps this occurred because of the concentration effect, since the population had grown dense enough to allow self-segregation of practitioners and teachers by special skills or interests and abilities. The structural needs of medical schools also drove the change. Organizing the growing corpus of medical scientific knowledge into teachable units led to grouping similar concepts and approaches into skill sets (microbiology, pathology, anatomy) and organ systems (neurology, cardiology, and pulmonary medicine). Teachers expert in a particular area became researchers in that area, and those researchers became that area's specialists. Research largely confined its efforts to a restricted field of investigational tools or endpoints, mostly focused on longevity and organ system function, both easily measured.[3]

In 1913 came the formation of the American College of Surgery, the first real specialty society, followed by the American College of Medicine in 1915 and, in 1930, by the American Academy of Pediatrics. Public funding of medical research began with a one-room laboratory in the Marine Medical Service (predecessor of the Public Health Service) in 1887, charged with protecting the public using bacteriologic methods to screen out new immigrants with infectious diseases. The enterprise grew slowly throughout the early years of the 20th century until the National Cancer Institute was founded in 1930. The National Cancer Institute, theoretically separate from the growing National Institute of Health (which was what that original one-room laboratory became) but built on the campus of the NIH, began funding research at academic medical centers in 1937.[4]

HEALTH POLICY FOCUS: FIGHTING DISEASE, EXTENDING LIFE SPAN

About the same time as Flexner, the health policy apparatus of the nation began to evolve and focus on fighting disease and extending life span. The American Lung Association was founded in 1903, followed by the American Cancer Society (1913), and the American Heart Association (1924), from precursor groups in major cities that had started in 1915. Then came the National Foundation for Infantile Paralysis (1937).

All these groups lobbied Congress for support of the activities of the new medical scientists, who turned their attention to specific diseases. The disease associations, charitable foundations, the medical schools and medical scientists themselves all pressed Congress for more. Their efforts paid off handsomely. The National Cancer Institute at the National Institute for Health began funding academic medical research in 1937. That funding grew from $4 million in 1947 to $1 billion in 1974 to $5 billion in 2003.[5]

At about the same time, a number of drug companies, followed by medical equipment makers, realized that the disease-conquerors and the longevity-seekers were pioneering new markets hungry for new products. Soon corporate bioscience jumped on board and gradually perfected marketing techniques to reinforce the notion that health was indeed longevity, appearance, and pain relief.

By the early 1970s, the research activities of pharmaceutical companies grew as the profit from drugs and other medical technologies and devices increased. For-profit companies soon began to fund the academic medical research enterprise along with government.[6] The actors, the doctor-scientists, move back and forth from government to medical school to for-profit pharmaceutical companies. Although these three different institutional groups assert some mutual checks and balances, whatever influence we might hope they would exert in the direction of the public's health usually goes unrealized. In fact, this academic-medical caste is a single culture of a single class of scientific entrepreneurs who have little responsibility for or involvement in the long-term care of individual patients or their communities. They have created a subculture, sometimes tagged the *medical industrial complex*,[7] anchored on health as longevity, with no training in or understanding of health as relationship or health as community.

The confusion of the urge to extend human life span with health was not intentional, of course. It was fallout from, and an unintended consequence of, the way we measure health, resulting from science's dependence on measurement, and the timing of medicine's switch to science. Life span and age at death, or years of potential life lost, are still measures that researchers can easily access, and have meanings that are generally accepted. Pain and comfort are harder to quantify and measure; well-being or happiness is difficult to measure in a way that has internal consistency over time, and the well-being of communities, and the ability of individuals to function in communities are, as concepts (sometimes called *social capital*, which we will discuss in detail in Chapter 16), more difficult to measure yet. The later concepts, however, may be more powerful statements about what we mean by health. Once infectious disease was conquered (or at least, markedly reduced) registries of causes of death stopped telling us anything about causes of ill health, but tell us only about the causes of premature death in the young, and the organ system failures associated with death in the old.

But though death is what can be measured, health, and the ability to function in relationship or as part of a community, is, as we explained above, very hard to measure indeed. The overwhelming majority of end-points and outcomes of clinical studies, the process by which medical science moves forward, involve either death, the occurrence of a disease affecting an organ, which in turn is known to cause death, or the impact on a measurable physiological state which has been associated with longevity or disease (cholesterol or blood sugar, for example). In fact, some of these outcomes are probably associated with functionality after all (control of diabetes prevents blindness and heart disease, which impact functionality; control of cholesterol prevents stroke, some of which impair functionality) but the magnitude of the effect on functionality is, in general, not known, so the public policy implications of medical science is not clear.

While there was an engine of growth for research (focused, always, on longevity and organ system function, which could be measured) there was little parallel engine of growth for medical scientific activities related to patient care, relationships or communities. Medical scientists quickly learned their professional success came from their ability to write grants and fund clinical and basic science research. There was no road to professional success in academic medical centers or medical schools for those who would concern themselves with the needs of communities, or the meaning of health as experienced by communities. True, there have been at least two attempts to build a community health center-based healthcare system in the United States. The first attempt, which occurred between 1910 and 1920, started as a way to coordinate public health programs, such as maternal and infant care clinics, vaccination clinics, venereal disease and tuberculosis clinics, with volunteer social service agencies in city neighborhoods, and then the approach was expanded to suggest a way to provide a number of health services in rural areas.[8]

The second attempt occurred in the 1960s, and survives today: A dissident civil rights activist and former science editor for UPI turned general internist named H. Jack Geiger and an infectious disease specialist named Count Gibson founded the community health center movement in the 1960s. The movement found its own path to federal funding as part of the Office of Economic Opportunity of the Department of Commerce, (later moved to the Public Health Service). But the community health center trend was essentially an afterthought, restricted to the care of the poor, and never developed as a creditable career path for researchers and medical scientists.

One only needs to scan at the public health and medical literature to see the huge impact that our spiraling obsession with longevity has on our medical culture. For example, Healthy People 2000 and Healthy People 2010 are comprehensive sets of disease-prevention and health-promotion objectives for the nation, constructed by the Department of Health and Human Services' Office of Disease Prevention and Health Promotion.[9] The documents have two overarching goals, namely to increase quality and years of healthy life and to eliminate health disparities. While there is a methodology for measuring health disparities, most of them relate to differences in life span resulting from variable access to care and the quality of care provided that result from race, culture or class. The notion of fairness as it applies to the allocation of healthcare resources is critical as we examine ethical frameworks for deciding who should get what publicly funded healthcare resources. But the lack of attention, in the Health People 2010 goals, to the existence of functional communities, and of functioning families, and of safe neighborhoods, and lack of attention to people having mental and physical time and space to spend with one another, all cries out for comment and critique. The "health" in Healthy People 2010 is a construct that will enrich pharmaceutical companies, and managed care companies, and through them a few wealthy stockholders, at the same time as this counterfeit "health" will impoverish, disable, and destroy families and communities. In the process it will damage the very real social and community health of millions, if we allow the "healthcare" market to proceed unchecked and unchallenged.

FROM CARE TO CURE, COMMUNITY TO LONGEVITY

Abraham Flexner's work, then, brought on an unanticipated outcome: changing the medical profession's understanding of health from care to cure, from community to longevity. With that redirection and the emergence of a more urban, materially successful American society, the role of the medical profession, the place of health and healthcare in American society, and American society itself, changed forever.

Flexner never intended his emphasis on the laboratory science of Virchow and Pasteur to be an end in itself, but that is what it became. Science, and the imperative to measure, pulled the focus of the healthcare system away from the world of small towns and small-town general practitioners, who were mom-and-pop small business people, there to provide comfort, reassurance, and occasionally aid to the towns and villages where they worked and lived. The healthcare system turned into a trillion-dollar business with a set of products: longevity, the promise of pain relief, improvements in appearance, and improvements in mood or the function of body parts, all to be sold in the evolving mass market that American society became.

Over the years, the ability to measure life span changed the orientation of the healthcare system. Because we could measure and influence the life span of the population, we began to direct all our energies *and* all our resources *and* even reorient our culture to focus on the single goal of longer life. That is the reductive trap: in order to study a phenomenon like health we reduce it to that which can be measured. We can often manipulate what we measure, using the scientific method to see what changes or improves our measurement, and creating a science that focuses on finding the things that improve what we measure.

The process of measurement itself causes our minds to close. What we measure begins to stand for the phenomenon we were trying to understand in the measuring process, and we trap ourselves into believing that what we measure is the same thing as what we were trying to understand by measurement. Before long, we devote all our attention, and all our resources, to changing, or improving what we were measuring, and the original phenomenon we were trying to understand falls by the way side. We come to believe that what we measure is the phenomenon itself, instead of an attempt to understand that phenomenon.

the trap is sprung

In the case of health, what we can measure is longevity. What we really mean by health, the ability of individuals to function in their families and communities, has fallen by the wayside. Promulgation of the new and – the authors believe – perverse sense of health rests on a chain of logical errors: a reductive trap. Before we enter the trap, health is a robust concept, encompassing broad social and physical dimensions. Then medicine adopts science and measurement as an operating principle, looks for something to measure, and finds life span and longevity. Measurement commences and the breadth of meaning begins to constrict – and the trap begins to close.

First comes the simple measurement of life span. Since the scientific method and positivist ethic hold that measurement is the only portal of truth, the next step into the trap is an inordinate emphasis on longevity. This second step is alluring because measuring life span is easy and because life's duration is, indeed, one of many components of the meaning of health. Third, because other valid components of health are less easily measured they are ignored altogether. Longevity masquerades as health. Marketers tout longevity as synonymous with health, and we get used to buying and selling health, as pills and procedures, inventing problems people didn't know they had because there was a treatment to be sold. And then marketing hijacks the entire medical services system, perverting it so that it serves corporate profit and, parenthetically, participating in a culture that undermines community, and making impossible the very construct – health as community – that medical science and the measurement of longevity set out to understand and support.

HORMONE REPLACEMENT THERAPY: REDUCTIONISM *PAR EXCELLENCE*

In the summer of 2002, the National Heart, Lung, and Blood Institute (part of the National Institutes of Health), prematurely ended the Women's Health Study. This multimillion-dollar, 15-year project included over 161,000 women aged 50 to 79 and studied the health effects of estrogen and progesterone, a combination of hormones taken by millions of women to prevent and treat osteoporosis and heart disease. NIH decided to publish results before completing its planned course of research because early findings showed substantial risk of heart disease and breast cancer in women taking the estrogen and progesterone combination.

Research about this hormone combination is interesting for many reasons, but especially because the study reveals how our culture views health and disease. We invest in research, treatment, and services that attempt to achieve longevity, pain relief, and improved appearance, all in the name of health, instead of providing services that build community while improving the well-being of individuals. Why does this happen? The answer is embedded in the history, sociology, and political economy of medicine and culture in America over the last century. The "treatment" of menopause is a telling instance of the treatment enterprise gone awry.

Three threads within the fabric of our culture have led us to "treat" menopause and its risks. First was the ancient tradition of ignorant sexism, which led us to classify the natural process of aging as a disease that proved, once again, the weakness and fallibility of female gender. Second, medical/epidemiological "evidence" purported to show that the treatment of this "disease" would both improve function and extend life span. The third thread was the profit motive, which increasingly places virtually every attribute of the human condition within the rubric of disease, from male pattern baldness to toenail fungus – diseases all treatable, for a price, and for someone's profit.

I was in practice when the use of hormone replacement therapy became most widely promoted within the medical profession. Although everyone understood that hormone replacement provided some benefit for the 15 to 30 percent of women who experienced symptoms of menopause – hot flashes, vaginal dryness, headaches and mood changes – those symptoms happened to relatively few women, and usually went away on their own. Women experiencing the symptoms of menopause sought relief of those symptoms. But physicians began to prescribe estrogen to *all* women who were going through or had gone through menopause.

The most convincing arguments for prescribing hormone replacement therapy in the early years of its spreading use were those related to life span.

There were lots of claims, made by reputable specialists who had done published, peer-reviewed research, that suggested hormone replacement therapy extended life span. This was due to reduced heart disease (which turned out to be increased heart disease when studied more rigorously), decreased mortality as a consequence of hip fracture, and diminished breast cancer mortality (which turned out to be increased breast cancer mortality when studied more vigorously).

But it was longer life span that was always the most compelling argument for long-term use of hormone replacement therapy. In my mind, and in the minds of most American doctors, longer life span was equivalent to health; without saying so, we believed longer life span was the major legitimate goal of our work. Let us examine the culture of 100 years ago, when we first started to believe that extending life span, and not preserving the function of individuals as part of family and community, is the goal of health workers and the healthcare system.

DESIGNING THE BETTER REDUCTIVE TRAP

William Howard Taft occupied the White House in 1910, steering the ship of state for about 92 million Americans who had an average life expectancy of about 50 (men 48.4, women 51.8) and who earned about $750 a year (nearly all men).[1] This was the age of immigration and reform, a hurly-burly time of great social upheaval, technological change, and American ascendancy. But the America of 1910 was a small-town and rural nation. Seventy percent of Americans lived in communities of fewer than 2,500 people, and 50 percent lived on farms. Of those in more urban places, most resided in villages and mill-towns – communities of exploited immigrants who had been brought to America as human fuel for America's exploding industrial machine, which sucked in labor and raw material and spat out cheap manufactured goods that saturated the world. Still, the social fabric was comparatively stable. There was a divorce rate of one in a thousand marriages and an expectation that people would remain lifelong in the cities, towns, and villages in which they were born and reared, or, in the case of the immigrants, would grow into the mainstream of the neighborhoods and mill-towns to which they had come.

In 1910, on the other hand, American medicine was in tatters. Although we were developing a scientific grasp of the complexities and interrela-tionships of cells, tissues, organs, and control of bodily functions, our real understanding of disease and its effective treatment were vestigial. We could set broken bones, warn people away from myriad dangerous or even deadly over-the-counter patent medicines, and try to protect people from hos-pitals, which, in those years, were deadly places in which infection ran riot.

At the turn of the 19th century, 20 percent of all women died in childbirth, and 50 percent of all newborns died before the age of one year. The first discoveries of scientific medicine – diphtheria antitoxin and arsphenamine (marketed as Salvarsan), a partially effective therapy for syphilis – were just coming into use. Insights in bacteriology spurred the public health initiatives such as water and sewage treatment and control of food-borne diseases by inspection and regulation of the food supply. Such measures markedly improved the public health, but they were only occurring in a few large cities that had progressive local governments. The development of aseptic technique and improvements in anesthesia were beginning to make surgery safe for the first time, but these developments took years to spread across the country, so that, in some places, poor sanitation, danger-ous hospitals, and life-threatening surgery remained the norm.

To make matters worse, most American physicians were little more than charlatans. Many practicing physicians had trained only as apprentices, before formal medical education was the norm. Still others trained at medical colleges that functioned as mail-order diploma mills. Most of the 162 medical colleges in operation in 1900 had no training requirements for entry. Most had no access to or relationship with hospitals. Many had no laboratories or libraries and no competent instructors and existed only to generate profit for their owners, as many were proprietary.[2–4]

Despite their educational shortcomings the physicians[5] of 1910 were, on the other hand, part of the fabric of life of small town America.[6] Though the science of medicine was very weak, doctors were the people who knew what to do in case of trouble at least as well as anyone else in town. They were who you came to for broken bones, or to tell you the cough was – or was not – consumption. They delivered babies (probably only a little more skillfully than lay midwives, if more skillfully at all) and patted the hands of the dying, assuring all that nothing more could be done (as in 1910, there was usually little to do). They were there to tell those with pneumonia that the crisis was coming on the seventh day, and there on the eighth or ninth day to tell those who had pneumonia and were still alive that there had been a miraculous cure. They were there to cut off the limbs of people who got gangrene, in the often vain hope of sacrificing a limb to save a life.

Despite the inconsistency of medical education, doctors in 1910 were still frequently the most educated people in small-town and rural America, as this was a time when only 10 percent of American adults had completed high school, and only two percent had a college education. They sat on the boards of banks, led the church choirs, and often became the mayor or the county judge, when people could not agree on anyone else they could trust. Many physicians were corrupt pill pushers, seeing 80 or 100 people a day just to churn income. Others were drunks and philanderers. But there were many others, who served as the social and moral consciences of the places where they lived and worked. There were enough of this sort to cement the notions that the small-town general physician embodied an un-self-interested advocacy and that of all the actors in the daily local drama of rural and small-town American life, the general practitioner was the most deserving of trust.[7]

This is an abiding cultural deep-structure. The sage archetype-doctor has lately morphed from Marcus Welby, the wise and generous, fatherly small-town physician of 1960s television, to Doctor Moonlight Graham, the character in *Field of Dreams* who personifies the kindness and humility, the decency and goodness of small-town American life. Then came the hip, angst-ridden but decent and caring doctor in the wildly popular *Northern Exposure*, who came from far away on a government grant to provide knowledge, acceptance and a commitment to the common good to a wild, chaotic town in the Alaskan wilderness.[8]

The ideal of the small-town doctor was a touchstone for all the virtues of American life: relationship and safety, trust, love and decency, kindness and intimacy, and, most importantly, the meaning of a *common life*. The archetype-doc lived not for personal profit but to bind together a community of people who shared common experience, common values and inhabited a place whose whole totaled far more than its parts.

For most Americans in small town USA in 1910, health was *that* ability – to live whole: with your family and in your place, among friends and neighbors.

The experience of immigrants and minorities was often different. Huddled in mill villages and stuffed in America's growing cities, industrial workers, who comprised up to a third of large-city populations in 1910, struggled to survive their workplaces and their environments. For them, health was the ability to survive to the end of the day, the end of the week, and the end of the month. The immigrant experience, both of life and of health, may well have fueled the cultural change in the collective focus of health away from community and toward longevity. Newly arrived immigrants focused on survival; the growing population of immigrants together with rapid technological change tipped the scales, and made the United States an urban immigrant place more than an agrarian, small-town place.

In 1910 America, however, the cultural mainstream still fed a network of small towns and neighborhoods whose health, well-being, and survival was assumed. The persistence and function of towns and neighborhoods, like the air we breathe and the water we drink, was thought an inevitable aspect of human ecology, taken for granted, unconsidered, unmeasured, and unprotected.

COMMERCIAL INTERESTS PROMISING LONGEVITY

The first report that ovarian extracts were able to relieve the hot flashes that occur after menopause came in 1897.[9] About 1900, the average life expectancy of American women approached, and soon surpassed, the average age of menopause, which now is 52 (but which probably was younger in 1900) and for the first time in human history, many women were living long enough to experience menopause.[10] The experience of menopause is variable from person to person and culture to culture, with many women in the United States experiencing temporary hot flashes and irritability, and many women in the United States and around the world experiencing little or nothing but relief from monthly menstruation and the burdens of childbearing.[11] Between 1900 and the 1930s, researchers isolated and looked for pill forms of estrone and estradiol, the active ingredients of ovarian extract, first obtaining these from the urine of pregnant women. Then, in 1942, when demand for the product had outstripped the ability to produce (and likely to collect) the substance in pill form, a pharmaceutical company found a way to produce an active estrogen combination from the urine of pregnant horses. (And you wonder why there are so many horses in the United States).

In the 1950s, Ayerst, the maker of Premarin, which is the trade name for conjugated equine estrogen, began a massive marketing campaign for physicians about menopause and its symptoms, and estrogen and its effects. By 1960, 12 percent of all American women who were postmenopausal used estrogen. In the late 1960s, Robert Wilson M.D., a gynecologist from Brooklyn, created a private foundation, funded in part by pharmaceutical companies, to promote the use of estrogen to the general population. Wilson's book, *Feminine Forever* (1966) became a best-seller, and laid the cultural groundwork for the acceptance of the notion of eternal youth – created by medications and prescribed by doctors – that could be bought for a small price at the local drug store. In the 1970s we came to understands one of the risks of using estrogen in a certain way, when estrogen alone was found to cause endometrial cancer, and the first well-controlled trial of the effects of estrogen was begun (30 years after estrogen began to be marketed!).

In the early 1980s, one study showed that women taking postmeno-pausal estrogen had a reduced risk of hip and wrist fractures, and the osteoporosis industry was born. Osteoporosis went from being a rare genetic condition found in infants and an inevitable x-ray finding which was thought to be part of normal aging to a potentially lethal, treatable condition which responded to medication. During the same period, studies began to be published about the effects of estrogen on cardiovascular disease, some which suggested an increased risk, and some which suggested a diminished risk. Studies were published showing ways of dosing estrogen and combining it with another hormone, progesterone, so that the risks of endometrial cancer were reduced or eliminated.

When I entered practice in 1986, one of the first medical controversies I remember was the estrogen and osteoporosis debate. It is curious and interesting to recall what I remember about the message of the time, particularly because I have always been critical of the role that pharmaceutical companies play in presenting and disseminating medical information. The "buzz" that was then current, spread mostly by the pharmaceutical companies at sponsored dinners in very nice restaurants after office hours, was that hip fractures posed a quantifiable risk of death, which "estrogen replacement" reduced, and that estrogen "replacement" lowered the risk of heart disease and breast cancer. Yes, estrogen replacement reduced the symptoms of menopause. But the sales "hook," the striking element, was always evidence that hormone replacement lengthened life.

The history of estrogen replacement therapy illustrates how commercial interests have used the promise of longevity – the most easily measured endpoint to evaluate the effect of therapy – to influence the market and sell their products. But before commercial interests, usually pharmaceutical companies, got involved, there had been a century of changing culture and language, as medicine donned the mantle of science. Science required measurement, and longevity was what could be most easily, and most relevantly, measured. In the process, we gradually eroded the robust definition of health – health as community – and replaced it with the denuded one: health as longevity.

how longevity kidnapped health

In his controversial but seminal study of the declining social involvement and interconnectedness of Americans, *Bowling Alone: The Collapse and Revival of American Community*, Robert D. Putnam argues that the loss of social capital in the United States has led to myriad pathologies, including lowered collective perception of health and happiness. Putnam sifts oceans of social and public health research data to substantiate his conclusion that living in a place that possesses or lacks social capital is as potent a predictor of longevity and function as is smoking cessation, lowering blood pressure or increasing physical activity.

> In recent decades public health researchers have extended this initial insight [that social connectedness matters to our lives in the most profound way] to virtually all aspects of health, physical as well as psychological . . . The more integrated we are with our community, the less likely we are to experience colds, heart attacks, strokes, cancer, depression and premature death of all sorts. Such protective effects have been confirmed for close family ties, for friendship networks, for participation in social events and even for simple affiliation with religious and other civic organizations. In other words, both marchers and schmoozers enjoy remarkable health benefits.[1]

Putnam further argues that along with a general decline in social participation over the past 25 years there has been a significant decline in self-reported health, despite gains in medical diagnosis and treatment. Although by many objective measures, including life expectancy, Americans are healthier than ever before, Putman contends that "these self-reports indicate that we are feeling worse."

This growing malaise suggests that Americans evaluate health and well-being using broader measures than life expectancy and the absence of disease and morbidity alone. In fact, the sum of Putnam's argument unites health and happiness as connected self-assessments of one's total satisfaction with life.

But as our research and medical training enterprise began to focus more single-mindedly on longevity, two counterbalancing factors to that shift – the integrity of small-community America, and the functionality of generalist medicine – were themselves slipping away.

By the start of the Kennedy administration, the shift from a rural America, a place where most Americans lived on farms or in small towns, to a suburban and urban society, where many people did not know their neighbors, had become irreversible. (The demographic tipping point is identifiable in the 1930s, with the cultural and social consequences lagging by 20 or 30 years). Today, 80 percent of the U.S. population lives in metropolitan areas. The social context for health, the small towns, and the viable neighborhoods of cities, began to vanish, taking with them the possibility of interconnectedness and relationship.

It is one thing, as Putnam observed, that civic participation has decreased. It is entirely another when the mass of the population simply does not live in places where relationships matter.

Along with the population shift came technological developments to support it. Previously, the economic and social dimensions of small places has necessarily been linked. The farmer bought feed from the locally owned grain mill, and the miller kept his money in the local bank, on whose board sat the farmer and the local doctor. People needed each other's services and knew each other well. There were risks that any advantage could be exploited and relationships often became locally unbalanced. Even in mill villages, where such unbalanced exploitation was common, people needed one another: the mill owner needed the mill workers (though tried to pretend that was not so) and the mill workers needed the store owner and the mill owner, even while being exploited by them.

As we evolved transportation and other technologies that made American society more efficient, more (locally) fair, and more productive, we lost interdependence. The farmer raised cash crops, which he sold in distant markets, and bought grain cheaply from a regional or national grain mill, so the local mill closed. With the mill's closure the local bank had fewer customers, and soon merged with first a regional and then a national bank. There was no longer a local bank board. A grocery store chain supplanted the town grocer; the local drug store was replaced by first a pharmacy chain and then by a distant pharmacy benefits manager to whom we mail away prescriptions. The local hospital closed. The local dry goods merchant was replaced, first by Agway, then by K-Mart, and then by Wal-Mart or Target. Big extended families atomized: networks of aunts, uncles, cousins, grandparents, great aunts and great uncles who had all lived close together spread out. Now most American families have relatives all across the country, and no one to watch the kids while Mom runs to the store.

Then nuclear families themselves started to disappear, so many people live alone, or in groups of two or three people, often unrelated except by choice. If health is a reflection of an individual's ability to function in relationship, the social and technological change of the last 50 years began to make that definition of health problematic because the context of relationship had begun to disappear. Places that had functioned as communities became just places to inhabit, and not places to interact.

THE DECONSTRUCTION OF PRIMARY CARE

As Flexner's legacy, medical schools came to focus on measurable outcomes and medical science. Before long, medical information proliferated, and needed to be compartmentalized so it could be effectively taught. This pigeon-holing of medical knowledge developed in two directions: one grouping – pathology, microbiology, surgery, and epidemiology – are more laboratory-based, and developed out of skills needed by the new doctor-scientists. A second grouping – neurology, cardiology, nephrology, hematology, immunology, psychiatry, and gastroenterology – focused on organ systems and their disorders and treatment. A few disciplines – infectious disease, oncology, and, to a certain extent, public health and community medicine – encompassed elements of both laboratory science and the clinical expression of types of disease involving multiple organ systems or multiple social levels.

Before long there were pulmonologists, cardiologists, neurologists, endocrinologists, neuroendocrinologists, radiologists, neuroradiologists, otolaryngologists, psychopharmocologists, orthopedists, hand surgeons, neurosurgeons, allergists, immunologists, obstetrician gynecologists, ophthalmologists and neuropthalmologists, pain specialists, dermatologists, dermatopathologists, geriatricans, gastroenterologists, psychiatrists, rheumatologists, addictionologists, hematologists, oncologists, vascular surgeons, thoracic surgeons, cardiothoracic surgeons, hepatologists, urologists, epidemiologists and pediatric versions of all of the above – so many different kinds of specialists that one has to go to medical school just to figure out who does what.

By 1960, there were more specialists than there were generalists, and the focus of American medicine had completely changed. Now, according to Rosemary Stevens, a noted medical historian, there are "24 approved specialty certifying boards" and more than 100 others "operating outside the system of certification".

To be sure, there has been reaction in an attempt to hold back the specialist tide, and to undo the damage it has done to American culture and American medicine. In 1947, generalists formed the American Academy of General Practice, an organization dedicated to preserving the role of general medicine in the United States. The AAGP developed the American Board of Family Practice in 1969, the certifying organization for what was to be considered the 20th medical specialty (though few people understood the pathos – and the extent of the generalist eclipse – inherent in considering generalism a "specialty"), and then morphed into the American Academy of Family Practice, in 1971.

There have also been generalist movements inside the specialties of internal medicine and pediatrics. The American College of Physicians gave rise to the Society for Research and Education in Primary Care Internal Medicine in 1978, and that became the Society for General Internal Medicine in 1988. The American Academy of Pediatrics, long the most progressive branch of organized medicine in the US, identified the need for a focus on Community Pediatrics as early as 1968, and by 1999 had created a task force and policy paper to strengthen the role of pediatrician role in the community, but even that work could not contain the specialist tide.[2,3] By 2002, only 43 percent of graduating pediatric residents planned to practice primary care pediatrics, and most knowledgeable observers believe that proportion has slipped further in the intervening five years, to no more than 30 or 40 percent.[4] By 2003, only 27 percent of graduating internal medicine residents planned to practice primary care internal medicine.[5]

Both the community health center movement and the development of HMOs can be understood as a reaction to the emergence of specialty medicine. Community Health Centers arose to care for segments of the population whose medical-services needs were not addressed by a disease, acuity, organ system, gender, or age-restricted service delivery system; HMOs were formed to redirect people to generalists after costs began to rise, when expensive procedures were employed to fix problems widely perceived to be easily, and more affordably, preventable.

Still, the specialist horse was out of the barn. Sixty to 70 percent of all practicing physicians are specialists. The remaining few generalists – pediatricians, general internists, and family physicians – practice in a specialty culture. (Indeed, in order to market the specialty, family physicians sometimes call themselves specialists: "the doctors who specialize in *you*"). Generalists have been forced by an evolving health insurance system to provide, bill for, and be paid based on "procedures". They record their work using a diagnostic system that evolved to track the work of specialists (whose work was covered by insurance companies before those companies paid for the work of generalists), since specialists saw patients because of a diagnosis usually made by a generalist. Most of the generalist's work is listening to people who perceive some problem with their health, and many of these perceptions are not really diseases, but instead are expressions of some alteration of the patients' ability to pursue their normal relationships. The insurance payment system, which mirrors the diagnostic coding system, assumes patients see generalists for a measurable unit of time that is concerned with the diagnosis of a specific disease. Instead, most generalists see people in the context of a relationship, to help their patients sort out perceived disruptions in their health. Few insurance systems support the full meaning of that relationship, or the role generalists play in their neighborhoods and communities.

Did specialization change the meaning of health? Specialization itself has little impact on what the healthcare system looks like, or how it functions. Any rational healthcare system has to include specialists adept at diagnosing and treating what is beyond the reach of generalists. Both generalists and specialists have important, complementary, synergistic roles in any healthcare system that balances access with effectiveness, and care with cure. Instead, the way our country began to use medical services, treating them as products from which profits could be made, is what radically changed our perception of health. Specialization changed the direction of the healthcare system, from a focus on the life of towns and neighborhoods to one aimed at lengthening life by selling products to treat disease.

The culture of generalist medicine, which was an economic and social bulwark of small-town culture, had no place in a metropolitan America, where, as Robert Putnam showed, two-career families, suburbanization, sprawl, the car culture, and television colluded to markedly reduce civic involvement. What went unnoticed as specialist medicine became dominant and as civic life in America eroded, was how much health itself depends on how people interact with one another. No one had connected the dots between the well-being of communities and the effectiveness of the healthcare system, which cannot create or sustain health if there is no civic life for the people it serves to be healthy in.

LONGEVITY AND POSSESSIVE INDIVIDUALISM

The final way longevity kidnapped health might well be considered an epiphenomenon – a subtle shift that happened over the years without our notice, not caused by the medical industrial complex but something that developed in parallel with it and made it possible. There has been, over the last century or so, a shift in American's self-definition, a change in our sense of our identity and what we think our life means. We changed from being members of community, people who put the family and community and even nation first, to people who put the individual first, and who consider life a property right.[6]

If people see themselves as individuals and believe that the goal of individuals in a consumer capitalist culture is to accumulate an estate of maximal value and to protect their property, and if they construe life as a property right, then it is logical for them to maximize the measured value of their lives. Because we measure life in years, it appears rational, if all the assumptions are correct, for individuals to want to maximize the length of their own lives.

This shift toward possessive individualism had its seeds in the breakdown of feudalism and the emergence of an individualist merchant and bourgeois class in Europe in the late Middle Ages. The cultural acceptance of possessive individualism was explained by philosophers like Hobbes and Locke, whose philosophies were incorporated in the founding concepts of the United States, in our Constitution and the development of our jurisprudence. They gained even greater influence during the last 50 years, when technology and culture made it appear that individuals in a place did not need one another economically or socially.[7]

This evolution in self-concept had many causes, which include the evolving technologies and distribution systems that free individuals from local economy and local culture, and enable them to see themselves as independent of community. Another cause is the need of a consumer capitalist economy to posit or create a possessive individualist "self" which can be the target of effective marketing.[8]

The shift from the primacy of people as members of a community to people as possessive individuals legitimized the shift in our understanding of health from health-as-relationship to health-as-longevity, just as the emergence of health-as-longevity appeared to legitimize the emergence of the possessive individualist self. The concept of humans as possessive individuals is not a full and adequate explanation of human feeling, desires and needs, and the notion of life as a property right does not really describe what we take life to be. So it is not surprising that a medical services economy built on these assumptions inevitably fails to fulfill our expectations of what services we want in a health system.

Longevity kidnapped health, but health is straining at her bonds, crying out for the freedom to be what she is.

11

medical services and communities

The town of Scituate, Rhode Island, has about 10,000 residents. It's a middle-class, exurban town, just 15 miles from Providence, a multi-ethnic city of almost 200,000. Scituate started as a farming community, became home to a number of fabric mills with mill villages surrounded by farms, and saw the mills displaced by the nearby city's need for reservoir space, which caused the mills to close and many farms to be replaced by the forests needed to protect a large watershed. Following that the town returned to farming for 50 years and now is working its way from a rural farming community to a bedroom town of commuters. Scituate once supported four or five general practitioners, one radiologist, and a part-time surgeon, an ear, nose and throat doctor and a psychologist, two or three drug stores with soda fountains, and a district nurse. Now the town has two doctors and one chain drug store. Visiting nurses from one of 11 home health agencies that serve the state come out from Providence when a local hospital sends them to see post-discharge patients, but the nurses typically change every day, and no one knows about or thinks about the poor or the disabled.

Scituate spends about $15 million a year on schools, and has three elementary schools, one middle school and one high school, about 300 teachers and other school department staff, two school bus companies, and three baseball and soccer fields. The school department creates lots of economic activity for the town, because money earned in Scituate is often spent there – at the barbershop or the hairdresser or the local supermarket. A fair amount of the life of the town is taken up with running the schools, moving children back and forth between home and school, discussing how and what the schools are doing and what they should be doing and how much money is being spent, and how it might be spent better.

On the other hand, about $80 million is spent annually by Scituate residents on health services, yet very little of that amount affects the

97

life of the town. As mentioned earlier, there are two doctors and their staffs, comprising in all about 10 people; a chain drug store that employs a few local residents, and one small nursing home for about 50 people, employing 30–40 mostly local staff. Though no one knows for sure, if national spending trends are replicated in Scituate, the populace spends some $40–50 million on hospital care, at hospitals 10 to 15 miles away; $15–20 million on medications, $10–15 million on specialists and tests, which are only available elsewhere, $8–15 million is spent on health-plan administration, and about $5 million on primary-care physicians and practices, but less than $1 million is spent on primary care in Scituate itself. To be sure, there are many healthcare workers who live in Scituate but work in other towns or cities, who bring back considerable income to be spent in the local economy; but that spending, though it helps the local economy, is not earned within the context of local relationships. That is, money is spent in the town but is not earned through local interaction of local people.

Contrast Scituate's situation, for a moment, with the neighborhoods surrounding any major academic medical center in the United States. From Boston to Providence, New York to New Haven to Philadelphia to Baltimore to Atlanta, Cleveland, Chicago, Denver, LA and San Francisco, the story is the same: gleaming buildings ringed by depressed or devastated ghettos. Doctors in white coats and patients from the prosperous white suburbs driving though boarded up streets, with men of color hanging out on street corners. This despite the very real efforts of the academic health centers to reach out to their communities, and work with neighborhood organizations to reduce crime and improve health. What explains this phenomenon? Do academic medical centers emit some toxin that injures the function of communities? Do academic health centers choose to locate in poor neighborhoods because real estate is inexpensive? Were most large hospitals founded many decades ago in locations where urban flight has tended to affect them more than newer facilities? Or, more likely, are neighborhood economic and social functions injured by the presence of academic medical centers, which suck up any of the medical services dollars that could give neighborhoods economic viability and the social capital that comes with it?

The way in which medical services affect local communities and the social capital of small places in the United States is the dirty little secret of the medical economy. The progressive centralization, specialization, and technological sophistication of medical services and medical culture have come at the expense of small places. Once, medical services comprised a substantial segment of the economy of small places. Now, medical services spending and interactions have, quite literally, moved out of town, undermining the relationships, integrity, and interdependence of small places in the process.

One interesting aspect of the history of the medical services delivery system in the United States is the apparently accidental way in which the centralization of services occurred. It did not have to be this way. In fact, there was a period in which it appeared the United States might develop a local healthcare system that supported communities as it provided medical services to individuals. Let's look at that history, and see what we can learn from it.

1969: COMMUNITY HEALTH IS GHETTOIZED

In 1966 and 1967, Congress created a system of community-based primary-care centers to serve poor rural communities and poor inner-city neighborhoods. Some health policy people, envisioning a healthcare system for the United Sates as a whole, thought these new Community Health Centers were the building blocks of a healthcare system that could support neighborhoods and rural places as it provided primary care and prevention for all Americans. Had this system been allowed to expand, it could have promoted health for all Americans and likely averted our current crisis. Instead, the American Medical Association fought successfully to limit the community health centers' ability to accept patients able to pay for care. Health Centers, restricted to the care of the poor, failed to become the national health service that the United States so desperately needs.

To understand the story of community health centers in the United States is to understand where we missed the boat, and how we might be able to get back on that boat again.

In 1957, H. Jack Geiger, M.D., a medical student at Western Reserve University School of Medicine in Cleveland, Ohio, spent six months with Drs. Sidney and Emily Kark in the Pholela Health Center in the Natal, South Africa, one of the most impoverished areas in sub-Saharan Africa. The Karks had created an approach to healthcare that recognized the neighborhood or community as a central broker of health. This social construction, called Community Oriented Primary Care, aimed at combining approaches to the health of individuals with the health and integrity of communities by developing programs that strengthened the integrity of the community as it addressed the health of individuals.

The Karks assembled care teams that visited people where they lived, and tried to understand the health needs people really had. They involved local people in developing ways of addressing their own care, educated local people to become health workers, and emphasized ways of addressing local health needs, which were defined by the community itself. Community

Oriented Primary Care aimed to keep control of the healthcare process in the community, as it augmented the civic life of the communities served by health workers by focusing on the things that mattered to communities, and using that focus to build and strengthen the relationships in the community.

Dr. Geiger returned home, finished medical school and trained in internal medicine on the Harvard Service at Boston City Hospital. He then got a job at the Department of Community Medicine at Tufts University School of Medicine and, in 1965, convinced the Office of Economic Opportunity to let him and his colleague Count D. Gibson, Jr., M.D., create the first two Neighborhood Health Centers in the United States, in the Columbia Point housing project, in Boston, and Mound Bayou, Mississippi. Both centers employed the principles Geiger had earlier learned in South Africa. The Neighborhood Health Center movement, now called the Community Health Center movement, created multidisciplinary teams of health professionals. The teams first included internists, pediatricians, obstetricians and psychiatrists. Soon family physicians – a newly minted specialty – pharmacists, visiting nurses, physical therapists, social workers, medical anthropologists, and community people trained to be the voice of community people in and among this group of professionals, enlarged the teams. With all these disciplines, the neighborhood health center teams had the breadth and depth to provide most of the services communities needed, conveniently and close to home and in a form the community could understand and make best use of.

The Neighborhood Health Centers were more than just places for one-stop healthcare services shopping. They were also designed to fuel local economic development, by bringing financial resources into the communities they served. They sought to spur the personal development of the people they served by helping them become the professionals who ran the centers. Finally, the centers encouraged community self-reliance, because community members governed them, a bold experiment in local democracy and community control.

This approach, of using health services to stimulate community-building and create community integrity, caught on very quickly. By the summer of 1966, eight health centers had emerged. Within a year the Office of Economic Opportunity and the Department of Health Education and Welfare funded another 150 health centers all across the United States. Plans were laid for 1,000 centers, serving 25 million people, by 1973. Many people inside the community medicine world understood the value of the health-center approach, and quietly planned to expand the health center model to develop a national health service system for the United States. Such a system would in some ways resemble healthcare systems in Britain and elsewhere around the world that focus on providing primary care to everyone, but the system would be uniquely American, locally controlled and democratic, and able to improvise solutions for the communities the health centers served.

What Geiger, Gibson, OEO and HEW could not have known was the direction American culture was going to take, and how important the health-center movement might have become in changing that direction. As Robert Putnam has observed, civic life in America was to wither over the following 35 years, a victim of the car culture, of television, and of the expanded working hours of now two-career families.

Although the Neighborhood Health Center Movement was aimed at low-income communities, we see, looking backward, how valuable these centers might have been to the survival of civic life in all communities and how they might have become a national healthcare system for the United States.

But 1967 brought the wrath of the private medical community. The private primary-care doctors, who then still dominated medical politics, correctly understood that the Neighborhood Health Center movement, if made national, would spell the end of the private entrepreneurial practice of medicine. For the private practitioners of 1967, the free enterprise system, and their ability to earn a living as small business people unimpeded by government, was a central tenet of their American faith. These private doctors, fearing the socialization of medicine, fought and almost defeated Medicare and Medicaid in 1964 and 1965. By 1967, they focused their ire on the Neighborhood Health Center movement.

Powerful, but not powerful enough to bury the health center movement entirely, the American Medical Association persuaded Congress to smother the movement by allowing the centers to provide free service only to the poor. Even so, organized medicine worried that the middle class, people with the means to pay for medical service or with health insurance, would use the health centers, and deprive the private medical community of their patient – and income – base. Two years later, in 1969, organized medicine persuaded the government to limit the health centers so that insured, or "paying" patients, could represent only 20 percent of the centers' patient populations. Although that limit was reversed in 1974, the health centers were marked forever as poverty programs, providing poor care for poor people – no others need apply.[1] Early evidence indicated that the health centers improved the health status of the communities they served and reduced cost through reducing unnecessary hospitalization and emergency room use. Because health centers are required to be accredited by the Joint Commission of Health Care Accreditation and private primary-care practices are not, and because health centers alone receive the Federal funding needed to create multidisciplinary teams and measure and report the quality of care they deliver, the best possible primary care happens in community health centers. Nonetheless, the business of medicine succeeded in eliminating the threat the health centers posed to it, and the hope that the health centers offered to the country as a whole.

In recent years, most knowledgeable observers note with a mixture of sadness and shame that the best primary care in the United States is practiced at the health centers, although most Americans still wrongly suppose that the Community Health Centers deliver the healthcare of last resort to people who have no other option.

the zero-sum game

Zero-sum game: A situation in which the success of one participant requires the failure of another.

Zero-sum game: When the gains made by winners in an economic transaction equal the losses suffered by the losers. It is identified as a special case in game theory. Most economic transactions are in some sense positive-sum games. But in popular discussion of economic issues, there are often examples of a mistaken zero-sum mentality, such as "profit" comes at the expense of "wages", higher "productivity" means fewer jobs, and "imports" mean fewer jobs here.

[Adapted from *Pocket Economist*[1]]

Back in the early 1970s Jim Peters worked on a series of TV commercials for a local meatpacker. The intended message of the spots was that hams and hot dogs lie near the core of the American experience: that they are spiritually enriching foods and that we should feel good about them and the people who make them. A church hall supper was the setting for one of the spots. The plan was to show a happy, hearty, attractive, multi-generational crowd enjoying each other and a delicious ham and hot dog supper. After several hours of planning shots and taping the floor for camera placements, the film crew briefed the congregation – the real one – about the need to wait for cues and cooperate with the filmmaking goings-on. "Yes, yes, that would be fine," the cast agreed.

The diners streamed into the hall and commenced to work their way through a supper of baked beans, salads and, of course, sliced ham. They behaved at first obligingly, pausing for close-ups as they speared slices of ham, nibbled bites of hot dog, and chatted animatedly and on-cue while ladling coleslaw. Before shot #4 was finished, however, the crowd had broken ranks and swept along in a raucous feeding frenzy to what should have been shot 10 or 12. Kielbasa was eaten indiscriminately and out of turn. Kids ran and screamed. Old ladies passed out pie long before the script prescribed. The church hall supper ran amok.

These hungry parishioners bring to mind the rough-and-tumble style of the American economy, which we might imagine as "The Gigantic All-American Zero-Sum Baked Bean Supper of the Mind," spread mile after mile along a single crowded table. At this event, all of us are players, but some possess more tickets than others. We do not follow much of a script. Some visit the table often, heaping plates to satisfy multiple appetites or deep cravings, while others mostly stand on the sidelines, some hungry, some sated, some uncertain, some too tired or too lazy to join in the fray.

It's a tough game. When we try to help ourselves to a portion of those things that interest us, we must usually elbow our way to our goals or go without. Many of us not only eat but sometimes prepare items for others to consume. The thing is, only so many dishes will fit onto the great groaning board of the economy. True, we do slip in some extra leaves from time to time, but that is slow work. We never seem to extend the table and its contents fast enough to satisfy the greediness of some and the hunger of others. Sometimes we remove leaves, making the crowding worse and the unfed more numerous. Because of the perpetually limited space, too many casseroles or baked beans leave less room for pies. When salads occupy more space, cold cuts have less. Diners who gorge on bread here make extra room for cheese there.

The economic potluck supper is an admittedly simplistic metaphor for the vastness and complexity of the process it attempts to sketch, but it does help illustrate that the economy possesses limited and only gradual elasticity. If medical services and military spending occupy a greater share, other sectors feel the squeeze. And within each sector, including medical services, which consumes about one-sixth of all our resources, a smaller scale zero-sum process prevails, in which some very curious allocations occur. We will discuss this a little later, when we briefly consider the various industries and interests that make up the huge medical sector and the relative distribution of resources to each of these.

For the total economy, among the consequences of the current configuration of our economic zero-sum game, education and housing, child care resources and infrastructure development, among others, occupy smaller and slower-growing portions of the nation's economy than the medical industry and the nation's military. America is the richest and most powerful society in human history, yet we clearly under-fund areas of significant societal need. With a revised set of priorities and given all our wealth, it should be possible to create, if not the ideal society, at least a better one. For example, with sufficient resolve and commitment our nation is unquestionably capable of:

 ▶ building better communities;
 ▶ improving education;
 ▶ making work more satisfying and rewarding;
 ▶ taking better care of our children;
 ▶ eliminating homelessness;
 ▶ redesigning the infrastructure to rely less on automobiles and more on alternative transportation systems, including foot power.

Any one of these aspirations presents profound challenges, and money alone, without a concomitant shift in attitudes and appetites, would accomplish none of them. But to the extent that we spend profligately in some areas – the medical industry highly notable among them – we surely lessen the likelihood that we will use our unique opportunities to the best advantage or see our way clear to finance available improvement in the American way of life.

The zero-sum game that we are speaking about here entails public spending priorities. There is general agreement that government at all levels should use taxpayer dollars carefully and effectively. Since the combination of Medicaid and Medicare represent over half of all U.S. health spending, the public has a clear right to question the assumptions and procedures that control these huge outlets of tax-financed spending.

From the outset, we should be clear about the distinction between personal spending decisions and prerogatives and spending decisions made by government. Collective, societal spending decisions, while they do not represent the largest portion of the economy, drive the social process in a more linear and understandable way than do individual spending decisions. We believe that the overall public budget should be reshaped in such a way that it invests more in community, education, housing, public transportation and the environment – and less on medical services that claim to improve longevity. Increasing investment in some areas necessarily means spending less in other areas, especially military operations and medical expenses that, in our minds, inappropriately allocate public dollars. Among others, these expenses include publicly funded efforts to provide curative – rather than palliative – treatments to people over 80 years old. We recognize that discontinuing funding for this practice and redirecting spending to more productive activities is a controversial position, but we believe that it is both rational and defensible and would allow a better system using the same or fewer dollars than are now spent by federal medical programs.

As for individual spending, how people choose to allocate their own spending is a matter of their own concern. Some decisions are prudent and wise, others are callous, wasteful or foolish, but, as the old Bessie Smith tune asserted, ". . . 'T ain't nobody's business if I do." This applies to medical expenses just as it does to any other spending decision.

Want liposuction, tooth whitening, or a prescription for that glitzy new anti-allergy medication you saw advertised on TV? OK, pony up the dollars and pay for it. Want surgery to repair great-granddad's aortic aneurysm? Fine, but Medicare (meaning the public) shouldn't have to foot the bill. We know, some people will be able to pay, others will not. Life is always inequitable; someone will always have more and someone less. Our premise is, however, that longevity is a consumer product and that society will never be able to shoulder the cost of sustaining everybody's longevity, regardless of quality of life, without paying short shrift to more important goals.

Even in the realm of personal decision making, we believe that most people would prefer to act as well-informed consumers, able to apply their own cost/benefit judgments to medical services as well as other buying decisions. However, consumers are at a great disadvantage in medical decision making. As has always been the case, today's medicine dons an intentional mantle of mystery, complexity, and aloofness. Like a priesthood or sacred society, medical people wear distinctive clothes, speak a distinctive dialect and interpret a deep set of mysteries for everyone else. To be sure, medicine is complicated, but the profession's tendency to obscurity is at least as much an age-old marketing ploy as a necessity of efficient practice.

The public, of course, largely buys into the mystical and ritualistic aspects of medicine. Many people want to vest their well-being in the hands of a shamanistic healer – they do not want to know too much because it might spoil the spell. Most patients accept doctors' instructions as immutable, unquestioned orders. Perhaps this is why we hear disquieting stories about old people eating pet food in order to scrimp together enough money to buy costly medications. What do these medications accomplish? Will the patient die or suffer without them? Often the patient has never asked nor has the doctor volunteered the answers to such obvious questions, even though "following the doctor's orders" has led to large changes in the patient's lifestyle.

Building community yields the highest payoff for public (and personal) investment. Yet even at the level of personal spending, the amount of money all of us must allocate to medical costs undermines our ability to buy more useful products and services. For most of us, the cost is somewhat obscured because it takes the form of insurance premiums often paid in whole or in part by our employer. The zero-sum game applies here, too, of course. The more employers spend on medical insurance, the less is available for higher wages. Whether we incur medical costs in the form of taxation (to fund Medicare, Medicaid and other programs) or as overhead in our employer's budget, or as a portion of our take-home pay, all of these costs inevitably must be counterbalanced by lessened resources to purchase other things. We are convinced that decoupling medical services and their costs from the workplace would do much both to clarify and streamline the medical system, and the relationships between employers and employees. It would also greatly enhance the bottom line for most businesses.

Spending by medical insurance companies falls between government spending and personal spending.[2] The medical insurance companies handle nearly as many health dollars as do government programs, yet, unlike government agencies and individuals, insurers do not play the zero-sum game. Their quandary is to balance marketing-spawned consumer demand for covered services and the need to be price competitive to their employer clients. In this process no hand guides the spending, and marketing driven consumer demand is unchecked by any serious consideration of public health policy or collective utility.

WHAT SHAPED THE AMERICAN MEDICAL SYSTEM?

It is fascinating to seek explanations for the particular configuration of the American medical system. In our nation's medical organization and cost of care we are very different from other countries. Here are four factors that we think help to understand how we got where we are:

1. Individualism

The American character of individualism has shaped many of our unique medical attitudes and approaches. America was the product of dissenters, rebels, outcasts, adventurers and escapees who sought to frame a new society and break the bonds of European tradition. Although by the time of the Revolution, most Americans had settled down into fairly staid and conservative communities, life on the frontier remained an adventure well into the 19th century and helped establish attitudes of independence and individualism as an American trait.

Frederick Jackson Turner proposed the notion at the Colombian Exposition of 1893 (when about 2,000 American bison remained on the open range) that the American frontier had played a fundamental role in the expression of the American character and experience. Events such as the Vietnam War and Watergate have served to reinforce both the value of the individual and the concomitant skepticism in large-scale planning and big government.

Given vast quantities of economic fuel, and unfettered by any moral governor placed on the engine of business enterprise, medical science and healthcare business in America have pursued every available marketing opportunity. So to some extent it is likely, we believe, that the collective value system of Americans helps to explain the relative lack of governmental involvement in the development of the medical system in the United States, contrasted with a high level of governmental policy involvement and planning involvement in the medical systems of Europe and other developed nations.

2. Positivism and scientific rationalism

The influence and consequences of positivism and scientific rationalism had a more profound and lasting impact in the United States than in the remainder of the developed world, even though positivism was developed in Europe.

3. American medical history

American medical history followed a course different from that in other countries. As the medical profession developed some effective technology and therapeutics and codified its training process toward the end of the 19th century, hospitals came to dominate the configuration and distribution of medical services. This role as the principal component in the medical system was strengthened as medicine grew increasingly specialized and technology-dependent and driven by the policies of huge government programs, most notable Medicare.

4. Postwar economic collapse in Europe

The economic collapse in Europe following World War II limited the resources available there for technological research and development and gave the United States an enormous comparative advantage in postwar science. Linked to that development was the immigration from Europe to the United States of many brilliant scientific minds, beginning with the rise of Nazism and extending well beyond the end of the war.

WHAT WE GET FOR OUR $1.7 TRILLION

On average, Americans live shorter lives and have higher incidence of some diseases than many countries that spend less on medical services. This comparative ineffectiveness results from many causes. We American are, for example, more financially diverse than many European countries, with a larger percentage of poor people who lack proper housing, jobs and access to preventive medical services. We also lack any system of guaranteed medical access, although hospital emergency rooms are legally constrained from turning away people who appear to be seriously ill. This results in an upside-down situation in which people obtain the costliest, least personal kind of medical intervention once they have become seriously sick.

In contrast to our fairly large poor population, our American middle and upper economic classes live to a damaging extent off the fat of the land – literally. They generally have insurance-based access to medical services (although an increasing percentage is uninsured) but this access is often offset by their way of life. Our national prosperity comes at a high price. Americans are increasingly stressed and fat and often hire doctors to make them relaxed and thin. The nation's rate of obesity is the world's highest, while the time we devote to exercise is the lowest. The stressful nature of our lives causes or worsens numerous somatic and psychological problems. The design of our cities and suburbs is automobile-friendly but pedestrian-averse. With all of these factors militating against physical and psychological soundness, it is hardly surprising that even using the "longevity = health" model, we're not getting a great return on our huge investment in medical services. Where is all that money going?

MEDICAL TECHNOLOGY

The proliferation of technology represents a substantial portion of medical expense. From cardiac surgical stents to PET scanners, thousands of new technological products enter the marketplace every year, most of them with very high price tags. Not only are they costly but they are also short-lived: medical technology becomes obsolescent very quickly. Two million-dollar MRIs or digital subtraction angiography systems are the very latest model at purchase time. Within a few years, their image quality, speed or other key features trail far behind the newest releases. Sometimes upgrades help bridge new advances, but before long, just like the four-year-old home computer, the medical hardware cannot cut it any more. The doctors who use it want the best, newest, most cutting-edge device available. The once shiny, remarkably fast, mind-bogglingly innovative technology heads for the scrap heap.

One might be inclined to argue that technology actually saves money, by simplifying care, sometimes shortening hospital stays or eliminating follow-up visits. On a case-by-case basis the argument is often sound. But simpler, faster, lower-cost medical treatments appeal to the consumer in us all. For example, where radial keratotomy seemed an exotic and rather frightening way to correct near-sightedness, its replacement, LASIK surgery, has grown by leaps and bounds: from 30,000 cases in 1995, to 950,000 in 1999, to an estimated 3.2 million in 2002.[3] Economies of scale and the effects of competition have reduced the cost of the procedure in many markets, but it still costs many hundreds of dollars per eye. Multiply that by millions and it becomes crystal clear that we're spending more overall on vision-improvement surgery. Is that so bad? Perhaps not. Perhaps eyeglasses and contact lenses are obsolete and should make way for something better, albeit more expensive. The point is, there is an added price. Multiplied by many such examples, technology adds cost. Sometimes the benefits are substantial; in many instances they are, at least, arguable.

THE "ABUNDANCE OF CAUTION" TRAP

During the course of their careers, many physicians still in practice have observed the entire sequence of clinical investigation and technological innovation that has produced today's implantable cardioverter defibrillator (ICD) technology, another example of technology that might potentially add much additional cost to the medical system.

Beginning in the late 1960s researchers identified the physiology and sites of origin of ventricular tachycardia, an excessively fast, dangerous heart rhythm that can lead to cardiac arrest, and other abnormal electrical activity of the heart that also cause the heart to stop suddenly, producing sudden death. During the following decade, miniaturization technology evolved and practical ICD implantation began to enter standard practice with the first FDA approvals in 1985. In the years since, significant advances in technology combined with the results from several large, prospective, randomized clinical trials, have bolstered the acceptance of ICDs as a first-line therapy for patients with potentially life-threatening ventricular tachyarrhythmias.

Late in 2002 a joint committee from the American College of Cardiology, the North American Society of Pacing and Electrophysiology and the American Heart Association issued a new guideline on the selection of patients for ICD implantation. The guideline states that heart attack survivors with an ejection fraction of less than or equal to 30 percent are recommended for an implantation of an ICD for primary prevention of sudden cardiac death.[4]

Approximately 10 to 15 percent of the one million annual U.S. heart attack survivors meet these criteria and would be candidates for an implantable defibrillator under the guideline.

Given this large patient market, ICD enhancements continue to flow steadily from the big manufacturers of these devices. Among the competing brands and models, physicians can select devices to control both ventricular tachycardia and atrial fibrillation. Generally each successive generation of the devices are more compact, longer- lived, and support more remotely programmable options, such as leadless ECG access and extensive telemetry, download and custom-control features.

With a large potential market of patients, medical technology firms will undoubtedly continue to enhance ICDs. Like so much other medical progress, these products will benefit specific individuals while prompting concerns about burgeoning costs of healthcare overall. As Dr. David E. Haines, a professor of internal medicine and co-director of cardiac electro-physiology at the University of Virginia Health System, noted in a recent news report, each defibrillator system costs $25,000 to $30,000. (Multiply that by 100,000, which is the lowball number of qualifying patients under the American College of Cardiology guidelines, and you wind up with at least $2.5 billion. It's not easy to determine just how much of that cost is incremental, but surely at least half is, and perhaps much more – for this one procedure. $2.5 billion will save lives, to be sure, but notice saving lives that might be lost is the total responsibility of the American College of Cardiology and its collaborating organizations. There is no one to speak for the effect that the loss of $2.5 billion has on families and communities.[5]

A recent large-scale study of ICD effectiveness[6] concluded that for every 16 patients with defibrillators, one patient's life was actually saved by the presence of the device. With hundreds of thousands of potential candidates for ICD technology, society must once again ponder not only the potential benefits of therapy, but its costs as well.

We think that the proliferation of ICDs is instructive for two reasons. First, these devices relate entirely to the theoretical benefit of extending life span; they have almost nothing to do with health. There is no useful data about how the installation of ICDs affects people's lifestyle or their ability to interact with the people who are important to them. Second, while ICDs are now a recommended therapy among a large number of people, their cost-benefit, in terms of years of life gained, appears very low: relatively few years would be gained for billions of dollars the devices and their support would require.

STATINS IN OUR FUTURE?

Let's look at another expensive technology, and see if we can see the confla-tion of technology, money and ethics into the therapeutic decision process as it plays out in the zero-sum game. HMG CoA reductase inhibitors, known as statins, are a class of drugs that lower cholesterol. On the one hand, statins are effective in lowering the cholesterol, and have only rare side effects. On the other hand, cholesterol lowering medications are commonly used, fairly expensive (between $60 and $100 per month, or $720 to $1200 per person per year. This is in a world where primary care itself costs $15 to $30 per person per month, and the entire cost of care ranges from about $4,000 to $8,000 per person per year), and eat up an ever increasing slice of the medical expenditures pie, and cost the nation an estimated $13.3 billion in 2002.[7] When you figure in the cost of doctor visits to prescribe and monitor statins, and laboratory tests to evaluate their effectiveness in lowering cholesterol (which is not the same as evaluating their effectiveness in preventing heart disease and death from heart disease, as we will discuss later) the yearly cost was $15 to $20 billion. Add medical cost inflation, and the more widespread use of statins since 2002, the yearly cost of statins probably approaches $25 billion.[8] Even at $13.3 billion, our spending on statins represents a fraction of what that spending could be. If we followed expert recommendations, we would increase by five or 10 times the number of people who get statins today; that is, millions of people who do not receive them now. This is because we are ineffective at distributing resources to the entire population who, experts tell us, might benefit from them. And also because the folks in the recommendation business, which is largely fueled by pharmaceutical companies sponsoring studies to which expert panels, made up of folks from academic medicine with many links to the pharmaceutical companies (the medical industrial complex), feel like they have to respond. This is a growth industry. Unchecked, we will soon be spending $50 to $100 billion on statins – and in a certain way, we are spending this $50 to $100 billion all because of a category mistake.

Category mistake? Here's the logic that underlies the use of statins. If we give statins to large numbers of people who are at risk for heart disease, we lower the risk of *death* from heart disease in the population of people who get the statins. (Note the concept that fuels the decision making here is the risk of death, not the ability to function in community.) We lower the risk a little, though not overwhelmingly, in a way that is proportional to the risk of death from heart disease before giving the drug. Here are some real world numbers: only about 10 percent of the population is at very high risk of death from heart attack, and that risk is 30 percent of dying over 10 years; in that population. Statins cut the risk of new heart attacks and deaths from heart disease by 20 to 30 percent in the high-risk group. Thirty percent! Sounds impressive. But the truth is working out the numbers, and understanding the actual science (as opposed to marketing science – remember, there are lies, damn lies, and statistics) and what it shows. Say we have a hundred people at high risk from dying from heart disease over ten years. Their 30 percent risk of dying suggests 30 people will die from heart disease over 10 years. The 20–30 percent reduction in that risk means 21 to 24 people will die of heart disease in this period, which means we will have kept six to nine high-risk people who would have died of heart disease from dying of heart disease during this period. Six to nine out of a hundred sounds pretty reasonable, though somehow not as impressive as a 30 percent reduction in the risk of new heart attacks and deaths.

But here is what the oft touted reduction in risk leaves out. First, the risk reduction is a population, not an individual effect. (That is the major category mistake – confusing a population effect with an individual effect to make an argument that sells a product.) That is to say, if a hundred high risk people take statins over 10 years, it is not possible to know who will get benefit in that group. Twenty or so people will still die. And 70 people will have taken a medicine for 10 years, costing someone $10,000 each, without receiving any benefit at all. And of the six to nine people who did not have a heart attack or die of a heart attack, some of them, and maybe all of them, will die of something else in that 10 years, given the yearly risk of death in people in their age group. In fact, even tens of drug-company-sponsored studies have not been able to show that the use of statins prevents stroke, or even that the use of statins reduce all-cause mortality, which means that statins appear to prevent heart disease profession and death but not death in the aggregate. (An early study actually showed that statins *worsened* all-cause mortality – that they made death *more* likely – but that finding has not been borne out by other drug-company-sponsored studies.)

Note that in order for these drugs to have their modest population effect over 10 years, everyone in the relevant population has to take them for 10 years. So all these estimates have to be tempered by the real world, by the likelihood that some people – often, the people at greatest risk: the people who are stressed, have diabetes and high blood pressure, and smoke – are not going to take the medicine and are not going to get any benefit at all. This limits the effectiveness of statins in the population who might be expected to derive most of the benefit. Two other factoids go into the mix: the effect is similar but more modest in people at lower risk, people who, for example, have only one risk factor for heart disease, like elevated cholesterol alone. And it is worth noting that 50 percent of all heart attacks and heart attack-related deaths occur in people with normal cholesterol. Lowering cholesterol does not prevent heart attacks or death from heart disease in individuals: it just reduces the numbers of people *in a population* who will have a heart attack or die of heart disease over 10 years. *There is no way to know how these medications will impact an individual.* All these medications do is change the odds for an individual. But there is no way to know if they are working for any one person, at any one time.

Our inability to know if statins are working for any one person at any given time is a major problem, and part of the category conflagration that allows our costs to rise without producing certain benefit, and creates the space in which marketing can sell medications very widely, though perhaps inappropriately. If we give someone with pneumonia an antibiotic, we can check that person for a clinical response, monitoring their condition and function daily, and can change the antibiotic if they do not respond – or add other therapies as necessary. We cannot do that with statins. We identify the risk, administer the drug, the drug company has a source of income for 30 or 40 years, and neither the person nor their doctors will ever have any clue if it is providing the individual patient any benefit, ever. That is, unless of course the person has a heart attack or dies of heart disease, at which point we declare that the heart disease was genetically determined, and is an inevitable effect of aging. The three-card Monte switch of longevity with health, the profit potential of selling a drug the effectiveness of which cannot be monitored, and the very American frontier mentality of doing what has never been done – preventing heart disease and death in the face of what we know about the actual human life span – have cooked a very expensive soup. The broth tastes like profit for some, illusionary hope for others, physical function improvement for a few, and incredible cost for the many, all while family and community are starving, and the future of family and community, which is the nectar of health itself, withers on the vine. Nero fiddles. Rome burns.

To be fair, we have also not been able to show that diet and exercise, which can produce reductions in total cholesterol and improvements in the cholesterol profile, have any impact on the risk of heart disease and heart-disease death. So from a population perspective, statins appear to be more effective than diet and exercise in preventing heart attacks and heart-disease deaths. But also from a population perspective, no one has ever shown that our spending on statins is better for our health and the health of our culture than spending on housing and education.

And there is a huge meaning to the difference between personal and population perspectives.

From the population perspective, it is reasonable to give statins to high-risk people, assuming they are affordable. Each life saved costs $25,000 to $50,000, about on par with costs we incur for saving lives and preventing deaths from other diseases. (There it is again, though – the way we measure, and what we measure, to make these decisions is a longevity-based calculus. Note we do not measure the effects of this treatment on family and community, something we will discuss later. If we took those effects into account, one wonders how the scale would tip.)

But from a personal perspective, would *you* take a statin, even if you were high risk? You get to take a medication every day, spend $10,000 over 10 years, and there is no way to know if it is helping you. Now compare diet and exercise. From a population perspective, we cannot prove that diet and exercise reduce risk. But you are not a population, you are a person. Diet and exercise have lots of added, intrinsic benefits, and they are free. True, we cannot get a 30 percent reduction in cholesterol from diet and exercise from the population, as the culture is not structured – but *you* might well get that reduction, if *you* work hard enough, long enough. True, we do not know if that will protect you against heart attacks and death, but truth be told, we do not know if stains will protect you against them either! We only know their effect on populations.

Now take the $13.3 to $25 billion we are spending, and let's see what happens if we spent it on housing or education. If we spend it on housing, we could build 100,000 two-bedroom apartments, if each cost $150,000, about the cost of building those units in the Northeast.[9] One hundred thousand units is housing for at least 400,000 people. That's about half the number of homeless people on one winter night across the United States.[10] For one year's worth of cholesterol-lowering medicine. And every homeless person who has a home has a roof over her or his head, as opposed to six to ten out of every 100 people taking cholesterol medicine not getting heart disease.[11] In three or four years of spending on housing, homelessness is practically eliminated.

We can run similar numbers for education. Spend $15 billion more on education? If we have about 60 million school-age children, that's an extra $200, or three to five percent, on education – probably not enough to make a huge difference, but surely a place to start. Unless . . . unless we used the money to guarantee every American child a college education. There are just under three million high school seniors in the United States.[12] That's about $5,000 per student. Not enough for the Ivy League, but most of a community college education for everyone. If we looked at all medical services spending this way, we wouldn't have to look to hard to find the cost of the best college education money can buy for every kid in the country. Which is better value for the future of America?

Regardless of value, let us examine where the money goes when we spend on drugs, versus when we spend on housing and education. If we spend on pharmaceuticals, some goes to doctors, who have to be paid for their time writing prescriptions. Some goes to pharmacists, who have to be paid for dispensing medications. Some goes to the owners and stockholders in pharmacy chains. But the bulk goes to the pharmaceutical companies, for overhead and profit. True, those companies have expense, for research and development, for distribution and production, for marketing. But pharmaceutical dollars get spent where the pharmaceutical companies and their stockholders are. Little stays in communities and neighborhoods.

When we spend on housing, on the other hand, some money goes to suppliers in distant places, the manufacturers of building supplies and lumber companies. But most stays close to home, supporting electricians and carpenters, laborers, plumbers and landscapers – all local. When we spend on education, the bulk of the spending is for teachers and ancillary staff, all local. Even when we spend on college education, the bulk of that spending is at local colleges, since almost every community in America has a college nearby, so the spending is, and stays, local, and contributes to the local economy of local "people, living together in a place and wishing to continue to do so."[13]

Of course, one of the confounding variables of all our medical-services spending decisions is health insurance. In addition to formal marketing (TV and magazine advertising) and informal marketing (endless cultural messages from government and the media that lowering cholesterol is what intelligent people ought to do), and direct instructions from personal physicians, health insurance is a major reason people are willing to obtain and use a chemical that is both costly and may not have any personal benefit for them.[14] Because health insurance obscures the immediate cost, people are more willing to "take" what appears to be a "benefit" they do not have to pay for, although that decision process is completely illusionary, since we all experience the cost as it is spread around and affects us all as rapidly rising health-insurance premiums. How many people would be willing to spend $1000 a year, or $10,000 over 10 years on anything without asking very hard questions about its value and the return on their investment. Since almost no one has to spend that $10,000 themselves, those hard questions are very rarely, if ever, asked.

Now, take that $10,000 *you* might spend on statins. Think about what might happen if *you* put it in the bank, where it can be used to invest in homes and business in *your* community, or put it toward *your* child's education, or build a new room on *your* house, using local carpenters and plumbers and electricians, who can then themselves put it in the bank, or use it for their kids' education. See how that money spins around in a community, making it more resilient and complex. Consider walking or biking in *your* town, and the people you will run into as *you* exercise. Consider talking to friend about the new recipes you use to eat more sensibly, and how conversations lead to other conversations – who is running for school board, what about the new middle school, hear about the new restaurant? *NOW* compare diet and exercise to statins. Any chance your blood pressure went down as you slow down, and talk to the people around you? Which is better for you? Which is better for your community? Which is better for all of us? Ever even heard the other side of the argument?

Health insurance, marketing, misconceptions about longevity exploited by marketers, the reductive trap that leads physicians to think about longevity because it can be measured, and no cultural imperative to think about the effects on communities – all these factors play into our medical services spending decision, and all together make us losers in the zero-sum game.

THREE PEOPLE, THREE AORTAS

The stories of three people, each with the same disease, serve to illustrate how people vary in the ways that they construe the value of life and in how much they fear, value, and desire medical services.

The aorta is the largest blood vessel, carrying blood from the heart to the rest of the body. It is the main pipe, the major highway, a critical piece. You cannot live without it, and you cannot live unless it is intact, uncut and largely unobstructed.

Thankfully, things do not often go wrong with aortas. A few children are born with narrow aortas and require surgery when they are young if they are to survive and grow. Some adults develop a weakness in the wall of the aorta that leads to a ballooning, like a bad spot on the side of a tire, which gradually expands, thinning the wall until the balloon pops, the aorta bursts, and the person dies suddenly.

An abdominal aortic aneurysm, a name for one type of this ballooning, is sometimes spotted in people in their sixties, seventies and eighties. For most of them the aneurysm grows slowly, at a rate of an inch every few years; the risk of rupture and sudden death is about five percent a year. This means that the people with aneurysms, everything else being equal, have about one chance in 20 of dying suddenly from their aneurysm in any given year.

There is surgery to repair aneurysms. Done as an emergency procedure, after the aneurysm has ruptured, the surgery is rarely successful, and 90 out of 100 people who survive long enough to get into an operating room end up dying from the aneurysm despite the surgery. Done electively, on the other hand, surgery to repair aneurysms is more successful, and 80 to 90 out of 100 people who have the surgery survive it. It is very major surgery, however, and involves four to eight hours in the operating room for a process called cross clamping the aorta (during which the surgeon ties off the aorta for a few minutes – as few as possible – but usually at least 15 or 20 minutes). This compromises the blood supply to the kidneys, which can cause them to fail as a result of the surgery, and places a massive strain on the heart, which can produce heart attacks during the surgery. Most people who have the surgery spend five to ten days in the intensive care unit afterwards, and many need an extensive period of rehabilitation (four to six weeks is common) to recover from the whole body assault that the surgery represents. Big, involved, and pricey, the procedure and all the related care costs about $30,000 without complications and perhaps $100,000–$300,000 if complications set in.

When someone has an aneurysm, they must make a couple of critical decisions. The first is whether to have surgery at all. It's a calculated risk. If you are 80 years old and we think you might live 10 years once the aneurysm is fixed, and your risk of dying from the aneurysm is five percent a year, does it really make sense to risk death and complications from surgery? Then there is the timing issue. The aneurysms that are at greatest risk of rupture are large ones, six centimeters or larger. But most aneurysms take years to grow that large. The people who do best with the surgery are younger people, in their sixties and seventies. So if you are going to have surgery, does it make sense to have the surgery when you are in your sixties, and the aneurysm is 4.5 to five centimeters? Or is it better to wait, and risk complications and rupture in the interval, until the aneurysm grows to perhaps seven centimeters when you are 80? Place your bets.

Bill Waters was a great moose of a man, hale, hearty and full of life at 76. He had run a family wire-making company, sold real estate, and served on the school committee and the town council and the Boy Scouts. He built his own house, set back from the road in a grove of 100-year-old pines and kept it immaculate. He lived a full life, surrounded by his children and grandchildren.

And then we found his aneurysm.

I do not remember how it happened, whether I felt it, rumbling in his belly like a Harley-Davison, or whether we stumbled on it in an x-ray which we got for some other reason, like an old shoe we tripped over in the dark. But find it we did, and off he went to the vascular surgeon: a 5.5-centimeter aneurysm in an otherwise well (except for having smoked earlier in his life and having a little hardening of the arteries) older man.

The aortagram was the first sign of trouble. This is an x-ray picture of the aorta produced by sticking a needle into an artery, slipping a catheter into the artery over the needle, and then gently navigating the catheter upstream through the arteries into the aorta itself, and finally injecting a dye that lights up on an x-ray. Then we take a picture of the dye as it flows through the aorta, and we get a pretty good picture of the inside of the aorta, its nooks and crannies, its bulges and narrowings, its rapids and the places where the flow is still. Vascular surgeons need the aortagram to tell them where to cut and what's at risk – whether they can cut and cure, or are more likely to cut and kill. It tells them when to go ahead, and when to still their hands.

Mr. Waters had a perfectly good and encouraging aortagram (5.5-centimeter aneurysm two centimeters above the renal arteries, little risk to the kidneys or the arteries that carry blood to the bowels or the legs), but then he had a brief disaster that no one could explain. He went into shock, without warning or explanation. His blood pressure disappeared, he stopped breathing, and his heart almost stopped. Thankfully, he was in a good hospital, with attentive staff. They poured fluid into his veins, put a tube into his throat, and put him on a ventilator and he spend the next two days in the intensive care unit. He recovered quickly. For the vascular surgeon, it was an unlucky complication of the aortagram, a chance allergic reaction, which meant he needed allergy testing before surgery. To me, it was evidence of a disaster waiting to happen.

Primary-care doctors have a different view than surgeons of what surgery means. For most surgeons, an operation is just that, a one-time thing, the chance to cut and cure. For primary-care doctors, though, some surgery is critical and life-saving, but most surgery is trickier than surgeons think. All surgery carries the risk of misadventure and death, a risk the surgeon encounters only at the time of surgery. I take care of the people and families who have the misadventures and sustain the deaths, and I know how even small complications can totally change a person's life and their family's fortunes. I know how deaths from complications live on as bitterness and failure in the hearts of those left behind. I'm pretty conservative about surgery. I want people to really understand the risks because I know they are real.

I live with the memory of a good friend who died at 39 of a massive pulmonary embolus, a rare complication of hernia surgery, which I once regarded as routine, almost trivial. I was in the emergency room with his family when his two daughters, three and six, came to say good bye. It was the saddest day of my life.

After Mr. Water's near-death experience, I sat him down and read him the riot act: the risks of surgery, with no sugar coating. The risks of his surgery, given what had happened during his aortogram. I did not know why he had a problem then. I did not have any evidence that would let me conclude that what had happened during the aortogram would happen again. But I'm a superstitious guy. My fear that he might have another allergic reaction, take together with the knowledge of the limited yearly value aneurysm-repair surgery for a guy his age, made me say, "Slow down and think." What if he died as a result of surgery, while, untreated, the aneurysm might not kill him for five or ten years? How would he feel if he had a big heart attack or major stroke during surgery?

I pushed hard to slow down, because my gut told me to be afraid for his life. But my words fell on deaf ears.

So, I sent him for allergy testing, because I was afraid he was allergic to latex, which probably would have aborted the surgery, but the test came back negative.

Mr. Waters was an optimistic fellow. He was sure he would do fine in surgery. The aneurysm scared him. With it unfixed, he would always be worried about an axe over his head, ready to fall. He would never be able to relax or have fun. He wanted not to worry, and he wanted surgery. (I did not have the heart to point out that the yearly risk from death of any cause for someone of his age was not much less than the yearly risk of death from the aneurysm, or remind him that there is an axe hanging over everyone's head.)

We were both right. Mr. Waters had the surgery, and he had the stormiest postoperative course anyone could imagine – worse than I predicted. (I suspect he had an allergy, and an overwhelming life-threatening allergic reaction, to something in the hospital environment.) For some days he had little blood pressure and suffered congestive heart failure, kidney failure and pneumonia. He remained in the intensive care unit for three months. His family came to say goodbye three different times. But, miraculously, Mr. Waters survived.

He survived, but in a weakened state, and on a ventilator. Once stabilized on a ventilator, we sent him off to a rehab center. I expected I would never see him again. Three months later, he was off the ventilator and out of rehab, a testimony to the amazing capacity of people to recover when they have the will to go on.

About eight months after surgery Mr. Waters was back to mowing his lawn. Six months after that he was dead of a massive heart attack (which he suffered while he was mowing his lawn).

Was it worth it? My guess is that Mr. Waters' hospitalization cost $500,000 to $1 million. Cost Medicare, that is. I very much doubt the process lengthened his life. In fact, I suspect, the process shortened it. Was it worth it? Mr. Waters thought so. I talked to him about it a number of times after he was home and off the ventilator. He was pleased as punch that he had the surgery, did not remember anything of the hospital stay, and was glad not to feel at continual risk anymore. His wife, who I saw recently, freely acknowledges how hard I tried to talk him out of surgery. Was it worth it? She thinks so. That way he did not have to live with an axe hanging over his head. Was it worth it? It is clear to me Mr. Waters was at risk, surgery or no surgery, and the huge expense and months of disability did not change the risk. In fact, when you consider that Mr. Waters learned about the aneurysm, and about the "axe", it might have been from a CT scan I ordered to look for something else. So I had probably put the axe there myself, and we spent a lot of money and months of a man's life taking it away. It was the most expensive treatment for iatrogenic anxiety I can image.

I am glad Mr. Waters died a happy man, but I am not so glad that the cost of his care could have paid for five to ten college educations of people who hadn't really had a shot at life yet. It may be that the price of Mr. Waters' happiness was at least some unfairness, and, writ large, a process that puts us on the road to social instability. Is it worth it? Only in a consumer society, where he who has the most toys – or the most operations, or the least anxiety – wins.

Mr. Burns had a whole different set of life experiences. He was already 80 when we found his abdominal aortic aneurysm, a vital 80, but a sad 80. Mr. Burns' life had been colored by illness and death. His wife, dead 25 years, had developed a degenerative muscular dystrophy that crippled her in her thirties, caused her to live as a complete cripple for 20 years, and then killed her when she was still young. As bad as that was, the mutation that killed her had been passed to three of their four children. Unlike the most common form of muscular dystrophy, which can be passed only to male children, Mrs. Burns' type could be passed to both male and female children. Mr. Burns had watched two of his children sicken and die in their thirties and early forties, and was watching the third child follow the path Mr. Burns and I now knew so well: dependence on a ventilator followed by death. Mr. Burns was living alone when he heard about the aneurysm, having recently ended a three-year relationship. He still had an unaffected son and an unaffected granddaughter, both of whom stayed close to him. He remained in good spirits despite a life of almost unimaginable sorrow, but he struggled quietly with depression. I did not think he would want surgery for the aneurysm, especially once I told him that it was just as likely to change the mode of his death as it was to lengthen his life substantially, which is the case when you have aneurysm surgery at 80 and have a pretty limited life expectancy anyway.

In fact, Mr. Burns did not want surgery, at least not at first. He was not the least bit interested. For him, life was good, despite the pain he had endured. Living every day was sweet, but he did not want to go to great lengths or entertain significant risks to prolong his life. It was a position that made sense to me and that I respected.

But then he talked to his son and granddaughter.

Mr. Burns' son and granddaughter were fiercely attached to one another. They had lost everyone else. They each assumed that they carried the gene for muscular dystrophy, even though many tests had shown that they had escaped. Both refused to have children because they were worried that the test results were wrong and that they had the gene hidden somewhere inside them, ready to be passed on to a next generation. Having only each other and Mr. Burns, they were as close a family as I have ever seen.

For the son and granddaughter the decision was clear-cut: Mr. Burns needed to have the surgery. He was their anchor, their sustainer, their hope. They could not imagine giving him up.

So he had the surgery, more for his little family than for himself. He had a pretty typical postoperative course, with a little kidney failure, a little respiratory failure, a little extra time on a ventilator, a little hallucinating. But he was expertly "managed" and survived the two-week hospital stay and three-week rehab hospital stay, and now is as fit as ever, walking around with no aneurysm. He does not remember his time in the hospital at all, and will tell you, cautiously, that surgery was the right thing to do. He still takes antidepressant medication, and, though he feels well otherwise, he reminds me of the Holocaust survivors I knew growing up. That is, he exists in a certain tenuous mood, as though he knows and will fiercely defend the value of life, but is not entirely sure he wants or deserves his own. I do not know how he would have felt if he had had a major crippling complication, nor do I know how long he would have lived without the surgery, or even how long he will live with it, and I'm not sure it matters. On the one hand, this person, who is so dear to a son and granddaughter, and who survived so much, can live with a little less fear. On the other hand, we see how strong is the pull to do everything we can to hold on to the people we love for every moment, even when the risks of trying to do so are no less than the risks of doing nothing, of watching and waiting.

Mrs. Kelly likes furs. Mrs. Kelly is a different person entirely. I met her a few years ago, as a perceived favor to someone politically well connected. Because I do a fair amount of policy work, I have the dubious distinction of being a primary-care physician known by members of our state legislature. The mother of a senior staffer of the House leadership had a cold. Her primary-care physician had retired and they needed someone to see her today. So I saw her today.

Mrs. Kelly turned out to be a delightful 69 year old with bleached blond hair pulled back in a ponytail, with lots of furs and jewelry, an omnipresent smile and an easy laugh. We had fun talking together when we first met and we have had fun every time we have gotten together since. Mrs. Kelly lives with her daughter, son-in-law and granddaughter whom she loves. They have a big RV, and enjoy going away for weeks at a time and driving off across America, camping and shopping.

So, Mrs. Kelly had a cold, from which she recovered. She also came with a six-centimeter abdominal aortic aneurysm built in. By "built in," I mean that the diagnosis had been made a few years earlier, when she had undergone the million-dollar evaluation, seen the best vascular surgeon in two different cities, been told about the likelihood of rupture, and had heard surgery recommended unequivocally by every doctor who ever came near her – and then she had told us all to go fish. Mrs. Kelly did not want her aneurysm fixed. She listened to us all discuss the risks and benefits a thousand times. She could quote the statistics and survival tables better than I could.

Mrs. Kelly just did not want her aneurysm fixed and that got me off the hook. Because the discussing and the informing and the warning had all been done a hundred times, I did not have to repeat the whole thing. I started, of course, but Mrs. Kelly cut me short. No aneurysm repair. She had an aneurysm. She knew it could kill her. She had lived 69 years. They were good years. She had a lot of fun. And everyone dies of something. When her aneurysm killed her, at least she would know what it was that was doing the killing, so she did not have anything to worry about. And by the way, she was going to keep smoking, thank you very much. That could also kill her, but it was one of her last pleasures, and, as she said about the aneurysm, nobody lives forever. The point is to enjoy life while you are here.

As far as I can tell, no one enjoys life more than Mrs. Kelly. She lives with the most passionate exuberance I have ever seen in anyone. It's all fun. No worries. Akuna matata. Life to the fullest. Maybe it is all denial, but it appears to me that Mrs. Kelly has more fun than anyone I know, and her willingness to have fun makes life fun for the people around her. Her daughter has fun. Her granddaughter has fun. Even her son-in-law has fun. (I have come to know them all over the years.) It is as if fun is genetic, or contagious.

Her spirit infects me too. When I'm with Mrs. Kelly, we have fun. I see her about every three months, and at each visit I double-check that she still does not want her aneurysm fixed. Then we chat for a while, I try to talk her into stopping smoking, refill her medicines, and we agree to meet in another three months. She usually refuses a mammogram, a physical examination, and a colonoscopy once or twice during each visit. It is totally unclear to me why I am paid for this opportunity, but that is another subject. What is interesting to me is how much I relax when the pressure to prolong life is gone. I do not have to worry about making a mistake or missing a diagnosis because longevity and the correct diagnosis that allows longevity are of no interest whatsoever to Mrs. Kelly. When I relax, we can spend a few minutes telling stores and asking each other questions, and we have a good time together. One day Mrs. Kelly will die. One day I will die. We can perhaps postpone but cannot eliminate death. In the meantime it appears that for Mrs. Kelly the point of life is trying to get everyone to live together happily and not doing anything that is bad faith, deviant and unnatural. So, left to ourselves, we relax with one another, and tell stories.

If there is a lesson to be drawn from abdominal aortic aneurysms, it is the lesson I learned from Mrs. Kelly. We all die of something. You can sometimes lengthen human life, but doing so can exact a cost, something more than money.

What went wrong in the U.S. healthcare system and why? We forgot who we are, what's important, and what health is. Why? Mistakes, money, greed, fear, alienation, distraction, and temptation. It just happened.

The point of philosophy, said Karl Marx, is not to think about the world. The point of philosophy is to change it. I am not a Marxist, but old Karl was right about that one. The point of all this talk about the meaning of health is not to think about health. The point of all this talk is to make health happen.

PART THREE

what health is

"By Community, I mean the commonwealth and common interests, commonly understood, of people living together in a place and wishing to continue to do so. To put it another way, community is a locally understood interdependence of local people, local culture, local economy, and local nature."

    — Wendell Berry

"Communities are collective associations . . . A community is more than just a place. It comprises various groups of people who work together on a face-to-face basis in public life, not just in private . . . Every life in community is, by definition, interdependent – filled with trusting relationships and empowered by the collective wisdom of citizens in discourse."

    — John McKnight

"Community is about the common life that is lived in such a way that the unique creativity of each person is a contribution to the other."

    — John McKnight

"And in the end, the love you take . . . will be just equal to the love you make."

    — John Lennon and Paul McCartney, "The End," *Abbey Road*

A. FIB

Atrial fibrillation is a disorder of the heart's rhythm that makes it beat faster than it should and causing it to pump poorly. The condition sometimes produces a backup of fluid in the lungs which we call heart failure (although it is really heart insufficiency, not failure). This abnormal rhythm creates a risk of stroke because when the heart is not pumping correctly blood pools inside it, can clot and pieces of the clot can break off, travel to the brain and block the small arteries there.

To prevent stroke, we often put people with atrial fibrillation on a medicine called warfarin, an anticoagulant. While warfarin prevents stroke, thereby saving a person's life, it can also be life-threatening because its correct use is very exacting. The dose has to be just right, and the right dose can change from day to day and week to week, a function of what a person eats, and sometimes, it seems, even of his or her mood. To regulate warfarin dosage, people have to get their blood-clotting capacity tested often, daily at first, then weekly or biweekly. If the warfarin dosage is too small, people can easily stroke from a blood clot that comes from the heart; too large a dose can cause bleeding, and a stroke from that bleeding inside the brain.

Quinnie Winkles lived in a peeling wooden two-storey house sandwiched between a twisting mountain road, a fast mountain stream and the mountain itself, as the road approached the top of a ridge on Clinch Mountain. Quin was 85 or so when I met her, and was one of the smartest people I have even known. She had an encyclopedic memory for people and places, stories and ideas, and she never missed a tack intellectually. When you talked to her, she was always two steps ahead of you. She knew where a story was going before it went there, and could weave her way in and out of the politics of the county like a hot-dogging 20 year old on a supercharged motorcycle in L.A. traffic.

She had never married, but instead had stayed home and cared for her parents as they aged, until they died and she became the person who needed care herself. She had a huge family, nieces and nephews, great-nieces and great-nephews and their families, with some teenager in trouble – one of those great- or great-great-nieces or nephews – always being sent to live with her, half so she could keep a watch on them, and half to take care of her, so someone would watch out for her. The watching out never happened either way. The young person entrusted to her care quickly figured out that she could not see or hear very well, and disappeared half the night, running hog wild in the county.

That meant no one really took care of Quin after all. She never could figure out how to get her medicine straight, so her atrial fibrillation was rarely in any kind of control, which meant her feet were always too swollen for her to get out to the outhouse (her house did not have indoor plumbing). There were always four or five bowls of her urine standing open in the kitchen or the sitting room that she could not remember to and probably did not have the ability to discard, waiting for someone to come home and toss out. She was often short of breath.

People in the county Health Department were always plotting to make her life better. We would drop by and clean up for her, and scheme over ways of getting her an inside bathroom built, and some welfare official was always trying to move her to a nursing home "for her own protection". She welcomed our visits but she steadfastly refused to change her ways. I spent months trying to convince her to go on warfarin but she always waived me off. The truth was that she was right and I was wrong, because the danger to her from the warfarin – from it causing a stroke if she fell and hit her head, or if she got the dose wrong – far outweighed any benefit she might have derived from taking it.

The thing I remember most about Quinnie, now, 15 years later, was her happiness. She loved people and loved being alive (though she had no interest whatsoever in my treatments or in any medicine designed to keep her alive). Her heart did not work and her eyes were bad and she was short of breath if she tried to walk and her feet were always so swollen they oozed. She lived in squalor in a house that smelled of urine and had more flies than anyone could count. Nonetheless, Quin loved the people around her, even the people who let her down. When I dropped by to visit once a month or so on my way back home over the mountain, she always had 40 pictures of family I had to look at and I felt as welcome there as I have ever felt anywhere.

Eventually, after I had left, they pushed Quin into a nursing home, where she died. I was not there, so I do not know what caused what. When you are sick and failing, death takes you because everyone dies of something, and sometimes we need nursing homes to take care of the people who just cannot take care of themselves, people who often like the company and support in a nursing home no matter how fiercely they fight going in.

But when she was in her own house, poor as she was, squalid as the house was, beset by chronic disease, despite the discomfort and disability, Quinnie was probably the healthiest person I have ever known. Quin had her place, and she had her memories, and she had her family, and she had people running in and out, and that was what she wanted – to be with the things and people she loved, because the being with was health for her. Not the living forever. The being with.

John Canterbury, on the other hand, was an industrialist. He owned companies. He lived in a mansion on a large piece of land in the country with his trophy wife, played golf, and jetted places. But he was really a very nice person despite all that.

John, who was in his seventies when I knew him, also developed atrial fibrillation. Worried about his heart disease, he had turned over the family business to his sons and was living out a dream by gentleman farming. It did not work out very well. The local people resented him and raised his taxes, so that he was carrying a large piece of the town's operating expenses. His wife strayed. His kids, busy with business and their own kids and more than an hour's drive away, did not have much time for him. Before long his greatest satisfaction in life was flying to Florida once a year to play golf with his brother for a week.

Despite the atrial fibrillation John was in excellent health. His heart rate was controlled by medication. His risk of stroke was limited because of warfarin, which he carefully regulated. He walked every day, was in great shape, and looked more like 50 than 74. He had strength and vigor.

But he was unhappy, and before long, that happiness turned into depression. We put him on medication which seemed to work for a time, but then he fell out of touch. I called him and he did not call me back. He stopped having his blood clotting checked. I tried to call him about that. I called his wife. After a while, he came in one day, assured me that he was feeling fine and promised he would have his clotting checked. Soon after that he was found unresponsive and unmoving. He had a massive stroke from bleeding into his brain caused by having taken far too much warfarin.

Quietly, and slowly, John had committed suicide with warfarin. He used his atrial fibrillation as a way out of a life that he could not make work and just did not want anymore.

Two people, one disease. Quinnie, who was sick, blind, nearly deaf, poor, and smelly, was healthy despite everything. John had everything but was sick of it all. So health is not the absence of disease, is not riches, is not age, is not medicine, is not science, is not freedom from pain.

Remember the elephant joke? "Question: How do you carve a statue of an elephant? Answer. Get a really big block of marble, and chip away anything that does not look like an elephant."

What's the nature of health?

We have chipped away at the marble in Part One, working through what health is not. Now we are going to pull out the jackhammer, look carefully at human history and human nature, and see if we can discover what health is.

what Webster thinks

In thinking about this book, we have come to believe that the crisis in our medical services system may stem from an incorrect premise – a wrong understanding of health. This is an immensely important error because how we define and understand health determines what the medical services system looks like and how it behaves. If we want to fix this system, first we have to understand, and agree on, what health is. Working toward this definition, the chapter will consider health by:

▶ probing the etymology and broad meanings of the concept of health;
▶ analyzing various definitions of health;
▶ discovering the contextual definition of health used in contemporary American society by exploring how we spend healthcare resources and what we measure to evaluate health;
▶ considering whether long life is an aspect of health;
▶ approaching a social definition of health;
▶ exploring the ways we use the concept of health as we think about the health of the individual, family, and nation;
▶ offering our own definition, from which a model for healthcare reform will later emerge.

THE BROAD MEANINGS OF HEALTH

Along with the vagaries of the weather, commonplaces about our health hold a near corner on the market of idle conversation. "How are you?" or "How are you feeling today?" or "How have you been?" are our most routine conversational gambits. These quasi-questions are such a matter of ritual and formula that we normally intend them as mere acknowledgments or vague assertions of affinity and empathy. We expect equally automatic and meaningless reciprocity: "Just fine, thank you" or "Not bad for an old fella", or "Pretty good, I guess." In fact, all but the most charitable of us tend to wince a bit when those we greet in this way choose to respond with a factual – and sometimes detailed – account their current medical condition.

Beyond the empty formalism of greeting, however, most people relish the opportunity to discuss their health and think of it often – especially when it is compromised by injury or illness. But is one's medical condition the same thing as one's health? Health, after all, is one of life's core issues – a powerful and pervasive reality that affects everything we do, that shapes our perception of and interaction with the world and that often determines both the course of our lives and our understanding of the meaning of life itself.

Our assessment and description of health delineates the extent of well-being in others or ourselves. "I'm in good health," or "She's radiantly healthy," or "His health has never been worse" all assert something basic and definitional about the described person. What is this condition of health, though? What are the attributes of health?

In classical Greek, the words *hugieia* ['υγεία] (n.), and *hugieinos* ['υγείνός] (adj.) serve as the approximate equivalent of our English words *health* and *healthy*, *hygiene* and *hygienic*. (Hugeia, also known as Hygieia, or Hygeia, usually appearing as the daughter of Asclepius on the Olympian family tree, was the Greek goddess of health, cleanliness, and sanitation. Her sister and healing partner was Panacea, the goddess of medical herbs and potions.) Use of these words ('υγεία, 'υγείνός) in classical literature makes clear that they apply not only to the biological condition of the body but also to a broader context of total individual well-being, including the physical, emotional and social environment in which each person lived. The Greek notion of *hygeia* implied that the body could heal itself if it were helped to do so, wrapping the body together with the environment and relationships that might help with healing.[1] That same expansive sense applies in Latin syntax, in which the verb *salveo (-ere)* (to be well, to be in good health) serves as the primary linguistic root of the concept of health. The present active imperative, *salve* (sing.), *salvete* (pl.), served as a common greeting, "Good health," and by extension, "Good day!" or "Good morning!" This same meaning appeared in the Anglo-Saxon expression *wes hal*, "May you be in good health," and migrated to English in *hail*, "Be in good health," or, more generally and commonly meaning, "hello," or "I salute you." Notice here that health and greeting often have the same root, as if health always references other people, and the human relationships between people.

Other senses derived from *salveo (-ere)* are worth noting: *salve*, "salvation," and *salvus, salva, salvum* (adj.), "well, unharmed, sound; alive; safe, saved." The Latin health-related root (*sal-*) also served as the basis of the Italian word for health, *salute*. This has been carried into English to denote a gesture of greeting or respect, but one that, etymologically, extends a wish for good health, just as does a letter's *salutation*.

The linguistic basis of the word *health* also lies deep in the rootstock of the English language. As noted above, its etymology stems from the Old English *hāl*, as well as from the Old Norse *heill*. In a millennium of transmutations through Old and Middle English, these root words have accreted a broad range of sense and nuance.

But here the meaning and use of these root words is related. Many words denoting health not only describe the condition of a person, but also express the wish for good health. These are relationship words, used in greeting. From their earliest etymological roots, words about health have described or referred to the relationship between people. Health and relationship have mingled in the origin of both ideas – the warp and woof of a primordial, complex and inevitable pairing.

Based on the work of philologist W. F. Bolton, English linguist David Crystal studied the many related words derived from the Germanic root of both *hāl* and *heill*. These include: *hail* (*hail from, hail fellow*), *wassail, whole* (*wholesome, wholesale, wholesome*), *holy* (*holiness, holiday*), *hallow* (*Halloween*), *hale, heal* (*healer*) and, of course, *health, healthy* and *healthful*.[2]

Dense, multi-tiered meanings for the notion of health operate in other languages as well. In French, for example, the word *santé* suggests temperament, constitution, well-being and hygiene. Synonyms include the notion of balance, order, equilibrium, and proportion, of calmness and security, strength and power, happiness and prosperity. Much of the same linguistic complexity applies to the German *gesundheit*.[3] All Western languages, in fact, appear to employ an extensive range of synonyms for their respective words for health. While the concept of individual physical well-being and proper functioning anchor the primary definitions of these words, all extend the sense of health to include dimensions of psychological, social, and material soundness, and all predicate the meaning of health on the relationship of an individual to some function, object, or other person.

The notion of health evokes a broad range of positive human conditions, in turn richly expressed in language. Vitality, vigor, well-being, alertness, fitness, energy, contentedness, strength, endurance, focus, happiness, capability, accomplishment, satisfaction – all serve as synonyms of and describe some aspect of what we call health, and all express the central idea that health is the state or condition necessary for people to be attuned to (or in relationship with) their world or community.

SOME DEFINITIONS

Most contemporary dictionary definitions of health are fairly limited in outlook, and fail to reflect on the etymological origins of the word and concepts from which our understanding of health developed.

The American Heritage Dictionary of the English Language, Fourth Edition defines health as:

1. The overall condition of an organism at a given time.
2. Soundness, especially of body or mind; freedom from disease or abnormality.
3. A condition of optimal well-being: *concerned about the ecological health of the area.*
4. A wish for someone's good health, often expressed as a toast.[4]

The first definition is incomplete. "The overall condition of an organism at any given time" might help us understand the organism, but would not enable us to understand its health. For that understanding, we must know something about the organism's natural history and habitat. We need to be aware of the normal function of the organism and what relationships it characteristically forms with its environment and other organisms like it. Definition number one does not require us to place an organism in the context of its relationships, but only to consider its condition – its individual momentary status. For human beings, placing the individual organism in her or his environment appears to be the first necessary attribute of a robust definition of health.

The second definition, "soundness of body and of mind", does not help much either. This definition is much like the *Oxford English Dictionary* definition: "Soundness of body. That condition in which its functions are duly and efficiently discharged."[5] Both definitions are artfully simple, but unsatisfying, as "soundness" begs us to ask, "Soundness for what function?" and the functions of the body demand that we know what the body's functions are, and to understand the requirements for those functions to be effectively carried out. *Soundness* again requires us to know how the body and person stands in relation to his or her environment and culture, suggesting again that it is relationship that defines health, not soundness *per se.*

What about *freedom from disease*? The absence of disease is not the presence of health, and the presence of disease does not mean the absence of health. A coal miner working in the pitch dark in 19th-century Wales might have been free from a disease for a period. Hands covered with coal dust, bent over in the bowels of the earth 12 hours a day, exploited by the ruling classes from the day of his birth until the day of his untimely death

– could he be healthy? A happy, hard-working diabetic, involved with family and embarking at new projects, has a disease but may be perfectly healthy at the same time. Health, we will suggest, is about functioning in relationships. Health is about hope and economic and political freedom, as much as it is about freedom from disease.

As to *freedom from abnormality*, if we are to accept this aspect of the *American Heritage* definition of health, we must assume that health is impossible for an abnormal person. But doesn't normality imply a social context? Nearsightedness was abnormal (and unhealthy) for a hunter-gatherer, but normal (and not unhealthy) for a middle-aged doctor. Intellects either far above or far below the "normal" range are, according to the definition, "abnormal" but is either suggestive of health? Normality and health are unrelated, but this analysis suggests again that health is about function, and, even more, about function in a social and cultural context.

Definition three, a *condition of optimal well-being*, is closer, but it also misses the mark. Optimal well-being implies both subjective and objective best function. It gets at the subjective sense of health, but does not explicate the functional, and relational, connotations of health.

Definition four, *a wish for someone's good health, often expressed as a toast*, is closest to the entomologic roots of heath because it includes the relationship implied in health, but is limited in scope to just a greeting.

The New Oxford American Dictionary definition, *the state of being free from illness or injury*, is the most limited of all.[6] As we discussed above, it is possible to have an illness or an injury and still be healthy. But perhaps, the notion of *a state* is useful. While it is possible to have illness or injury and still be healthy, being in the state of freedom from illness or injury implies just that, just and exactly freedom. People who are not healthy are consumed, in some way, by their illness or injuries. People who are not healthy are constrained; they cannot go about their lives as they choose. They cannot have the relationships they value, or those relationships are limited by their illness or injury. People who are not healthy are not free to go about their lives because of the loss of some body function. And people who are healthy *are* able to function *and* have relationships that are important to them.

The World Health Organization definition of health is: "Health is a state of complete physical, mental and social well-being and not merely the absence of disease or infirmity." This comes closer, but still does not get at the need for functionality or relationship.[7]

Well-being appears to be a necessary condition for health, yet it does not provide a complete definition. Social well-being, for example, is a function, not of the individual, but of his or her community and environment, and from this observation we learn that the health of an individual is meaningless without an understanding of the health of the family, community, and society. We learn again that health is about relationship, not just well-being.

Notice, in all these definitions, that long life, or longevity, did not appear even once. Our understanding of the meaning of health does include much about function and relationship. Our understanding of the meaning of health does *not* include anything about longevity.

TOWARD A NEW AND BETTER DEFINITION OF HEALTH

With the above definitions, an individual human body is set forth as the unit by which we can grasp the meaning of health, but we quickly discover that we must add the relationship between a body and the social environment in which that body lives. In addition, although soundness of body suggests functionality, it does not denote the subjective well-being of a human in her or his own context. Relationship, soundness, and functionality are clearly aspects of health, but by themselves these aspects do not define health, but merely contribute to its definition.

Here, then, is a more robust definition of health, one that we believe meets the tests of etymology as well captures what most Americans mean by health: *Health is the biological, social, and psychological ability that affords an equal opportunity for each individual to function in the relationships appropriate to his or her cultural context at any point in the life cycle.* Health is not the mere absence of illness or disease, nor is it an entirely physical state. In fact, like an ocean wave, health has an ambiguous, momentary, and situational reality. Health is the conditional manifestation of the ability to function in relationship. Health as a condition can be limited by pain, be limited by mental disorder, or limited by physiological dysfunction – but implied in that condition, and necessary to give that condition meaning, is the existence of the superstructures of family and community. In order for health to be actualized, there must be relationships, and those relationships have necessary conditions, contexts, in which they can exist and be stable over time. The predicate of relationship is the gorilla in the room, the definitional piece present in the etymology of the word health, and missing in all the definitions, including the oft-cited WHO definition, that we have critiqued above. But not only is the predicate of relationship missing from the dictionary, it is missing from medical services, and all our healthcare spending. Without providing the context, without attending to the superstructure of relationship, without making sure family and community are functional, health becomes an absurd concept, and we can spend all the money we have and hope to have, still not achieve the health we want, and always lack good health outcomes. What other countries have (but, like us, are losing) that we do not have is the context, the stability of family and community.

The notion of equal opportunity for function is also important to health, and brings in the relationship between individual health and population health, which we first described in Part One. Individual health, you will recall, is a subjective state, that comes out of a person's beliefs about lifestyle and medical services choices, and involves some negotiation between the need for function in relationship, the desire for discomfort control, and an interest in life span as a consumer good, as well as the existence of functional families and communities. Population health is the collective expression of the health of the individuals in a population. But it is also a reflection of the collective ability of individuals in a population to enter and sustain relationships without social impairment. It is also a reflection of the resilience and added meaning that the population as a whole brings to individuals, recalling that a population in a place, as an organism, as a whole, can be greater than the sum of its parts. Population health is measured by measuring some aspects of the health of individuals, and collating those measures, with frequency of occurrence of a specific finding, circumstance, disorder or trait being the numerator of the measure, and the number of people in the population being the dominator. We currently measure population health inaccurately, using measures which are easy to obtain but which do not adequately reflect the meaning of health; that is, we do not measure function in relationship, but measure mostly longevity or the occurrence of disease in a population.

Equal opportunity to function in relationship is important to the meaning of health because of the extent to which social interference, and not just mental or physical function, can impair or impede relationships. The social impairment of relationship is no less ill health than physiological impairment. It was no better to be physiologically well in Sarajevo during the disintegration of Yugoslavia than it is to have cancer in the United States, was no better to be a poor black kid in central Harlem in the 1990s than it is to be a 10 year old with juvenile onset diabetes in the suburbs of Des Moines, and maybe worse, from the perspective of health and life chances. Where social structure impairs relationship, where there is significant inequality, social conflict is certain to result, social conflict which undermines the integrity of family and community, the necessary conditions for health.

There is no ontological or immutable fact or state of health, but rather a set of conditions that, in their conjunction, yield a condition we call health. This condition implies a certain amount of freedom that is social and political, a certain amount of mental and physiological well-being, some freedom from the encumbrance of disease and injury, and implies the existence of family and community for the relationships that give health meaning.

When one considers the sheer size of healthcare literature and health policy, it is striking how little attention is devoted to understanding health, and to agreeing on an adequate definition of health on which to build a healthcare system. It is as if we decided to spend 16 percent of our budget on a service that we are unable to define or describe and to order it before we have decided what benefit we expect from it. It is as if we had decided to devote a huge portion of our income ordering from a catalogue, without either having the catalogue or being able to look inside it.

IF HEALTH IS RELATIONSHIP, WHAT IS HEALTHCARE?

Collectively, we spend billions of dollars on information about, and services and products to promote, the individual quest for health. The fact is, though, that the vast bulk of health-related expense is transacted within what we have come to call *healthcare*, or perhaps more fittingly, the *healthcare industry*. Healthcare implies the involvement of others to support an individual's or the public's health. For us to talk about the ways in which America pursues health or directs its investments related to health, we must consider not only individual activities but the vast enterprise of medical services. As we will soon see, the same muddiness and confusion that surround the meaning of health also bedevil our definitions of healthcare, and, hence, of its actions and priorities.

The American Heritage Dictionary of the English Language, Fourth Edition, defines healthcare as, "The prevention, treatment, and management of illness and the preservation of mental and physical well-being through the services offered by the medical and allied health professions."[8] This seems a curiously shallow definition, in that it confines healthcare to the tasks of managing illness and preserving well-being. This definition assumes both that health is the absence of disease and that services offered by the medical and allied health professions are effective in preserving mental and physical well-being. Both are important and worthwhile pursuits, of course, but the definition ignores the fundamental sense of the term, namely to provide services that create or reinstate health. Indeed, the definition assumes that all healthcare is subsumed by the services of the medical professions. But if health relies on the existence of families and communities so that individuals can have relationships, and if the action of the medical professionals focus only on providing services that prevent, manage, and treat illness and preserve well-being, then a more robust definition of healthcare must reflect on the need for functioning families and communities, and must anticipate more participants than just medical professionals and their allies.

An alternative definition might look something like this: *Healthcare is the promotion and recovery of function by individuals, and the strengthening of families and communities as the context for that function, through services offered by medical and allied health professionals, and organized by private and government organizations and institutions.*

old villages, new lives

By considering its etymology and definitions, we have concluded that the meaning of health (and, thus, the proper role of healthcare) places the individual within a broader social context. Health is in a dance with community – health cannot exist without community; communities cannot exist without healthy individuals. How and why did this come about? Is health a function of community because the role of the individual is as a constituent part of the community, because the machine does not work if the parts do not work? Or is health a function of community because individuals cannot be healthy unless there is a family and community context for their relationships, unless there is a community for individuals to be healthy in? If health and community are intertwined, what sense can we make of health in the 21st century, when our understanding of family and community is at least changing, and at most breaking apart? To answer these questions we must consider the course of humanity's social and cultural history from the very beginning.

Our evolution and history give us valuable insight into the meaning of health because they show us two important characteristics that make us who we are, that make health what it is, and that come into conflict, and create real challenges for health and society in the 21st century. Those characteristics are:

▶ the fundamental social character of the human project – our relationships with one another which produced thought and language;
▶ what some have called the cut-and-measure, or cut-measure-and-control approach of the human intellect, our proclivity for breaking large tasks into small ones and to address the world piece by piece, instead of holistically.

In the vortex of human evolution, a number of strands interacted, and intertwined as they interacted. We stood on two legs, and viewed the world around us. We evolved physically, responding to both the changing environment and progressive incremental change in our bodies. We developed the ability to communicate with one another, with great sophistication. We developed the ability to think. We learned to use tools. And we developed the ability to teach one another about the tools we developed. Essentially, we evolved culture, a way to spread and perpetuate our tool using that was separate and distinct from one person's physical body, making the whole greater than the sum of the parts. But tools and their use had an additional impact on the human condition. Our ability to make and use tools made us social beings, whose evolution and meaning depended on one another, but the tools themselves configured the way we think and who we are.

Early tools were edge tools, made by chipping small pieces off a stone until an edge was formed. Mounted on lances, spears, and arrows, these sharp edges allowed us to bring down prey with lessened risk of losing our own lives – and made us more successful as hunters. With sharp-edged stone axes, we could skin the prey, cut the meat and prepare the hides. The same edges enabled us to cut wood for fire and to escalate the violence and efficiency of battle with our neighbors.

In order to make these edges, our ancestors learned to break down a complex task that could not be accomplished with a single movement – the fashioning of an edge – into a series of very small tasks – the removal of stone fragments – by repeatedly striking the latent edge with another hard, small stone. In time, we folded this process, called *cut-measure-and-control*, into our human makeup as a profound epistemological predisposition, a hard-wired intellectual apparatus with which we *naturally* approached problems. Once inculcated, this "cut-measure-and-control" approach influenced all human thoughts and actions and determined our interaction with the natural world. Everything that our intellect enabled – written language, counting, differential calculus, quantum mechanics, and even chaos theory – emerged from this cut-measure-and-control epistemology.[1]

But at the same time as we were developing a cut-measure-and-control approach to thinking about tasks, we developed the social and community character of human beings, which drove thought and language, and it is thought and language that incidentally allows – and constructs – consciousness. Our ability to interact, to be in relationships with one another, powered the development of thought and language, and it was thought and language which took the cut-measure-and-control method of approaching tasks and turned it into a culture which developed and spread increasingly sophisticated tools, and which achieved progressively more control over the environment. Without thought and language, there would be no tool development. Without thought and language, there would be no spread of tool using, or, as we call it now, of technology. Without thought and language, there would be no culture. And without relationships there would be no thought and language at all.

Of course, it is not possible to divorce the dancer from the dance, to separate out the contribution of thought and language – and the primacy of our social being to the human project – from the contribution of technology to making us who we are. But the connection of that social being, and of thought and language, to consciousness, argues for the primacy of that social character in the construction of our self-concept, and the primacy of our social character to the meaning of health. At bottom, we are cut-into-pieces, talk-and-teach creatures. The cut-into-pieces way of thinking propels our changing culture. But our talk-and-teach nature is really the center of who we are, or, at least, who we have been up until now.

However, as we shall argue later in this part of the book, the cut-measure-and-control mechanism by which thought and language operate would create a conflict for humanity in the 20th century. The culture that gives humanity meaning would be threatened by the process of thought, which allowed human culture to succeed in our evolutionary niche but now threatens to cut the human experience itself into small unrelated parts, breaking communities apart in the process. Health, the expression of the effective function of human culture, would be caught in this vice.

toward a social definition of health

Rene Dubos and Ivan Illich are both theorists who have written critically about health and health policy, and both use remarkably similar, promising, but ultimately wrong-headed, definitions of health. Daniel Callahan, an ethicist, has pointed out what health is not, and illustrates the danger of confusing health and happiness, and confounding both with individual need. It is John McKnight, the great community organizer, who is not a health theorist or a health policy expert, who points the way to a usable social definition of health.

RENE DUBOS

Rene Dubos, biologist and early health-policy theorist, believed that health, the ability of the individual and species to adapt to a changing environment, is impossible – a mirage – because of the incessant striving of the human spirit: "Health and happiness are the expression of the manner in which the individual responds and adapts to the challenges he meets in everyday life."[1] Dubos' critique relies heavily on his broad understanding of biology, and refers to biological models. For him health is both the ability of people to *adapt* to changing environments and social situations, and the product of that adaptation. For Dubos, health exists only during the brief periods when neither environment nor culture change very much. Even then, because it is the unique capacity of human beings to strive toward a better world, their striving changes the environment, which means there is never a quiet place for health to happen, and health becomes a goal to which we aspire but will rarely if ever reach.

The definition of health was not the center of Dubos' argument, which mainly sought to understand the human spirit from the perspective of biological (as opposed to social) models. Still, the strength of Dubos' argument is that it argues for health as an ability, not a condition, which is consonant with the common-sense understanding of the meaning of health. It is in its use of the notion of adaptation that the Dubosian view fails. Adaptation is an ability of species, more than of individuals, and the definition of health as the ability to adapt is really a definition of the health of the species, not the health of individuals, who may occasionally need to adapt but mostly need to function in a set of environmental conditions that do not change much over time. Still, by referencing the environment, Dubos hinted at a contextual definition for health: one is not healthy in the abstract, one is healthy *in reference to* an external set of conditions (in this case, in reference to adaptation to a changing environment). The contextual setting is important in understanding health – but Dubos got the context wrong. The context health refers to is the context of the relationships important to an individual in a particular time and culture, and at a particular stage in her or his life cycle, and *not* the context of a changing environment.

We can also fault the Dubosian view for its reliance on Dubos' assertion of two aspects of the human condition. Dubos termed them humanity's *restlessness* and humanity's *commitment to ideals that transcend life itself.* These aspects of the human condition do not reflect on the meaning of health but only on a human paradox: the impossibility of realizing health, which results from the drive to improve conditions that determine health.

Still, the Dubosian definition is useful because it argues that health has meaning only in reference to a set of external relationships (to the physical and social environment), essentially, that health is ability to function in relationships. And though Dubos argues that health is a mirage because of inadequacies of the human spirit, his argument is useful to the extent it can be turned, so that health is possible because it relies on the ability of human beings to be in relationship with one another.

IVAN ILLICH

Illich uses a similar definition of health to Dubos:

> Health designates a process of adaptation. It is not the result of instinct, but of an autonomous, yet culturally shaped reaction to socially created reality. It designates the ability to adapt to changing circumstances, to growing up and aging, to healing when damaged, to suffering, and to the peaceful expectation of death. Health embraces the future as well, and therefore includes anguish and the inner resources to live with it.[2]

However, Illich was engaged in a very different project. Health for Illich *is* adaptation, but it is also culture, and it is more than culture. It is the human ability to suffer and recover from suffering, with recovery occurring because of a set of rituals and behaviors in the culture, with suffering being necessary to give health – and human life – meaning, and culture the overarching context in which health, suffering, and individual life have both meaning and value.[3] Illich also believed, as we do, that the dominant culture has expropriated the goal of health in a way that strips authenticity from human life. Health has been *medicalized* and packaged for sale in the service of the few and at the expense of the many. Indeed, Illich believed that medicine has become a tool of the industrial machine, manufacturing the idea of illness which requires treatment, producing treatment which requires dependency. Thereby it undermines the existential meaning of health, which is closely tied to the autonomy of individuals who are in relationship with self, each other, and the whole of human suffering, which Illich believed gives health, and all of the human experience, meaning.

Again, as a definition, Illich's model of health falls short. Illich under-stood health to be an ability, and he even understood the importance of the cultural context, but he was focused on his view of authentic human existence and consciousness. This, for Illich, implies suffering and the recovery from suffering, an existential view of the human project that is not widely shared, and is much broader than most people's view of health as a concept. Still, Illich's view helps us understand the social context within which one might view health.

"To a large extent, health and culture coincide."[4] His social construction, which he called *cultural iatrogenesis,* suggests there are ways in which our social organization, or its failure, may undermine health. Cultural iatrogenesis is an incredibly useful idea that we will return to over and over again in this book. We believe that the evolution of postmodern culture, and the deconstruction of family and community that is part of postmodern life, undermines health. Illich believed that it is the expropriation of health by consumer capitalism and the medical industrial complex that undermines health, and clearly, that expropriation has contributed to our cultural malaise around the notion and nature of health. But whatever the cause, it is clear that the culture contributes mightily to the meaning, perception, and possibility of health, a contribution first understood and articulated by Illich.

Thus, in considering the work of Dubos and Illich, we can conclude that health is not the status of an isolated organism but rather an ability and a condition that encompasses one or more organisms that operate within the context of relationship. Notions of soundness and capability are also part of the meaning of health, but the definition must reach beyond individual condition to include capability to participate in relationships and to adapt to the social environment. That adaptation can be perilous indeed, since human culture can as easily undermine health as support it.

DANIEL CALLAHAN

Daniel Callahan, healthcare ethicist, philosopher, and co-founder of the Hastings Institute, has struggled with the meaning of health, correctly understanding that an adequate definition of health is a necessary condition for the creation of a healthcare system. Callahan is critical of the WHO definition of health for confusing health, happiness, and well-being, and for being the basis for an inappropriate expansion of the medical into the rest of the human world. Callahan is also sensitive to the confusion between health and longevity.

> To be happy is not necessarily healthy, and to be healthy is necessarily to be happy. That is what the WHO definition, and its accompanying philosophy, failed to concede. That definition, while sensitive to an important truth about health, also embodied a view of the relationship between health and human well-being in general that is not simply wrong. When joined with the idea of meeting individual needs it also adds a burden to our thinking about health policy that is bound to increase demands for health beyond prudent boundaries, and even the pursuit of which takes us down a hazardous road.[5]
>
> Good health does not guarantee a good life, or a longer life necessarily a better life. A good life is compatible with some degree of poor health, and a life obsessively dedicated to good health can be neurotically miserable . . .[6]

We are all indebted to Callahan's thinking for introducing the kind of ethical analysis that this book draws on, for his keen observations about the social causes of illness, the need to balance medical services spending with spending on other areas that improve social function, and the need for health policy to achieve fairness in life chances. But Callahan was never able to write a robust definition of health. He struggled with the relationship between health and happiness, and the relationship between good of the body and good of the self, sensing that relationship was central to health, but never explicating the kind of relationships that health presupposes.

JOHN MCKNIGHT

What relationship does health presuppose? The answer to that question is suggested in a definition offered by community organizer/builder John McKnight, a friend and colleague of Illich's: "Health is the unintended side effect of citizens acting powerfully in association."[7] The substance of McKnight's argument is that individual health relates to the totality of what people in communities do together – more a function of democracy than medicine – and not merely to long life or freedom from pain. For most disconnected, 21st-century Americans, this idea of health may, at first, seem very far from their previous personal experiences. Still, the notion that health is a condition and an ability in which individuals have the soundness of body, mind, culture, and society to enter into associations with each other, in family and community, seems a closer description of health than any definition we have otherwise encountered.

Again, we believe health is both the equal ability of an individual to function in the relationships appropriate to his or her cultural context at any point in the life cycle, and is the condition which results from that ability.

What about the meaning of the health of families, communities, and society as a whole?

health and community together

"Monday," recalled 66-year-old Angie Martocci, "almost everyone in town ate spezzati [a spinach and egg soup]. Tuesdays, it was spaghetti and gravy [tomato sauce]. Wednesday was roast chicken and potatoes. Thursday, spaghetti again. Fish on Fridays, of course. Veal and peppers on Saturday; and antipasto, meatballs and spaghetti on Sunday."[1] Roseto, Pennsylvania is a town of about 2,000 people, near the New Jersey border, about 75 miles from Philadelphia and New York City, a town surrounded by slate quarries and blouse factories. Roseto's mostly Italian-American population is descended from people who came from the same village in southern Italy. They were a close-knit group, with much in common: churches, sports, scout troops, a newspaper, a labor union, and, for many years, little to pull them apart. Most people did the same kind of work (slate mining for the men, sewing in small blouse factories for the women), earned the same income, and ate the same kind of food, which was anything if not high in fat content. Many smoked. But few people in Roseto developed heart disease. In fact, when compared to their neighbors in surrounding towns in the years 1950–1980, the people who lived in Roseto were different in only two ways. First, their heart-attack rate was half that of their neighbors. Second, the extent to which people from Roseto were interconnected, the extent to which they spent time together in church, on the football field, in living rooms or on their front porches, was greater than the interconnectedness of people in surrounding towns.[2,3]

The idea that social structure – the extent to which people living together in a place are interdependent – can influence the health of individuals (as both the ability to function in relationships, and to attain longevity), is centuries, and perhaps millennia, old. Surely, that notion underlay early legal codes in Babylonia, in the Inca and Aztec lands, in Africa and in Greece. For the notion of law itself, a structuring of rules allowing people to live together in a place in relative harmony, had to come from the need to create peace in order to allow people in more densely populated cultures to have relationships and to prevent death from violence. The use of social organization to promote the health of individuals is deeply entrenched in the Old Testament, which contains a moral and legal code that structured concepts of ritual purity, as well as the attempt to create peace between people living together in a place. Ritual purity appears to come from concerns about infectious diseases like leprosy and sexually transmitted disease, and an early understanding of the need for food purity, understandings which reflect the perception that there is a relationship between social organization and health. The relationship of social structure to health appears again and again in the work of many late second-millennium thinkers, from Malthus to Marx, from Virchow to Durkheim and John Rawls.

Is there something we can learn about health from exploring what is known about social interconnectedness and how social interconnectedness predicts population health? In this chapter, we will review what is known about social interconnectedness and health, hoping to get at two concepts: the degree to which social interconnectedness (social structure) is a necessary condition for the health of individuals and populations, and is part of the meaning of health. At the same time, we will explain three additional "meanings" of health: what we mean when we talk about the health of families; what we mean when we talk about the health of communities; and what we mean when we talk about the health of society as a whole. We will be looking for the connection between health and social organization as we go.

One warning: these are slippery ideas. If health is, at least in part, the ability of individuals to function in relationship, and social interconnectedness is the sum of all the relationships of individuals, there is a risk that these concepts can slide into one another as we talk about them. Hopefully, defining these terms before we start will give us the intellectual clarity we need to understand how health and social interconnectedness are related, how they overlap, and how they are not the same idea.

THE DIFFICULTY OF MEASURING SOCIAL INTERCONNECTEDNESS

As we have described, health appears to be related to social interconnectedness, and social interconnectedness may be a necessary condition for health. Our ability to *measure* social interconnectedness is just developing, and our understanding of the extent to which function (itself rarely, and poorly, measured) and longevity are related to social interconnectedness is just being understood. The level of, or degree to which, social inter-connectedness exists in a place is called that place's *social capital*. Measures of social capital include levels of interpersonal trust, income equality or inequality, the degree to which people report they give and expect help from neighbors, and the number of voluntary associations people report belonging to. These measures of social interconnectedness are relatively new and are not supported by widespread consensus about their value or validity.[4] Moreover, measures of social capital that are being developed are applicable only for large places; that is, in places large enough to support millions of people, places large enough to be compared statistically, with measures drawn from survey or economic data, and which require a large population for the data to be considered statistically meaningful. Indeed, the measures we do have are often tested to fine associations with proxy variables for health – usually for infant mortality, all-cause mortality, and predicted life span at birth and five years of age. These proxy variables often reflect the economic level or function of *society*, in terms of its ability to provide adequate nutrition or medical services to its people (infant mortality). Or they reflect the panoply of social influences on body function (economics, environmental exposures, social discrimination, the risk of death from violence) with a little genetics mixed in (measures of all-cause mortality and life span). Most, with the exception of infant mortality, measure longevity and not health, so we must take great care to understand these associations correctly, as there is substantial risk of finding that what appears to be an association is really a self-referential or circular observation. (The notion that income inequality is associated with poor health, for example, must be understood very slowly and carefully: income inequality is associated with reduced population longevity, but reduced population longevity can result from or be associated with low income. In this way, income inequality and population longevity may not be truly independent variables, and the association may be in some degree circular or tautological.) The measures of social capital have not yet been tested against measures of individual function, so the associations between health and social capital need to be approached with some care.

Worse, we have little or no ability to measure or compare the social interconnectedness of small communities, the places in which real relation-ships between real people happen or do not happen, and count toward the perception and meaning of health for the people who experience those relationships. John McKnight, the noted community organizer, describes the ability of people in small communities to care for one another as "community regenerative power", as "stories and friendships, obligations and wisdom".[5] It is not at all clear that the social capital of small places, the web of relationship of communities that give communities resiliency and value and are the wellspring of health itself, will ever be effectively measured.

Social capital and measures of population health

Disclaimers aside, let's now look at the relationship of social capital and health as we measure health. How is social capital related to our usual measures of population health? The best studies focus on mortality and self-rated (and self-defined) health, and clearly tie state or national level measures of social capital to improved longevity and the perception of well-being: *You live longer and you perceive yourself to be healthier when you live in a state or nation in which you and your neighbors trust one another, spend time together, and do not have large disparities in incomes.*

Here are the data: there have been a number of studies that tie social capital to mortality and, hence, to longevity in the United States. Kawachi et al. compared responses to the General Social Surveys conducted by the National Opinions Research Center in 1986 and 1990 by the residents of 39 states to state-by-state mortality rates. People who reported not trusting others (by saying the statement "You cannot be too careful in dealing with people" was true) were more likely to live in states which have higher age-adjusted mortality rates, and higher rates of coronary artery disease, malignant neoplasms, cerebrovascular disease, unintentional injury and infant mortality. In addition, people who belonged to more voluntary organizations were more likely to live in states with lower age-adjusted mortality.[6] Shi et al. compared smoking rate, income inequality, and a state's number of primary-care physicians per 10,000 people – all state-level measurements which arguably reflect the degree of social connectedness or social isolation – to state-by-state mortality rates. They found that people who lived in states that had more social connectedness (more primary-care doctors, fewer smokers, less of a disparity between rich and poor) had lower rates of infant mortality, cancer, and heart disease, and lower rates of death from all diseases taken together.[7] Kawachi and his colleagues also compared individual self-rated health (a rating obtained from survey data, which itself has been independently shown to predict longevity[8]) to a number of state-level measures of social capital, all also drawn from survey data. These included trust ("Most people can be trusted"), a sense of confidence in other people ("Most people are helpful") and membership in voluntary organizations. The researchers found self-rated health was best in states with the most perceived trust, helpfulness, and reported volunteerism, and lowest in states with lowest perceived trust, helpfulness, and perceived volunteerism.[9]

HEALTH AND INCOME

One major measure of the relationship between social capital and health is a measure called income inequality on the one hand, and longevity and infant mortality on the other hand. Income inequality is exactly what the name suggests, a measure of the difference between rich and poor in absolute dollar terms. In some countries, the richest 20 percent of the population may earn five times the incomes of the poorest 20 percent of the population. In other countries the richest 20 percent may earn 100 times the incomes of the poorest 20 percent. Income inequality may, and often does, change over time. The change in income inequality in one country over time can be seen as a measure of the relative social cohesion of a place at different times in the history of the place. The greater the income equality, the greater the social cohesion of a place at any given time; the greater the income inequality, the more likely it is that people in a place are not taking care of one another and, worse, more likely to be in conflict, or risk conflict emerging. In the same way, income inequality can be used to compare places: if one place has more income inequality than another place, the place with more income inequality is the place where people are more likely to be in conflict (and to perceive themselves as unhealthy, and to have shorter life spans).

The relationship between *income* alone and *longevity* is well known, and intuitive. "Poorer people die younger and are sicker than richer people; indeed, mortality and morbidity rates are inversely related to many correlates of socioeconomic status such as income, education, or social class."[10] Income helps predict the length of life of individuals, although it is not entirely clear that income always causes better health. Some ill people are poor because they are ill, and some wealthy people are wealthy because they have lived long enough to accumulate wealth and earning power, so their wealth comes from their longevity and not the other way around. The statistical association between income and longevity exists in all societies and across all ages, and appears compelling.[11] The association between income and longevity makes biological sense. This is because poor people work harder, so their bodies wear out faster; sometimes live in violent neighborhoods more at risk for environmental exposures, are exposed to toxins in the workplace; are more likely to serve in the armed forces and be killed in war, and are more likely to smoke or commit suicide because of the stress of poverty itself.

Health as longevity, and income

But wait! We just learned something new about health! In Part One of this book, we argued that longevity is a consumer good, a property right, when viewed from the perspective of what people want, and that longevity is not health. We have just learned, on the other hand, that longevity may be determined by the cumulative effect of social influences on a person's function, on a person's health. Longevity may not be health, but health is a necessary condition for longevity, and the impact of social conditions on health (as function) determines longevity. Buried in the notion of health are these complex relationships: social conditions impact health; health is a major determinant of longevity. Even more, health and social justice are *intimately* related (although different): social injustice worsens health as function, and shrinks longevity; social justice improves health and improves longevity. Ideology aside, the health of individuals and populations *always reflects* social structure and always almost always determines longevity. We cannot say the word health without implying something about social structure or about the prediction, however subtle, of longevity.

In a consumer capitalist society, an association between longevity and income is more compelling yet, because such a relationship appears to reinforce the central value of the culture, and communicates the idea that the goal of all human activity is the accumulation of wealth, and that accumulation is rewarded by longer life.[12] Indeed, this association, between longevity and wealth, underlies many social movements, which seek to change how wealth is distributed. Why should some few powerful people get to keep all the earth's resources, including the right to have a longer life?, critics ask. Let's change society and redistribute the goods more fairly, then everyone will have an equal shot at long life, and justice will be served.

But the key to the fallacy of the argument that wealth and health together are the reward of virtue and all virtue is directed at accumulation is found in the slippery slope between longevity and health. If health is relationship, and not longevity, and higher income only buys longevity (sometimes) but not health, the argument that all human activity should be directed toward accumulation falls apart, unless one accepts that longevity alone is the goal to which all human activity should be directed. On the other hand, there *is* an association between income and longevity. But it is not clear how strong the causal connection is between income and *health*, so is it not clear that the goal of human society should be to redistribute income itself (until it can be shown that income redistribution improves relationship) – unless achieving equal life spans is considered adequate justification for income redistribution.[13,14] By this logic, longevity appears to be more like a property right than a measure of function or attribute of well-being, and the argument that justice as fairness requires the equal distribution of longevity is neither stronger nor less strong than the argument that justice as fairness requires the equal distribution of wealth.

Considering longevity a property right helps us draw a distinction between property rights and functional abilities as we reflect on the meaning of health. Health is more a functional ability than it is a property right. Health may *enable* a property right – such as longevity, or wealth – but we should be careful to parse the difference between the property rights that health enables and health itself, particularly because property, as quantity, lends itself to measurement, while function does not. Still, there is something important about the ability of health to enable longevity that appears to be built into the meaning of health – which is different from the way health enables wealth or political liberty. Health predicts longevity in a way it does not predict either wealth or political liberty. You can have wealth and liberty without health, but you cannot have longevity without health, which is likely the reason longevity is used as a proxy indicator, or outcome measure: the "what we can measure" for the health of populations. Health, then, references longevity because it is a necessary condition for longevity, but health and longevity are not the same: health is an ability to function in relationship. Longevity is a property right which results from health and a number of other, mostly social and natural, conditions over time – the absence of war and interpersonal violence, the safety of the environment – which might reduce longevity and/or impair health. It may be worthwhile to reflect that essential reference as we round out the meaning of health.

Health as relationship, and income

But what of the association between health as *relationship* and income? As we have few measures of relationship quality for individuals, and fewer measures still for the quality or quantity of the relationship network of communities, it is difficult to measure the association between relationship and income, although there is data that support a relationship between interpersonal trust and economic growth in transnational comparisons.[15] But interpersonal trust is very different from the ability to function in relationship.

INCOME INEQUALITY AND LONGEVITY

What can we measure? Understanding the reductive trap that measurement entails, we can measure income equality or inequality in a given place, and compare *that* to our proxy indicators of health status. That measure, of income equality or inequality, suggests much about the extent to which people in a place think about justice, and it suggests much about the quality of the relationships between them, the quality we have already referred to as social cohesion. On the other hand, income equality or inequality may predict social stability or instability, since big gaps between rich and poor are likely to create jealousy, and jealousy is likely to lead to conflict and violence. The association between income and longevity is about the impact of social stratification on the cumulative effects of that stratification on individuals. In the same way, the association between income equality or inequality and longevity is, at the end of the day, *really* about the quality of relationships in a place, on the one hand, and the cumulative effects of social structure on well-being of individuals on the other. Income inequality is a proxy variable for the quality of relationships in a place, and that is why researchers find it so compelling a measure.

As we have argued, most of what we know about income inequality is its association with disease and longevity itself. Richard Wilkinson, who was among the first to note the association between income inequality and longevity, observed that there is little relationship between the longevity of wealthy countries and their incomes, although within a given country there is a strong relationship between income and longevity regardless of which country is under analysis. That is, when you compare countries by income, countries which have the same income may not have the same average life span. However, if you look at each country individually, longevity increases with income (although the extent to which increases in income produce increases in life span levels off at a certain point, suggesting there is a biological limitation on life span that increases in income or material wealth do not change). Wilkinson then observed that the variation in life span between countries not explained by income itself could be explained by the presence or absence of income inequality. If a country had less income equality, it was likely to have shorter average life spans.[16]

Wilkinson's work has been the subject of heated debate among epidemiologists, sociologists, and economists and has stimulated a very careful and precise statistical picture of the social determinants of longevity, which include income equality and inequality, but also include the population composition of larger places, household composition, wealth and taxation, class, occupational and environmental exposures, gender and race. Wilkinson, Michael Marmot, Ichiro Kawachi and Bruce Kennedy, and many other noted theorists in this arena, have been able to develop the statistical argument and carefully, even elegantly, show how income inequality is associated with longevity.

The data have been reviewed in detail and well summarized by Kawachi and by Wilkinson, and involve both cross-national studies and within-country investigations.[17] Despite critiques that focus on the validity of the measures used to make comparisons and the potential for confounding variables (the so-called like-with-like comparisons), there appears to be a strong relationship between income equality and longevity: people live longer in places where they share resources, as if health as relationship is its own reward.

The most confusing study is one which looked at the relationship between income inequality in developed and developing countries and infant mortality, by looking for an association between infant mortality and gains in income in people in the upper five percent of income households.[18] One might expect no association between upper income earners and infant mortality or, perhaps, a slightly positive association between the two (if the trickle-down theory of the social benefit of upper earners income gains is correct), so the results of the study were surprising – there is a negative association between upper earners gains and country-wide infant mortality. When rich people make more money, the infant mortality rate of a country gets worse. What's happening here, and what can we learn from the meaning of health?

On further analysis, however, the association between upper earners' income gains and infant mortality rates makes perfect sense. Infant mortality is a different kind of proxy health indicator than adult mortality or one of the longevity measures, which reflect the cumulative effect of social and genetic influences on body integrity and function. Instead, infant mortality reflects the nutrition of pregnant woman, the adequacy of prenatal care, and the integrity of maternity services, and little else. As the wealthiest sectors of society accumulate more money, there is less left in that society for the poor and for publicly provided prenatal and intrapartum (during delivery) maternity services. Poor people exist at a morbidity tipping point, which rich people never see. That is, if we take one dollar (or peso or shilling or dinar) from a poor pregnant woman, and one dollar from publicly provided maternity services, we push poor women over the edge of health in pregnancy, and when that happens across a population, we increase the infant mortality in that population. If we give the same two dollars (or pesos or shillings or dinars) to a rich person, there is no equal but opposite effect on the infant mortality of the rich, since their infant mortality is likely maximized in the culture already, and birth rates in that population are generally lower.

What does that tell us about the meaning of health? When used the term "health in pregnancy" what did we mean? We meant the ability of a pregnant woman to produce a healthy newborn, an ability which we said depends on two factors, nutrition and access to prenatal and intrapartum maternity services, both social conditions promoted by interconnectedness – and look, it happened again! Every time we use the word health, we reference necessary conditions for health, which are inevitably social, and promoted by social connectedness. Health is about the ability to function, to be sure, but health always references the social conditions necessary for function. Social interconnectedness is not health, but it is a necessary condition for health. Longevity is not health, but health is a necessary condition for longevity. *Now* we are getting somewhere! Social interconnectedness is a necessary condition for health, health allows individuals to function in connected societies, and function in connected societies allows longevity! Think of Haiti, the South Bronx, or Somalia, or Zimbabwe or Bosnia or Romania or Bangladesh. Widespread infant mortality. Governments in disarray. Gangs and warlords feuding with one another. Life expectancies as short as they were in primitive culture. Now think of Britain, Cuba, Japan, Scandinavia, and Singapore, places where healthy individuals can function together. The successful cultures of the contemporary world work from a certain expectation of equal life chances, and build a culture in which we can together take advantage of what we have learned together. In *those* places, the places people have learned to live together, we take advantage of what we have learned, and get longer life as the reward. *Now* we are beginning to connect the dots.

EXPANDING OUR DEFINITION OF HEALTH

Let's expand the definition of health we suggested in Chapter 4, taking into account the thinking of Dubos, Illich, Callahan, and McKnight, and adding to it what we learned from thinking about the relationship of social capital to health, measured as infant mortality and longevity. Health is the equal ability of individuals to function in the relationships appropriate to their cultural contexts and place in the life cycle, and the condition that results from that ability. Social interconnectedness is a necessary condition for health, and health is a necessary condition for longevity, which is the result of the impact of social, biological, and genetic factors on an individual's ability to function over time, as well as the chance avoidance of natural and human trauma. Because of these associations, thinking about health always denotes some thinking about both social interconnectedness and longevity, though health is not the same notion as either, and though these three interconnected concepts are frequently confused and confounded.[19]

Kawachi proposed three ways in which income inequality affects mortality and, conversely, longevity. First, places with income inequality have more wealthy people, who do not need social services, and whose influence on public policy leads to less spending on social services, some of which, like education and housing and access to medical services, allow the mass of people to live longer. Second, income equality and social cohesion may be associated with a protective effect or factor, perhaps biological in action, which itself extends the life spans of individuals but which is lost when the social fabric of a place is disrupted. Third, income inequality may lead to jealousy and conflict, which in turn produces frustration and stress, which, in turn, may be a risk factor for illness and death, in ways that are psychologically (through violence and suicide) and biologically (through hormones and blood pressure effects, for example) mediated.[20]

As important as the income-equality argument is for its ability to suggest a relationship between social cohesion and one health-related outcome – longevity – income inequality also reveals much about biases shared by many researchers and theorists about size and policy. These biases are due to the process of analysis itself, which requires the study of large numbers of people in large places in order to find valid statistical associations.

Here, the reductive trap raises its head again. Relationship does not happen in large places. Relationship happens among small groups of people, groups which exist under the radar screen of statistical significance. But policymakers deal with large groups and big numbers, and it is rational for researchers hoping to influence policymakers to focus on large group aggregations and comparisons.

It is reasonable, then, to cede the point that income equality and inequality is statistically associated with mortality and longevity, and to recognize that the measurement of social capital, though it is early in its development as a measure, probably provides an important insight into a necessary condition for health. But we must also recognize that there are some theoretical limitations in the ability of statistical analysis to explain the meaning of health as relationship, a recognition that provokes an understanding of an important paradox.

If we cannot study the function of relationship well in small places, and cannot draw statistically valid conclusions about those relationships, yet we believe that the character of relationships in small places is what health is, does that mean we must abandon our attempt to create health as relationship from the perspective of public policy? Or shall we use the *suggestion* of epidemiology and statistical analysis, and the *conclusion* of the language use and social analysis of this book – that relationship *is* a predictor of longevity *and* relationship is the necessary condition for health – to design policy which creates the correct environment for relationship in small places? In short, instead of being blinded by all the statistical analysis, which shows some (relatively weak) associations but arrives at no firm conclusions, can we combine statistical analysis and common sense to help us decide what we as a society should do? Even though we cannot be sure that any one particular strategy aimed at small places works (because we lack the analytical tools to measure the social cohesion of small places) it still appears worthwhile to invent ways of making relationship happen in small places. This is because the social cohesion of large places is a product of the social cohesion of many small places aggregated. We can still test the effectiveness of an intervention in small places by studying the cumulative effect of many small-place interventions on social cohesion in larger places, but we should not let our inability to measure get in the way of what looks to be a rational way to proceed.[21]

Because we can apply analytical tools effectively with large populations, and because large populations have economic and political power, contemporary society has forgotten about the importance of relationships of small places, and forgotten what health is. We believe that the goal of medical services ought to be supporting relationships in small places, and the goal of health policy ought to be creating an environment in which the support of relationship in small places happens most effectively.

Notice how all the measures of social capital relate to longevity, and not health as we have defined it: the equal ability of an individual to function in relationships appropriate to that person's age and culture. Part of the failure stems from the absence of measures of an individual's ability to function in relationship at all. Part of the failure to tie social capital to the prevailing definitions of health arises from the lack of consensus about social capital as a measure, and the difficulty of defining and measuring social capital at multiple levels of social organization – at the family, neighborhood and community, city and regional levels. Essentially all we have are state-level measures, which are really just crude survey data guesstimates, and not precise or sophisticated measurement tools at all.

DISTINGUISHING SOCIAL CAPITAL AND HEALTH

Underlying this difficulty of measurement is another conceptual problem: in a way, the notion of social capital seems to slip inside our definition of health, and seems indistinguishable from it. Social capital is a measurement of the richness of associations. Health is a measure, if you will, of the ability of individuals to function in associations. How do we tell the dancer from the dance?

The dancer and the dance distinction is, in fact, the solution to the conceptual problem of the distinction between social capital and health. Health is a predicate of individuals, of dancers. Social capital is the dance, a predicate of social organizations, of groups and communities and populations occupying places. Social capital is a social measure of the extent to which individual health exists among groups of people in a place. Health is the ability of individuals to enter into relationships; social capital is a counting of the number and intensity of those relationships existing in groups of people.

To some extent, emerging measures of social capital function as measures of public health and may provide more important measures than those we use now, which just tell us how long people live and why they die. What should we know about social groups and places? Knowing how long people live and why they die is nice, and a good way to detect infectious diseases and prioritize spending so that those diseases can be controlled. But knowing how well individuals function in relationship in a place, knowing how effectively social organization and the environment are collaborating to foster relationships or conspiring to isolate people – knowing social capital – really tells us about the meaning of human life in a place. It provides us with the information we need to think about the success or failure of our attempt to live together. Social capital is not health. It is, however, a new way to talk about the necessary conditions for health in the public arena, and a new way to think about whether our social organization is creating the lives we want and need, or leaching those lives away.

Still, the correlation between social capital and health does not mean we can create health by building social capital. That is a theory that is yet to be formally tested. Similarly, the notion of building social capital by building a primary-care infrastructure, which we will argue for later in this part and Part Four, is also untested, however rational it may seem. That's the task this book lays out, the gauntlet we mean to throw down: can we build social capital *and* health, by redirecting our existing health spending to build a primary-care based healthcare system that focuses on the health of people in small places (small towns and urban neighborhoods) first, builds an infrastructure to support that delivery system, *and* leverages our health spending to support and improve small places, all at the same time?

health and fairness

> Justice is the first virtue of social institutions, as truth is of systems of thought.[1]

Health reflects on, and refers to social interconnectedness. Social interconnectedness reflects on and refers to social justice. Is there something about social justice that can tell us more about the meaning of health?

Social justice means many things to many people. To some, it means only the effort to improve the lot of the poor. To others, social justice speaks to the perceived need to redistribute resources, so everyone owns common resources, eliminating any inequalities in income and wealth. To still others, social justice means an attempt to equilibrate life chances, so everyone has an equal ability to makes something of their lives, and then we leave the "something" up to the individual, letting people knit what they choose from the raw material of life chances. To still others, life is intrinsically unfair, with genetics and social position always causing/resulting in the unfair distribution of opportunities. According to this philosophy, social injustice is inevitable, a meaningless illusion, and the suffering and early death of the poor is nature or God's way of improving the human race, and is not to be or cannot be tampered with.

There are both utilitarian and ethical wellsprings to the interest in social justice, as well as to the position that social justice is an illusion. The ethical argument can be made theistically and atheistically. The theist argument that we come from dust and return to dust, that all people are equal in God's eyes, and all people deserve an equal part of God's providence, and have an equal ability to join the Kingdom of Heaven (noting, in the Christian tradition, how unlikely it is that a rich [white?] man will find himself there). The atheist argument is similar, though (often) strays into utilitarian territory: we are all created equal, and if one man has a dollar he did not work for, some other man worked for a dollar he did not get. At its base, it is violence or the threat of violence that creates inequalities, and violence is inhuman and undemocratic; inequalities are also likely to result in social unrest, which endangers the well-being of rich and poor together.

The play to social stability and instability is the centerpiece of the utilitarian, or rationalist, argument. If society allows inequalities to exist, the people who perceive themselves to have been shorted will get angry, and that anger will turn to violence, which, once it starts, is hard to stop. A society run by warlords gives us lives that are brutal and short: a society of law and democracy is more effective at insuring that people can cultivate and sustain the relationships that are important to them over time, and is far preferable to the world of the knife, club, and gun.

JOHN RAWLS

John Rawls was the most articulate of the many people who have contributed to our understanding of justice, developing a theory of justice out of an understanding of the social contract (itself developed out of classic utilitarian and rationalist arguments that underlie both social contract and modern economic theory). Rawls believed that society "is a cooperative venture for mutual advantage," that individuals are rational and make rational choices; and that justice is the operative principle, providing the umbrella of social stability that allows both the society as a whole and individuals to flourish.[2] Justice for Rawls is fairness; that is, if we assume that we could begin a society all over again, justice is the (or a) set of rules that insures that every rational person would choose to follow, since those rules would balance the interests of all. Proceeding from a point of the basic and fundamental equality of persons, justice distributes the benefits of society, as the protective umbrella, equally to all. Rawls' theory of justice thus permits the existence of social and economic inequalities only to the extent those inequalities can be shown to provide social and economic benefits for all. But Rawls does not believe that just societies can intentionally set about providing the greatest good for the greatest number as an operating principle. This is because that classic utilitarian position results in social instability, and harm to all at the end of the day.

To the very limited extent Rawls considered health, health is part of the "initial position," the place of theoretical equality at the beginning of society, without which rational persons cannot make the rational decisions that lead to the social contract, and the set of rules that flow from the social contract as justice.[3,4] The notion of the need for the equality of the initial position is a crucial one for the definition of health, and is useful across the wide range of thinking about the social contract that underlies our thinking about democratic society in general. *Health is necessary for the rational participation of individuals in society.* Health is a necessary condition for the social contract. Without the health of individuals, there can be no justice.

RAWLS, DANIELS, AND HEALTH

Healthcare, for Rawls, is essentially an afterthought, a problem of "extension": how members of society extend the unifying theory of justice into areas that are not central to its formulation, like international law, and our relations with animals and nature.[5] Rawls believed that healthcare was a practical not a theoretical problem, which just needed to be worked out in the legislative arena: you measure what resources need to be expended to make people functional as rational participants in society, and you devote the resources needed to do so, balancing the need for those resources with other societal needs.[6] (If only it were so simple!)

It is Rawls' student and colleague, the philosopher and medical ethicist Norman Daniels, who has worked out the application of distributive justice to healthcare with great elegance. Daniels distinguishes between healthcare *needs* and healthcare *preferences* in sorting out what a just society must distribute fairly in order for individuals to function rationally within a social contract, and considers as well the role of justice as fairness in sorting out and fairly distributing *opportunities* for life chances.[7] For Daniels, healthcare is a special social good, because health itself is a necessary condition for an individual to share in the normal opportunity range in society, and that ability to share triggers the rational engagement in the social contract, engagement which actualizes the process of justice.[8] Daniels works through the fairness of different schemes of the distribution of healthcare resources, one of which (similar to part of the healthcare system we will propose in Part Four) determines that no person over a certain age (age 70, in Daniels' example) will receive high-cost, life-extending technologies. In Daniels careful analysis, in which he very seriously considers the problem of whether such a scheme represents age discrimination, such a scheme might be considered just because it represents the distribution of goods and services across the various stages of life, and not among competing age cohorts.[9] That is, through such a scheme we use institutions to create and maintain fairness in the distribution of goods and services over time, and institutional policy is guided by an understanding of the need to protect life opportunities for individuals across all the stages of life. In such a scheme, we are maximizing the life chances of individuals during their lives, not taking resources for one age group unfairly to subsidize the needs of another age group. We are, from a societal perspective, understanding the needs of individuals at each point in the life cycle, and distributing resources to protect the opportunities of individuals in the social contract. We are insuring that more people will reach old age, instead of insuring that those who survive to old age will have equal access to life-extending technologies or other resources at any point in time. Viewed from the perspective of justice as fairness, insuring that people have equal life opportunities to participate actively in the social contract is vastly more important than insuring those who have survived have equal access to resources. Perhaps the converse is also true: that giving those who have survived to old age access to resources in a way that might deprive those who have not attained old age is patently unfair, and demonstrably unjust.

Here we see the complexity of the interrelated ideas of justice, health, interconnectedness, and longevity. Interconnectedness is a necessary condition for health. Health is a necessary condition for justice. Justice potentiates interconnectedness. Health is a necessary condition for longevity. Justice requires us to attempt to distribute resources in such a way as to produce more equal longevity. The meaning of health percolates deep in this matrix of interrelated ideas. It provides the nexus between the desire of the individual for life and the pursuit of happiness, the function of a just society in permitting that life and that happiness, and the ability of individuals and society together to survive, grow, and prosper, as the whole becomes greater than the sum of its parts.

EXTENDING OUR DEFINITION OF HEALTH

To this end, it is time to make one small addition to the definition of health we have developed in preceding chapters. We need to add the word "equal" to the definition, to reflect the social need for a population of individuals who can participate equally in society, and generate justice by their interaction with one another. Health, then, *is the ability of individuals to function in the relationships appropriate to their cultural context and place in the life cycle, and the ability to function as equal participants in the social contract.* Equal participants, so people can help maintain society. Help maintain society, so there is a context for their relationships. Context for relationships, so there is a reason for there to be justice. Maintain justice, so they can live long and happy lives, and the whole can be greater than the sum of the parts, so everyone can live happily ever after, after all.

AMISH BOY

The relationship between health, illness, self, and community was first suggested to me in 1981, when I was a third-year medical student, working on the pediatric ward of Rainbow Babies and Children's Hospital in Cleveland, Ohio. One night we admitted a four-year-old Amish child who lived in one of the many Amish communities east and south of Cleveland. The little boy had a very fast-growing tumor in his abdomen, and a surgeon at a community hospital, thinking the child's pain was caused by appendicitis, had operated. He found a mass that turned out to be a Non-Hodgkin's lymphoma, and was presented with a dilemma: by the time the surgical wound had healed the tumor was likely to be widely spread. Desperate for a solution, the surgeon sent the child to Rainbow, one of the best children's hospitals in the country, to see if anything could be done.

Nineteen eighty-one does not seem that long ago, but it was relatively early in the history of children's cancer care and the medicines we had and methods we used were relatively primitive by today's standards. This tumor was especially challenging because it was very fast-growing, doubling in size every few days.

The oncologists at Rainbow worked incredibly hard to find a solution, but the options were not good. They could try chemotherapy, but everyone understood that the surgical wound might never heal and the child might be disabled because of it. Even so, there was no more than a 40 percent chance that the child would survive.

I was in the room when an oncologist told the parents what the team thought would be the best course of action. Amish people do not drive, and it had been difficult to arrange for both parents, who had five other children, to come to Cleveland together. They had brought friends and family to listen. Conference rooms in hospitals are always too small and always too brightly lit. Crowded into the room were the child's mother, surrounded by four or five other Amish women, the child's father, a farmer, standing with another Amish man, and an earnest medical team that included an oncologist, an oncology fellow, an oncology resident, an oncology medical student, a pediatric attending doctor, and a pediatric intern. I was standing in a corner, close enough to see the sweat on people's faces and involved enough to feel everyone's grim determination, but an observer, not really a party to the interaction.

The parents were young and simply dressed in the plain, unbuttoned style of Old Order Amish. They spoke accented English carefully and stared straight at us as the oncologist spoke, as if searching our souls to make sure what they were hearing was the truth.

The oncologist was kind as she spoke about the dangers that lay ahead. She described the chemotherapy and its possible complications carefully. She described next steps in a way that communicated confidence in the face of danger, never hinting that there was anything to do but to try treating this tumor.

"What was the likelihood of survival?" the boy's strong, square-shouldered father asked, his blond-bearded jaw set and his teeth clenched.

The answer was repeated, "Forty percent."

"What will the boy's life be like if he survives?"

The chance of disability was discussed again, as well as the kind of complications that accompanied chemotherapy in those years: pain, hair loss, vomiting, infections.

There was silence for a few moments.

"We will talk to our community," the father said.

I was in the boy's room the next day when the answer came back from the parents. I'm sure the answer was expressed in words to the oncologist, but I did not hear the words. Instead, I saw the answer as it unfolded.

From the moment the boy had been admitted to the hospital there had always been people, his mother and perhaps four or five others, sitting quietly or circling quietly around his room, offering their company, or taking care of his parents.

Now, suddenly, the four or five became 20. All of a sudden, stacks of folded black sheets, mourning clothes, began to appear and were placed about the room. All of a sudden, the role of the people in the room changed. The parents, who have been resolute but passive observers, and the others, who had been caretakers for the parents, became caretakers for the child again. The nurses, engines of quiet efficiency, backed away and became assistants, there whenever needed but otherwise withdrawn.

A great peace entered the room. The anxious determination disappeared. The parents had decided not to treat the child and were making ready for his death.

I remember a few moments of angst or worry and confused responsibility among the more junior members of the medical team. Was the failure to treat child abuse? Should we call the state's child protective team, go into court, and compel treatment?

Thankfully, calmer, older, and wiser heads prevailed. They knew the limitations of our treatments. They saw the value of a community taking care of its own.

The boy died a day later. He died a peaceful death, surrounded by the love of a family and a community that had great faith in God and one another. There is value in individual life and tremendous value in young life, but there is also value in the ability of people to be together, and peace in their ability to care for one another with faith, love, and humility.

what's next?

"The definition of insanity is doing the same thing over and over again, and expecting a different result."
   — **Albert Einstein**

"Either we'll find a way, or we'll make one."
   — **Hannibal, as quoted by Saul Alinsky**

who gets what?

CHANGING WHAT WE THINK AND DO IS NOT EASY

It is easy to point out that public spending on healthcare, social services, and the military must play by the rules of a zero-sum game. When we spend $100,000 on the care of a 92 year old with an illness that he or she is very unlikely to survive at such an advanced age, we no longer have the $100,000 to spend on the education of poor kids from South Boston, South Providence, or the South Bronx. Somewhere within the great calculus and world economics, when we spend $80,000 on a smart bomb dropped in Iraq or Afghanistan, we do not have $80,000 to spend on the medical school of Moi University in Eldoret, Kenya, which is almost enough to educate an entire class of 100 young doctors in training for a full year.

It is easy to point these things out; it is not easy to change what we do.

We behave and make the choices that we do because of the intersection of a number of beliefs, public policies, assumptions, and incentives. In the case of the 92 year old, here are some of the imperatives at work: the primacy of the individual, individual rights and individual autonomy is central to our culture and our economy. In general, we protect individuals' right to life, liberty, and the pursuit of happiness they already have, although we vary in the extent to which we provide life, liberty, and the pursuit of happiness to those who do not have those freedoms. The central tenet of medicine as a profession is the notion of un-self-interested advocacy – the notion that physicians and the healthcare system should put the interests of patients in front of their own interests.[1] Then there is the economically and reductively driven social drift to redefine health as longevity, instead of the ability to be in relationship with others, which we have described at length, that has reduced a patient's interest in the preservation of life as the only operative value. Then, our medical culture is designed to protect life first and ask questions later, a bias which comes out of a realistic understanding of the world of advocacy and legal responsibility. (You have to save a person's life if you are going to be able to ask meaningful questions about the way they define their own interests.)

Another factor is the deconstruction of family, community, and relationship, which means there are many 92 year olds who cannot speak to their own interests because of age and its attendant disabilities, and have no one who can speak for them. When they become wards of the State, the State falls back on the only definition of a person's interest it has access to, which is focused on the preservation of life. When family is present, many surrogate decision makers choose to attenuate life long after life can possibly be meaningful. They do this, fearing death and loss, having no way of measuring how their decision making affects the patient in terms of pain and dependence, and having no sense of how the financial implications of decisions about what to do for whom (remember the zero-sum game) will affect themselves personally or society at large – and having no other value on which to base decisions.

In addition, the positivist bias of our culture hints that life could be endless, given the right technology. Deeply held biases around the denial of death and its universality also color the way people make decisions for themselves and their families. We are a diverse society, and many people have a religious perspective that hews to the central value of life, defined simply as heart beat and blood flow. Finally, there are a number of economic incentives to doctors and hospitals, which appropriately reward life-saving behavior.[2]

Of course, everyone dies of something. And once you realize that longevity above the average life span is a consumer good, and that we focus on longevity because we can measure it, and that longevity is not health, you realize that we do what we do for no particularly good reason beside the self-interest of the players.

It is not easy to change how we think, or what we do.

On the other hand, we also have a number of deeply held beliefs, public policies, legal precedents, and assumptions that could be combined in a different way, to create new incentives, different choices, and to achieve different outcomes. In particular, if we can resuscitate the meaning of health we can make a very different set of choices, which will produce very different outcomes. We do this if we remember that for most of us health is about relationship and not longevity alone, if we remember the critical role that fairness plays in structuring our society, and recall that our culture revolves on the cult of personal responsibility of decision making (another, more Rawlsian, way to look at our individualism). If we could re-evaluate our choices from the perspective of justice as fairness (do our choices create a society that is fairer, and yield lives that are more balanced and satisfying?) as well as from the perspective of individual rights, we might be able to use our social spending to create a better collective life. In doing do so we can make health possible, instead of spending only in the service of the protection of the individual right of longevity, which is what we do now.

Let's highlight that dichotomy for a moment. Now we spend on the *perceived right to longevity*, a notion that is an artifact of the way our measurement technology commingled with a broad set of commercial interests – spending which is demonstrably self-defeating, because it is one of a number of factors that has diminished social capital. And social capital, you will recall, is associated with improved measures of health and improved longevity, improvements we are failing to see because of our focus on longevity itself. We have seen and can measure a certain failure to improve U.S. population health (as we measure it), and have not realized health as we understand it. If we spent our resources on *health as relationship*, however, we would expect to see improvements is both health as we measure it, *and* health as we understand it.

Let's focus on fairness for a moment. In our current construction of "fairness," everyone has access to primary and secondary education of varying quality, and access to essentially unlimited medical services toward the end of life. If we could recalibrate our notion of fairness, defining it as everyone having the same access to social supports (housing, education, public safety, and medical service) for a certain number of years, we might be able to leverage a change in our spending choices, and hence in the outcome of the zero-sum game. As Norman Daniels has argued, such an approach is both fair and just, because we would be creating equal life opportunities, by insuring that everyone can be an equal and active participant in civic society.

THREE POLICY APPROACHES

Here are three ideas that, in our estimation, would be extremely helpful in developing a more rational and just approach to healthcare services in the United States.

1. Everyone gets primary care and hospital care until they are (about) 80 years old. After 80, everyone gets primary care, and all the hospital care they want to pay for on their own

What would that approach look like? In terms of medical services, it would mean that everyone would get the same access to needed medical services up to the average expected life span. Everyone would get health insurance up to, say, 80. For folks over 80, we might cover expense related to comfort, but not those related to life extension. Our 92 year old could still get whatever services he or she wished, but would have to pay for some of those services.

Now that sounds pretty draconian, until you turn it on its head for a moment. Under this proposed system, for example, we would have 84 year olds dying of heart failure, because they could not afford their water pills; and 92 year olds with bad lungs dying of emphysema, because they could not afford oxygen, and 85 year olds with abdominal aneurysms dying of the rupture of those aneurysms, when today we have a 40 to 90 percent chance of repairing those aneurysms, laying aside the issue of cost (paying for each one costs about $100,000).

But what do we have now? Now, we have all the water pills we need (which are actually pretty cheap, and were not covered by Medicare until 2006 anyway) and all the oxygen we need and all the aneurysm repairs we might ever need for 84 year olds. But we do not have a decent life for poor kids, and it is fundamentally unfair to preserve the lives of very old people at public expense when we are sacrificing the lives of many youngsters to poor schools, broken homes and communities, and unsafe streets. To this point, here are some numbers from Geoffrey Canada:

> . . . 760,000 children in New York City live in poverty. Barely a third (39.3 percent) of the city's elementary and middle-school students meet or exceed grade level on state and city math exams, while only 35.3 percent meet or exceed grade level on city math exams. Twenty percent of the city's high school students drop out before graduation. Citywide, roughly 215,000 children between the ages of six and thirteen are unsupervised by a family member in the after-school hours – the same hours, studies show, when children and youth are most likely to use alcohol, tobacco, or drugs, or commit a violent crime.[3]

And that's just New York. The same story is played out in every U.S city – thousands and thousands of kids, killed by gun violence, or brought down by street life, because we will not spend $10,000 a year on kids who are 8 or 10 or 12, but we will spend $50,000 to $100,000 a year keeping the adults they become in jail, and we will spend $100,000 repairing the aneurysms of 84 and 88 and 92 year olds. These old people had an 84- or 88- or 92-year shot at life. The 12 year olds get nothing. Is this fair?

But it's not just the inequitable financial distribution that constitutes the unfairness of our current medical services spending. It's the money we spend collectively on treatments that are really consumer goods, on treatments that do not support the ability to function in relationship, that increase our medical services spending unnecessarily in a way that contributes to the split between rich and poor, the undermining of community, and the progressive impossibility of health. There is no role for insurance coverage of cosmetic plastic surgery, just as there is no role for insurance coverage of Viagra, or insurance coverage of treatments for runny noses. Take the case of Viagra. A 40 year old on Medicaid can request and be prescribed 30 Viagra tablets a month, at a cost to the public of $3,600 a year. That's about the cost of providing primary care to 20 people, affordable housing for a family for three to six months, or perhaps 10 percent of a college tuition for a kid from the inner city. A similar analysis works for the treatment of runny noses, which might cost $2,000–$3,000 a year.

In our current system, insurance companies cover these treatments because drug-company marketing campaigns make runny noses and male impotence seem like a health concern (in turn because there is a medicine to treat it and a diagnosis which describes it, not because of its public-health impact). The insurers' marketing people, not wanting to alienate potential subscribers, cover these medications in order to preserve their market share, and simply pass along the increased cost to their customers. Because every insurer functions in the market in much the same way, and experiences the same market pressures, they also all behave the same way, so these costs just get wrapped into the increasing cost of health insurance, without a process for deciding who gets what, and what is essential for the maintenance of health. For public programs, a number of factors work to inflate cost and extend benefits. Medicare, as a public program, is subject to pressure from industry, disease-oriented interest groups (many of which are industry supported), and specialty physician groups (many which are also enjoy industry support both as groups and as individuals). Combined they produce a welter of advocates, putting pressure on legislatures and regulators alike, who hear only a chorus of positive voices and do not have to pay the bill.

Consider drug-eluting stents as a case in point. This common treatment for narrowed arteries is only marginally better than previous therapies, but is three to six times as expensive and costs the nation over a billion dollars a year. Worse yet, the Medicare program decided to pay for stents before the treatment had been rigorously tested, triggering a debate about its safety. There was little debate, however, as to whether the marginal benefit obtained at a cost of one billion dollars (and virtually certain to increase from year to year) was worth the money. Nor has anyone voted that we should spend money this way, instead of on a program to improve elementary education or to build affordable housing.

A similar problem exists in the Medicaid program, which is funded by a combination of state and federal dollars but administered at the state level. Medicaid is subject to the same sorts of pressures as Medicare, from industry groups, political factions and various advocates. The legislators and regulators who control the Medicaid programs have little evaluative methodology to determine if a treatment serves the public interest, especially if a diagnosis and a treatment are linked and are covered by commercial insurance. At the state level, however, legislators and regulators do have one powerful constraint: the need to balance budgets. Their inability to print money is something the federal government can do to fob off the responsibility for today's expenditures onto tomorrow's taxpayers. Instead, the administrators of the Medicaid program have grown adept at all sorts of financial manipulations, inventing rules and changing policies frequently to keep their creditors at bay. But it is a rare state that has developed a calculus for looking at the costs and benefits of new treatments.

One state, Oregon, made a brave attempt to rank the value of treatments paid for by its Medicaid program. This approach was effective in controlling cost increases, but it involved a very complicated public process which affected only the portion of the population served by Medicaid, and was unable to extend the process of deciding about the comparative usefulness or value of various treatments for the state as a whole. Oregon's Medicaid experiment shows the difficulty of sorting out who gets what and, in particular, shows the impossibility of beginning that process for a small part of the population, instead of for the population as a whole. Buffeted by constituents, special interests, and legislators, it is no wonder that the Medicaid administrators want to pay for 30 Viagras a month – there is lots of advocacy for doing it and little restraint against it. It is easier, at budget time, to just cut 10 or 20 percent from all Medicaid suppliers (and 20–50 percent from the politically weakest suppliers – usually the primary-care community – than it is to have to work through a rational approach to decide who should get what. But there is a way out.

2. Everyone gets a medical savings account and high-deductible health insurance

The way out is to narrowly define medical services that are in the public interest, directly fund those services, and transfer the responsibility of deciding whether any other specific medical service is desirable (and worth the price) to the individual.

What would such a process entail? It would have to include a publicly funded primary-care system and a hospital system. (Hospitals in the United States are heavily funded by federal and state monies already; the combination of the Medicare and Medicaid payments represents around two-thirds of the total revenues of most hospitals.)

This approach would also require tax-advantaged, annually capped individual savings accounts that could be used only to pay for discretionary medical services, coupled with high-deductible major medical insurance. These accounts could be used for other things once the individual reaches a certain age, probably the age of average life span. The high-deductible insurance component would help pay for discretionary costs once a person's medical expenses have exceeded a defined amount. In this financial system (which is a way to pay for services, and as such is not a "healthcare system"), people with Medicare and Medicaid coverage would use the same basic approach to medical decision making, but the money in their savings accounts and the money to pay for their high-deductible insurance plans would come from public funds.

The first notable benefit of this approach is that everyone in the country gets treated equally. Second, we would get insurance companies and government out of the "who-gets-what" game, and leave medical expense value judgments to each individual. The third benefit is that we would put the power of personal responsibility to use, employing it where it is relevant and can be used in a balanced way, by asking consumers themselves to weight the costs and benefits of treatments that are discretionary. Because, in this architecture, we have committed ourselves to universal primary care, we have given everyone in the country a coach, a trained eye and a listening ear, someone who can help a person sort through the white noise around treatments that someone else is going to profit from.

Naturally, this approach raises many questions. What about adverse selection and the concentration of need? Critics of medical savings accounts have long argued that this approach will appeal only to healthy people, because the ill, who consume 60–70 percent of all medical services expenditures, will go through any money in their medical savings accounts quickly; while well people will not get the routine preventative care that will help prevent illness of the future. And what will prevent someone who wants more medical services than the average from intentionally exhausting their savings accounts, forcing themselves into the high-deductible insurance plan? If lots of people were to do this, wouldn't insurance, even with a very high deductible, soon become unaffordable? Posing the question another way, how does this system deal with the drug-eluting stent problem, in which the bulk of the costs of an expensive new technology are shouldered by the high-deductible insurers. Wouldn't they experience the same pressures that insurers, Medicaid and Medicare, face today?

First, once the entire nation is moved to such a system, adverse selection will not be an issue, because everyone would be treated the same way. What happens to 10 percent of people who account for 60–70 percent of costs is more complex. Some of those costs will vanish as we stop using public funds to pay for life-prolonging care for people over 80. Some costs will be markedly reduced, because some of that 10 percent are people who seek medical services that are unnecessary and unhelpful. And the care for the large majority of the 10 percent, who have real medical needs, will stay the same or drop somewhat, because this funding approach would encourage them to ask questions about the real benefits of the treatments they now receive.

How about people who do not use preventative services that are now covered by health plans? That is the easiest objection to counter, because primary care and prevention will be publicly funded and population-based. Included in that public funding can be inexpensive generic medications, which means few people will go without an effective medicine because of inability to pay. When primary care and prevention is publicly funded, there will be no financial roadblock to using it. When primary care is population-based, there would be a good multidisciplinary health center for every community of 10,000 people, a health center that is required to know, see, and care for everyone in that population. We will have a mechanism to get prevention to the people who need it most, to meet people where they are, as they are, and make sure everyone has equal access to primary care and prevention.

The most difficult objections to counter involve the risk of people driving themselves into the high-deductible category because they want more services, and the decision process for including new technologies like drug-eluting stents in the list of covered services. There is, however, a secret, powerful, and effective method of preventing people from driving themselves into the high-deductible portion inappropriately, and a similar method for making good decisions about new technologies and controlling their costs at the same time. This tool is called managed care.

Despite the hated position managed-care companies now occupy in the minds of the public and physicians alike, managed-care companies do bring skills which add value to our ability to manage the costs of expensive medical services for the high-deductible major medical insurance portion of each person's medical services-funding arrangement. In addition, we believe a major portion of hospital funding should be assumed by government from tax revenues, reducing the amount of money that managed-care companies put at risk.

There are two opportunities for managed-care companies to help constrain the cost of the high-deductible portion of each medical services-funding arrangement, and profit in the process.

One managed-care approach involves the certification of spending from each person's medical services' discretionary account. It is unlikely that all spending from that tax-advantaged account should, or ought to, "count" toward fulfilling the deductible requirement, because some of that discretionary spending will be for consumer goods that do not influence function, like the treatment of runny noses or spending on plastic surgery. How much of that discretionary-account spending qualifies can be determined by contract between the seller of the high deductible and the individual. And how much qualifies will be a major determinant of both the marketability and the cost of the high-deductible insurance. If it is easy to fulfill the deductible, the deductible will be popular, but costly. If it is difficult to fulfill the deductible, the deductible will be harder to sell, but more affordable. Managed-care companies will compete on the design of the deductible, as well as on technology they employ to qualify, or disqualify, expenses as meeting the deductible, with ease of use aiding the marketability of their products.

The second opportunity for managed care in this new system is for managed-care companies to have a major role in the adoption of new technologies and controlling their costs. Want to sell us drug-eluting stents? Convince us that there is adequate return on investment for those stents before we shell out a billion dollars in new spending for them, and rest assured that, as soon as someone else can produce a better stent for less money, we will buy the better, cheaper models. Managed-care companies have the ability to perform this kind of technology assessment, and have been able to use their market power to constrain cost inflation, as long as their regulators make sure that they are profiting only from technology assessment and utilization review, and not claims processing and administrative-overhead manipulation. In this new environment, with managed-care companies providing the high-deductible major medical insurance for the entire nation, we can develop a buffer, so that government itself is not involved in the decision making. The decision making is a process that has shown itself to be very vulnerable to manipulation by the sellers of technology and their ever-present groups of academic, specialty, and disease-centered fellow travelers.

Managed care companies that provide high-deductible insurance will, of course, need to be carefully regulated. It will be necessary to insure that they fairly reimburse critical services, that regions of the country, or social, racial, and other demographic groups, are not inequitably served, that the companies honor their contracts and remain fiscally sound, that their marketing is accurate and ethical. It will also be necessary to insure that the marketplace is not dominated by one or two large entities capable of driving out competition and eliminating product differences which provide the consumer choices that will help preserve the function of the market in spreading access and containing cost.

So, despite concerns about the ability of the medical marketplace to build a healthcare system, we believe a balance of government regulation of the market, and the market itself, is an effective method to pay for certain medical services, promoting equity as it creates access and constrains cost. One additional advantage of the architecture we have described is that it expands but focuses the role of managed-care companies. That changed but expanded role is likely to make managed care less resistant to the process of changing the system, a political consideration that is justified because of the ability of the market and of managed-care companies to add value to a reimbursement system, instead of profiting by exploiting their market power unfairly.

3. Everyone gets to pay co-pays, which help balance need and responsibility

It may seem odd that we discuss co-pays in a chapter called "Who Gets What?", because co-pays are about giving, not getting. But co-pays, and giving, are about the distribution of fiscal responsibility, another way of saying that in order to get a healthcare system, we also get responsibility for choices we all make, and that responsibility has a financial side.

Co-pays are an effective way to balance access, responsibility, and utilization – a concrete method of letting people know what things cost. They are an effective way of reminding us all that we are participating in a zero-sum game, and that unnecessary consumption of medical services will keep us from building the community we need to make health both a possibility and a reality.

When General Motors designed a medical services system for its employees and set the co-pay too low (they set it at $3), their employees used so many services it made General Motors uncompetitive. This was because they had to load the costs of that healthcare system onto each car they tried to sell, and that made the cars more expensive, and more difficult to sell. If we set the co-pay or cost of services too high, on the other hand, people will avoid using any services at all and will not benefit from appropriate treatment and prevention. Co-pays help us enable access for those who cannot otherwise afford services while imposing restraint and rational choice for those who might otherwise needlessly consume. The trick is to design a co-pay structure that is based on evidence, one that encourages people to make appropriate choices, so our financial arrangement for medical service mirrors our understanding of behavior that makes health, as opposed to medical services, available to everyone.

In the past 30 years, lots of research has shown the medical and economic advantages of a primary care-based system, and the adverse health and economic consequences of a system that is specialty and hospital dominated. Designing an intelligent co-pay structure is easy, if we follow that evidence. We forbid co-pays for prenatal care, well-child care and yearly preventative examinations performed by primary-care physicians, because those services have value as a social good. We establish low co-pays for other primary-care visits, so people think about their utilization. Here low but not insignificant co-pays would work best, in the range of $10 to $20, enough to encourage people to think about their real need for service, but not so high as to discourage use when people really need to use service. We set much higher co-pays (in the $50 range) for specialty care, to encourage people to use their primary-care physician first, so that there is someone who knows each person coordinating that person's care. And we set co-pays for un-referred emergency-room care highest ($100 to $200) to discourage emergency-room utilization for anyone who does not really need it.

Some medical services have social value; others are consumer goods. If we pay attention to who gets what, and design a financial support network for medical services that promote health, we can provide medical services without cannibalizing our health and our culture, and create a healthcare system that is rational, personal, and just.

how should it look?

Say we could rewrite history using some of the principles and ideas developed in this book, and create a healthcare system from the ground up. What principles and ideas would we use? What goals and objectives would the redone healthcare system have? What would be the system's moving parts? What would it look like? Who would it serve, and how would it serve them? Who would be health workers, and how would they be selected, paid and trained? What would it cost? How would we pay for it, and how would we know if we were actually getting the health we want and paid for?

We would argue that the new healthcare system should be founded on a single principle, which we have articulated in our definition of health. This is: that health is the ability of individuals to function in the context of relationships appropriate to their culture and stage of development in a normal human life cycle, *and the ability of individuals to function as equal participants in the social contract*. An individual's ability to function in relationship depends, it would appear, on two secondary organizing principles – access to technologies that facilitate that function, and an environment in which relationship can happen. That is, the new healthcare system would have to provide equal access to the tools we use to prevent, diagnose, treat, and cure disease, but such a healthcare system would also need to address the culture of relationship, the social context in which relationships are either emphasized and facilitated, or are discouraged. We have argued that income equality helps create social capital, a clear correlate of longevity, and that social capital, or social cohesion, is a measure of trust, and is associated with improvements in self-reported health.

More important, we have argued that a just healthcare system is one that enables the equal and full participation of individuals as participants in society – and, in addition, that health depends on free society as the guarantor of relationships, the structure that makes relationships possible.

So it would appear that equal access to many medical services is necessary for a functional healthcare system under this rubric. That is, equal access to many medical services is necessary to have a *functional* healthcare system. But equal access to medical services does not mean equal access to *all* medical services, because, as we have argued, other areas of social spending need to be publicly supported as well. So spending on medical services needs to be carefully limited, in recognition of the limitations imposed by the allocation of resources needed to promote social capital. Spending on medical services needs not to trump spending on housing, education, or public transportation, because health as we have defined it relies on a rich net of social interactions in many spheres, a rich net that is built with carefully parsed social spending, so we grow communities which have many different areas of social interaction.

By definition, then, a new healthcare system would have the growth of social capital included in its "mission statement," together with a focus on promoting the ability of individuals to function in relationship, and an awareness of the need for individuals to function as participants in civic society. The need for equal access provides a check and balance on the drive toward longevity, as resource allocation decisions could be balanced on that principle. In practical terms, that means we spend public money on infrastructure and technologies that promote individuals' ability to function up to the national average expected life span, and leave spending on longevity and function for people older than that expected individual life span up to the private sector.

Not spend public money on medical services for individuals who are older than the expected individual life span? A healthcare system that builds social capital? That's exactly the reverse of what we do now, where some 30 percent of all medical services expenditures are made for the last 30 days of a person's life, and social capital is never on the medical services agenda! Such inverted priorities would turn the healthcare system on its head! What would such a turned-around healthcare system look like?

POPULATION-BASED PRIMARY CARE

Population-based primary care is that system of healthcare distribution that assigns every person in a geographical area to a primary-care practice accessible to that geographical area, and makes every primary-care practice responsible for the primary care of every person in that defined area. We have never seen population-based primary care in the United States, and have no concept of what it looks like. Population-based primary care looks more like public libraries, public schools, and local police stations than it does like the hodgepodge system of private practitioners stacked in medical office buildings that we have now. Each neighborhood, town, or village of 10,000–20,000 people would have a primary-care center, providing robust primary care that includes 90–95 percent of the medical services used by that community's inhabitants.

Population-based primary care imagines a vibrant, open, broad, reaching-out primary care, with practices that include physicians, visiting nurses, midwives, mental-health workers, nurse-practitioners, physician assistants, health educators, nutritionists, dentists, pharmacists, and physical therapists, able, with this breadth and a multidisciplinary team approach, to care for 90 to 95 percent of the medical services' needs of communities. Population-based primary-care health centers staffed in this way can be open 12 hours a day, eliminating the need for urgent care centers and limiting the need for hospital emergency rooms for all but life-threatening emergencies. Population-based primary-care health centers use new ideas about scheduling, called open or advanced access, which allow such practices to accommodate anyone who wants medical services when they want and need those services, open under the tag or banner of "sick today, seen today".

The orientation, putting many services in one building, serving one population, meeting people where they are, as they are, providing what they need when they need it – and doing outreach – will encourage much of the population of a place to choose one health center. In this way the health center staff, instead of trying to serve who comes through the door, is able to think more broadly, about the needs of the entire population of people living in a place. The health center itself will employ local people and capture many more health dollars than physician practices now capture in the suburban communities where the bulk of the American population now live. It will provide a place where busy people will see one another regularly, as they come to the health center for services, build social capital, trust, and pride: this is something we do together for ourselves.

Because of size of the practice and the charge of this policy direction, population-based primary-care practices can reach out to the communities they serve, and become public health practices. They can bring screening and prevention to those people who do not seek them for themselves. They can arrange for home-based care in a coherent way, coordinate the home services with the medical team that manages a person's care, and bring less-traditional health promotion services, such as exercise classes or health education, to community groups and organizations like schools and senior-citizens housing.

In addition, by putting many services now disbursed over a region or centralized in urban centers, often to teaching hospitals, back to a local community, population-based primary-care practices helps build the social capital of a place in two ways. First, they put a dense network of medical services that serve a single population (primary care, mental health, physical therapy, dental care, nutrition, visiting nursing, maternity care) in a single place, tying the people of that place more closely together. When the people who live together in a neighborhood or town have to come to the same place for many services, they see each other more. People run into each other in the grocery store. In a population-based primary-care system, people run into each other in the health center as well.

Second, population-based primary-care practice secures the economic value of those services to the place and people served, so the wealth of that place stays in that place, as money circulates many times among the people who live there. So by organizing medical services in a population-based primary-care way, we both improve the ability of individuals to function in relationship while we are strengthening the environment for relationships to function.

In addition, a population-based primary-care system would go a long way toward eliminating disparities in longevity and function due to race, class, culture, and geography, disparities that mock any claim to effectiveness made by the current marketplace and market-driven delivery system.

A QUICK PREVIEW OF THE COST

We haven't detailed the costs of the system or the financing mechanism to support those costs, areas we will explore later in this and the next chapter, once the service-delivery model has been laid out. But here is the painful preview of the cost analysis, which nails down the value of the population-based primary-care approach. In 2003 dollars, we estimate population-based primary care to cost $500 per person per year or less, including dental care, primary-care laboratory and imaging, mental health, visiting nursing, nutrition, physical therapy, common generic pharmaceuticals and public health services, with costs dropping if a more integrated business model can be achieved. (By integrated business model we mean one in which all services are provided by the same business entity, and all payments, with the exception of per-visit patient co-pays, are provided by a single source paying in a timely manner.) By comparison, in 2003, the per person per year cost of health insurance was $4,000–$5,000 if people over 65 are included, of which 10–20 percent, or $400–$1,000, was consumed by the cost of administration of this market-driven system. Put another way, we are wasting a huge amount on the administration of an unnecessarily complicated marketplace, as much as twice the cost of providing care to everyone who needs it (the cost of Medicare administration is less than four percent). Moreover, that administration is not getting the services to all the people who need them, nor is it even recognizing the need to build community as services are delivered. So it is undermining community, and making the health it claims to care for impossible for the people who need it to get.

WHAT ABOUT SPECIALIZED SERVICES?

Even if a population-based primary-care system can deliver 90 percent of the medical services a population needs and wants, that leaves 10 percent of services unaddressed. These specialized services, which support the function of the many people who are ill from diseases and conditions as diverse as kidney failure to heart disease to cancers of all sorts, are critical to the security of the millions of affected individuals. They are also critical to primary-care practices, whether population-based or market driven, helping those practices care well for people in communities, and teaching those practices new techniques and new approaches to health and disease.

In the current medical-services supply system, the availability of specialized services is a market-driven phenomenon. It is squeezed between the willingness of consumers to pay a high price for services, and barriers to entry of new practitioners supplying those services imposed by the willingness and ability of the specialty organization "guilds" to train more practitioners, increase competition, and lower the cost of service. Supply and demand in the specialty services sector is actually quite complex. Contributing to the supply and pricing of specialized services is government support for training, and the overlapping expertise and turf of the specialties. Another contributor is the pressure of marketplace actors such as equipment suppliers and pharmaceutical companies – actors who reach for a larger and larger market by finding ways of making medications and procedures originally confined to the specialty arena available to primary-care physicians for their use.

A population-based medical-services system would take a lesson from the U.S. managed-care experience. In this, private organizations hoped to profit from the chaos in the medical-services supply markets by trying to measure need for service (and eliminated payment for services that it found "not medically necessary"), consolidated kinds of services into purchasing pools, and purchased needed services for the best price, achieving economies over unmanaged purchasing by applying management principles to these service purchases. The U.S. managed-care companies, of course, were motivated only by profit, and served just a small segment of the population – the segment with employer-provided health insurance whose employers were clever enough to use their market leverage to dominate markets and control prices. From the managed-care experience, we have learned that it is possible to measure the need for specialty services and go about purchasing those services in an organized way. However, we can also infer a huge societal benefit, if the managed care kind of analysis and market leverage can be used in the service of a medical services system that is population based, equitable, and focused on the common good, instead of profit.

In the population-based medical services system environment, that means regionalizing specialized services into area community hospitals (in Europe these are known as polyclinics) that serve the population of affiliated population-based primary-care centers. This kind of regionalization, which exists in a constantly twisting, disease-oriented way in the United States now for some diseases and conditions (trauma, cancer, and neonatal intensive care come quickly to mind), can easily be made system-wide by analyzing the incidence and prevalence of disease, and considering geographical and transportation barriers, to determine size, scope and location. Specialists ought to practice at area community hospitals, which means they will be accessible to people in communities and the population-based primary-care practices they exist to support. Our guess is that one area community hospital will be required for every 100,000 to 200,000 people, and support 10–20 population-based primary-care practices; but the population base of area community hospitals is also a function of geography and the incidence and prevalence of disease. We might need one area community hospital per 200,000 people in a part of the country where the incidence and prevalence of disease is relatively low and where geography and culture are not a barrier to access. But we might need one area community hospital per 50,000 people in a part of the country where genetics, economics, and culture have collided, causing lots of disease in a culturally complex place which struggles with the geographic isolation of its communities. We have adequate science to sort out who needs what. We just need the social commitment and a health services system with adequate resources and enough political independence to site our hospitals correctly, and then get out of their way, and let them do the jobs we ask them to do.

Of course, some diseases and conditions occur with very limited frequency, and will require more hierarchical regionalization. Regional hospitals, charged with caring for diseases and conditions which occur with frequencies less than 10 per 200,000 people, for diseases which occur more frequently but are present in unusual severity, and for the rare complications of more common conditions, might serve regions of 5–10 million people. They might support 50 to 100 area community hospitals, and through them 500 to 1,000 primary-care practices. As such they are the ideal setting for the nation's medical schools, which, if they associated with the regional hospitals, would have an unrivaled clinical base of patients with rare conditions, area community hospitals, and population-based primary-care practices. They would provide the clinical setting with which to teach many stripes of health professionals the knowledge base of single disciplines as well as the teamwork and collaborative skills needed to be part of a broadly based healthcare team. In addition, regional hospitals could serve as the nation's research infrastructure for new technologies, providing the backbone of research and development that needs a clinical base.

And some diseases are very rare indeed. Five to 10 national hospitals, serving people with these very rare conditions, and a population base of 50 to 75 million people, would care for people with these conditions, and would support five to 10 regional hospitals, 250 to 1,000 area community hospitals, and 2,500 to 20,000 primary-care practices. (The population base of each level of care is fictionalized for demonstration purposes. Much more planning, involving studies of the incidence and prevalence of disease, local and regional variation in disease incidence and severity and age and gender balances, as well as transportation challenges provided by geography, would go into decisions about the service area and scope of hospitals at various levels. Politics would invariably play a part, but like districting and redistricting, the need for a fair distribution of resources and social cohesion often balances self-interest and advocacy. Excluded people fight back.)

GOVERNMENT SUPPORT

How would a population-based medical services system need to be supported by state and federal governments? Both would need Health Authorities, with different powers and responsibilities than with the U.S. Department of Health and Human Services, or most state Departments of Health, currently have.

At the federal level, the U.S. Health Authority would have the responsibility of seeding the development of local health authorities. These authorities themselves would be responsible for organizing and overseeing population-based primary-care practices, assisting states in planning for and assuring the funding of area community hospitals, organizing and funding regional hospitals and medical services training schools, and organizing and funding the national hospitals. In addition, the U.S. Health Authority would be responsible for research and development and for control of infectious disease, as it is today with the National Institutes of Health and the Centers for Disease Control of the U.S. Public Health Service.

The process of seeding local health authorities, while complex in practice, is simple in construction. First, the U.S. Health Authority needs to work with the State Health Authorities to plan for the location and staffing of each authority. Then, the federal government would fund the building of each population-based primary-care center, using the time-tested model of low-cost federal loans to autonomous or semi-autonomous local health authorities, themselves brought into existence at the behest of local government with the support of federal funds for planning, and federal loans for building. These federal loans, modeled after those given water-treatment authorities, libraries and local schools, could be extended in a rolling way, with the loan repayments coming back from the first cohort of primary-care centers being used to pay for each successive cohort, until everyone in the population has access to population-based primary care.

Two additional roles for the U.S. Health Authority would be to measure and eliminate disparities in longevity and function due to race, class, culture, language, low social capital, and geography. Measurement of disparities could be, and should be, done state by state, encouraged with matching federal dollars, with the federal government responsible for supervising the methodology, to allow state-by-state and locality-by-locality comparisons. Then both state and federal governments could help eliminate the disparities identified, by grants in aid to population-based primary-care centers operating in areas that have poor longevity and function compared to the mean.

State health authorities would have five primary functions:

▶ planning of population-based primary-care practices;
▶ planning, oversight, and funding of area community hospitals;
▶ the measurement and reporting of health disparities;
▶ quality measurement and assurance for population-based primary-care practices and area community hospitals;
▶ the design and implementation of state-wide campaigns to deal with public health problems identified in the quality and disparity analysis.

The existence of a population-based primary-care practice infrastructure would give state health authorities much greater reach, from a public health perspective, than state departments of health, which are essentially regulators instead of organs of public health, have now.

Local health authorities, the real cornerstone of a population-based medical services system, would have two primary functions: organizing the actual distribution of primary care as it is delivered in communities, and keeping the process of its organization democratic. Here's what they would do: structured as private-public partnerships, the local health authorities would apply for federal loans and grants, which they would use to lease or build space for population-based primary-care centers. Then they would contract for services, working with existing primary-care practices and providers, or seeding new primary-care practices that were broad enough from a multidisciplinary perspective, to deliver the service that each community needs. The local health authorities would have a supply of primary-care physicians, providers, and practices to contract with. This is because of:

- low-interest federal loans;
- the numbers of patients likely to be drawn to the primary-care practices by breadth of services and by the access to care that the health authorities bring to the table;
- other incentives worked out between state and federal governments to promote primary-care practice where it is needed most (scholarships, low-interest educational loans, loan paybacks, and tax incentives are the kind of incentives in use today, and a primary-care service requirement as a prerequisite for specialty training has been used in other countries with great success);
- because the existence of population-based primary care, which is the kind of medicine most primary-care physicians and other providers actually want to practice.

Using the incentives just mentioned, the local health authorities would be in the position to create service-delivery standards as a prerequisite to provider contracting. By using incentives (and likely, as a condition for state and federal support), local health authorities could require practices:

- to remain open extended hours;
- to see anyone who is ill the day they are ill;
- to keep waiting times below a certain target;
- to include mental health workers, visiting nurses, laboratory and simple x-ray services, physical therapists, nurse midwives, nutritionists and dentists and dental hygienists as a part of their practices;
- to engage in the measurement and improvement of the quality of the work they do and the services they offer;
- and to provide services to all community institutions, like nursing homes and schools;
- and to offer a variety of health promotional activities, from exercise classes to hypertension screening to diabetic classes, to the community at large.

If the local health authority found service-delivery standards were not being observed, it would be able to not renew, or in the case of extreme malfeasance, to cancel the contract of the practice providing service to the community.

This distribution of roles – the local health authority which controls the building and the incentives for practicing in a community-oriented way, and the professional practice, which is responsible for the delivery of care – achieves an appropriate balance of oversight and input (the local health authority) and professional integrity and independence (the professional practice). This is a balance that the closest existing model, community health centers, lacks today. Community health centers are controlled by executive directors who are often not health professionals, and governed by community boards which are requited to be at least 51 percent consumers. But the executive director, community board model breaks down in a number of ways. First, as most community health center funding is public grant funding, and does not follow individual patients, community health centers often pay closest attention to what their federal handlers ask and want of them, instead of concentrating on what their patients and communities need. Second, executive directors and their administrative staff are often the only permanent staff. Health professionals, often paid below market rates, come and go, so decisions are made, not on the basis of professional imperatives but to serve administrative or political ends. And the community boards, titularly 51 percent community members, are often composed of community members hand chosen by the executive directors, and thus have as their first commitment loyalty to the executive directors, and not to the needs of the community that is served. Politics, patronage, and protectionism often rule the day at community health centers, and it is this imprisoning structure that has contributed to our current situation, in which community health centers are marginalized to the care of the poor, instead of being the flagships of the healthcare system they were intended to create.

The local health authority, on the other hand, would be in the position to insure that the overall governance of the health centers remains democratic. How? By making sure the board members are elected! Because the health center, in this construction, serves or is available to serve everyone in the community, everyone in the community has a interest in how it runs, and the simplest way to choose its board is to elect it, just as city council members and school board members are elected. (There are other ways of choosing board members, of course, from having them appointed by local officials to having the local health authority be a private non-profit corporation, like a charity or the board of a private college. Boards of charities or private colleges usually have existing board members choose new members, and select either volunteers with special abilities needed by the organization, large donors, or loyal alumni.) But the direct election model has much to say for itself, both in terms of keeping the health center focused on its clientele and in terms of making sure people in each locality pay attention to what the health center is doing, and develop a feeling of appropriate ownership for it.

The existence of a population-based public-health infrastructure would allow us to influence the incidence and prevalence of disease in a coherent way. Imagine an influenza vaccine campaign, for example, in an environment where we can identify every citizen at risk, where we have a clear and consistent way of reaching every citizen at risk, where we command the resources necessary to purchase and distribute vaccine, and where we have a community-based way of administering vaccine. Now imagine the same infrastructure, focused, led, and funded for public health interventions by the state health authority, working away at cigarette smoking, exercise, cholesterol lowering, lead poisoning, or TV consumption. Imagine a network of health workers of all stripes, fanning out over a community in which all the health workers are known members, and using the rich network of community life, from the hairdresser, barber, coffee shop and IGA, to the churches, synagogues, and mosques, to the library, to the public school, to the zoning board and tax collector, to deliver messages that promote health. Imagine how health messages might circle the porches and church suppers. Imagine a common life.

how should we pay for it?

Perhaps the most significant of the many tail-wags-dog phenomena in current American life is the endless debate over healthcare financing, in which we try to decide who pays for what we all actually pay for together, before we have decided what it is we are paying for. We have no consensus about what the healthcare system is or should look like, but we struggle endlessly over who should pay for this expensive monster we cannot afford.

A population-based primary healthcare system opens the door to intelligent and equitable distribution of costs. It gives us a shot at actually matching resources to needs, instead of the current system, in which we essentially throw an armload of money into the air, and hope it lands somewhat near the people who need it, and allows them to buy the services they need to buy.

BUILDING THE NEW HEALTHCARE SYSTEM

Let's begin at the level of the local health authority, as it makes most sense to build this healthcare system from the ground up.

As we said in the last chapter, local health authorities will require federal grants and loans to support building and organizing primary-care centers. This economic stimulus comes appropriately from the federal government, as it is in the interest of the nation as a whole to see such a system up and running, as we are and will be unable to sustain the cost of medical services in an environment where there is no guiding principle allowing the matching of resource to need. Federal grants and loans give us the ability to develop and use large capital flows for the new investment this system will initially require, but to do so in an equitable way, insuring that new investment is fairly distributed from a geographic and economic perspective. It also insures that the emerging health centers meet quality and sustainability standards in their organization, and insures representation, consideration of the population-base, and professional breadth and quality.

But operating funding for the primary-care centers can come from patients themselves, in a radically redesigned health-financing scheme. It would be one that uses traditional indemnity health insurance, patient savings accounts and direct funding of primary-care centers brokered by municipalities and their local health authorities, to create a financing scheme that aligns incentives correctly as it assures adequate funding for what is needed.

How funding would work

Here's how it works: every person gets a tax-protected savings account, which exist in current tax law as medical savings accounts, health savings accounts, and health reimbursement accounts. Deposits into those accounts can come from a number of sources: a person's employer or her/his parents'/spouse's employer, a person her or himself, or from state or federal governmental sources, through the Medicare or Medicaid programs. Withdrawals from those accounts can be made in two ways: mandatory withdrawals, for both required participation in the primary-care centers and for high-deductible health insurance (also known as catastrophic insurance), and via a smartcard, like a credit card, which can be used by patients as they pay for medications, tests, or specialty care. Money left in the savings accounts becomes the patient's own property, earns interest, and grows from year to year, finally becoming deductible at retirement or when the account grows larger than preset limits, for the patient's own use.

Most experience with high-deductible major medical insurance suggests the high-deductible major medical insurance component consumes 40 to 50 percent of the health insurance dollar, or $1,600 to $2,000 per person per year for people under 65, and $2,400 to $3,000 for people over 65. Our estimates of the per-person per year cost of primary care suggest it costs $200 to $300 per person per year. Combined, the mandatory withdrawals from each person's medical savings accounts will be $1,800 to $2,300. This leaves $1,700 to $2,200 per person per year in each bank account for people under 65 (if we start from an average current health insurance cost of about $4,000 per person per year) and from $2,700 to $3,400 for people over 65 (if we assume the average yearly cost for people with Medicare is $6,000). Because no health insurance company or government forms processor has to administer the funds that remain in the medical savings account, we might expect an immediate savings of $150 (for people with Medicare, where the administrative costs run about five percent) to $400 (for people with commercial health insurance, where the administrative costs run as much as 20 percent). True, the fixed administrative costs may not shrink in so scalable a manner, reducing the impact of the savings, and there is likely to be some administrative cost in running all these medical savings accounts. However, it appears that some of the cost of the new primary-care center system might be funded out of existing administrative expense that contributes nothing to the actual delivery of medical services at a community level, and contributes less than nothing to the leverage of medical services spending to build social capital – something the primary-care centers can and will do.

What this model delivers

The magic of this architecture is its ability to do so much with relatively little.

- It gives us a funded primary-care medical-services delivery system for the first time, and with that, creates our ability to make prevention happen, because it allows us to address the entire population.
- It provides universal and equal access to the most important medical services – the primary-care services.
- It helps us redirect resources so we use our medical-services spending to build social capital, reversing the trend of the current system.
- It very likely saves money, because it gives each person an incentive to be careful about their spending on medical services, because people are spending their own money when they purchase services.
- It provides choice, as anyone can go to see any medical provider, and gives them some money to pay for that.
- It funds prescription drug costs, as it provides every person with a certain amount of money they can spend, or save, any way they wish.

Addressing the critics

This model addresses many of the criticisms voiced by social progressives of medical savings accounts (long the favorite of the Republican right); criticisms which faulted medical savings accounts for abandoning prevention and creating a phenomenon called adverse selection. People with "classic" medical savings accounts (savings accounts which require only a tax-advantaged medical savings account and a obligatory high-deductible major medical insurance policy, but not a contribution to or membership in a primary-care center) would abandon prevention, progressive critics argued. They thought this would occur because regular physical examination, and preventative technologies – such as pap smears, mammograms, cholesterol measurements and the like – cost money, and the medical savings account structure so strongly incentivizes individual responsibility for health expenditures that people with medical savings accounts would not be willing to spend on these simple technologies. Then, it was argued, when these same people became ill with preventable illness, they would not have enough money saved to care for themselves, would likely become impoverished by illness, and would throw themselves on the public dole, through Medicaid or Medicare. Any savings appreciated by individuals, these critics argued, would be eaten up by public expense, and would represent cost shifting from the private to the public domains, with a net increase in cost to tax payers.

Adverse selection is a similar critique. Progressive critics argue that the only people choosing medical savings accounts would be the young and well, who have little medical expense. The old and sick, these critics argued, would remain in traditional health insurance plans and HMOs, and the costs of their care would be spread over fewer people. This would boost the costs of these plans, making them unaffordable for anyone. Employers would then abandon the old and the sick to the public domain, allowing private savings only at the cost of significant new public spending, as the costs of caring for the old and the sick were transferred to tax payers. Although medical savings accounts might provide the illusion of cost savings or cost reduction, those savings or reductions would come only at public expense.[1] These critiques are fallacious in a number of ways, and any weakness in the medical savings account structure is repaired by the modified medical savings account structure presented here.

The progressive critiques, while theoretically interesting, cry out for any evidence in support of their accuracy. First, there is no evidence that prevention actually saves money when viewed from the perspective of a population over time. Remember the reductive fallacy? Preventive technologies have been evaluated individually, with endpoints like disease-specific morbidity (breast cancer, heart disease and stroke) and both disease-specific and total mortality. In this way each technology appears useful when viewed in isolation from all others. (It is sometimes only marginally useful – the value of mammography is in much dispute, and has been abandoned in Great Britain; and the value of cholesterol lowering most clearly established only after heart disease has occurred, in people at risk for heart disease, with no prospective study showing a cost benefit, and no demonstrable benefit in terms of total mortality). There has never been a true cost and benefit evaluation of a range of preventive technologies used together in a population of people over time. Indeed, while there may be a longevity advantage to prevention, the relationship and cost advantages are likely to be complex, as everyone dies of something. By postponing death (which is what some say all prevention really achieves) at great collective expense and creating a longer period of aged frailty for all, what we may be doing is enslaving ourselves to corporate America. All our youth is fast becoming devoted to preventing our own deaths and caring for the frail old, so we do not have either the time or resources left to have relationships with one another, so that we do not enjoy the flower of youth, but suffer, in a slavery of our own making, into the twilight of the dependent old. Viewed from this perspective, the progressive fears of transferring cost savings from the private to the public domain is a straw-man argument indeed, and those same progressive critics are providing us the ultimate Hobson's choice: choose some slavery now, or more slavery now and longer dependency later.

In any case, the modified medical savings account/population-based primary-care structure makes the prevention argument disappear. This architecture gives the first hope of making prevention real by making it population based. It is the first hope of using these technologies to fundamentally alter the incidence and prevalence of disease. What people choose, and what they do, when we empower communities in this way is unpredictable. Communities able to make medical-service choices as communities may decide to go down a totally different path, and weighing the relatively poor evidence, not choose to do prevention at all.

Lack of evidence for false-economy arguments

Both of the false economy arguments – failed prevention and adverse selection – cry out for evidence to support their occurrence. If anything, experience with medical savings accounts in the marketplace suggests the converse: early in their life, and with limited use, there is no evidence that false economy actually occurs. Most private employers who use medical savings accounts or their look-alikes experience full voluntary adoption with no adverse selection, over three or four years. The reason for that is twofold. The first reason is what we call the casino mentality. All the casinos in America are filled with the old and poor, who have done little but lose at life's game for their entire collective lifetimes – but they keep playing. We are a nation of gamblers, a nation of people who have irrational hope in the face of overwhelming odds. People who are old and sick are not likely to run a precise economic calculation. They are likely to gamble on beating the odds, hoping against hope that there will be a little money left over in their medical savings accounts for them to use on a good dinner out or a trip to the Caribbean. The old and the sick will choose medical savings accounts regardless of the odds, and regardless of the economic calculus, which shows no clear benefit making that choice, because of the sliver of irrational hope that it built into us all.

And the old and the sick, in doing so, understand what the health policy pundits do not understand: the structure of health insurance in America makes everyone a loser. Because of deductible and co-pays, cost shares and employee contribution, the out-of-pocket cost of health insurance in the United States in 2007 is very similar to the out-of-pocket costs which might be incurred in a modified medical savings account environment. In fact, few traditional health plans, in 2007, have a pure out-of-pocket upper limit, and few have any reward for not spending money, two features of most health savings accounts: there is upside risk, and no downside benefit. The money you spend on traditional health insurance is just gone, while some of the money you put in a health savings accounts stays yours, if you are lucky, healthy, and are a smart consumer. But choose traditional health insurance or HMOs, and all the money spent under your name is gone to someone else's pocket. Choose modified medical savings accounts, and you have some money in your pocket, at least for a while, and some hope of hanging on to it, if you can see through the medical marketing machine designed to pry that money away.

The first false economy argument – that ill people will spend through their deductible, become ill, and fall onto the public dole – is no more true than the notion that traditional health insurance is any real protection or security. Fall ill in today's world, and you lose your job and your health insurance with it, and fall onto the public dole just as fast. The difference is that, with a modified medical savings account/population-based primary-care environment, we will have built a community to take care of you when calamity happens. In today's world, you are on your own. The progressive critics do not get the way in which they have become apologists for medical capitalism and the medical services profiteers, and by trying to prop up the current health insurance system, they are working to enslave us all.

KEEPING THE SAFETY NET SAFE
Financing area/community, regional, and national hospitals and medical schools

So imagine a world in which everyone has a medical savings account that's linked to a population-based primary-care practice. Does that make the world a better place? Can the high-deductible major medical sustain hospitals?

One of the great modern myths is that hospitals can live on fee for service dollars: that hospitals, with their huge overhead costs required to sustain essential services which are both very expensive and have varying need and demand, can and should somehow spread these fixed costs over everyone who needs hospital services. The way the system works, you pay (through the nose!) for hospital services when you use the hospital if you are sick and you pay to sustain hospital services if you are not sick. This is because of the way increased hospital costs are spread to everyone who has insurance, because the people who really pay these fixed costs are insurance companies, which pay the bills and pass the costs on to all their insured.

Of course, such a structure creates all sorts of inequality and maldistribution across the system in which not everyone is insured. The first sort of inequality is the effective tax on the insured, who have to pay for the uninsured, who do not have to bear these costs. This kind of cost shifting pushes up the cost of insurance, and has made insurance progressively unaffordable. This creates what is sometimes called the death spiral of health insurance, in which more uninsured causes increases in insurance cost which causes increases in the number of uninsured, and so on, until the system inevitable collapses, something that hasn't happened yet, but will. The second inequality caused by asking the sick and their insurers to bear all hospital costs is healthcare profiteering; highly reimbursed services, originally provided in a hospital, and priced to spread the hospital's fixed costs over sick people and their insurers, are suddenly being performed out of the hospitals by various physician entrepreneurs, who collect higher than reasonable fees but do not have to support the hospitals costs. This process, which involved radiologists, surgeons and gastroenterologists, has pushed up the incomes of some specialties, as it has impoverished hospitals and left too few dollars for primary-care practice development.

The third kind of inequality is called cherry picking. Many insurance companies, usually those that sell high-deductible health insurance, engage in a practice called cherry picking – they insure only well people, and cancel the insurance of the ill as soon as they become ill, leaving public methods of paying for health service to pick up the cost of all illness. The "cherry picking" insurance companies profit, having charged people for the cost of illness which the insurers then do not have to pay for, once the illness occurs. Cherry picking increases the cost of health insurance for those entities left holding the bag – often government programs and health insurance companies that do not engage in the practice – because the responsible players have fewer well people over whom to spread the cost of the illness of the ill.

Reducing the risks of a high-deductible system

One of the great risks of a population-based primary-care system funded by a high-deductible insurance program is that hospitals and medical schools will be underfunded, and crippled, if high-deductible insurance companies cherry pick their insured customers.

There are two ways to reduce the risk to healthcare institutions from a high-deductible system. The first way to reduce the risk of a high-deductible system is to require that everyone be insured, with insurance funded by either a state or federal tax, since state and federal governments already collect tax universally. (Local government, which might be a more trusted tax collector, does not usually collect tax from everyone, but only from homeowners, and it would be burdensome to design a new tax collecting authority while there are existing government agencies that can do the work.) The second way of reducing the risk to healthcare institutions from a high-deductible major medical system is to carefully regulate health insurance companies (which are heavily regulated now) to require community rating. That is, in this new environment, people would buy their health insurance through their communities, and insurance companies would have to agree to accept all community members when they write high-deductible policies available to members of population-based primary health centers. Communities, which would come to the table with the ability to purchase for large numbers of consumers, might be able to force community rating in this way, without regulation, since purchasing pools of 10,000 to 100,000 people are very attractive to insurers in the current marketplace.

Using this approach, state or federal government might have a role in supplementing the budget of communities which had an unequal burden of illness, and a higher cost of community-rated catastrophic insurance, until the primary-care practice was effective in eliminating the disparity in the incidence or prevalence of disease. (One can imagine a situation in which government provides reinsurance for very high-cost situations, a concept that is being tested now in New York and a few other states, as a way to reduce the risk to health insurance companies and level the playing field in the competition between them, in order to allow them to remain community rated and keep health insurance affordable. However, the transfer of financial liability does not really make insurance any more affordable, it just spreads the risk of those expensive situations to the largest possible risk pool: taxpayers. The effectiveness of such an intervention is still unknown, but early reports are positive.) The second way to reduce the risk of a high-deductible system to healthcare institutions is to rethink how we bill for hospital and other expensive services.

We now often use unit billing or case rates to pay for hospital services. That is, when someone is in the hospital, they are billed for every identifiable service and supply, from aspirin to the time of a highly skilled surgeon. These separate charges often look like the itemization of a bill from the Pentagon – $12 for an aspirin, $20 for a box of tissues – because the hospital has no other way to recoup its operating costs, other than by spreading those costs over each service. On the other hand, government and some insurance companies sometimes pay hospitals case or day rates, paying them a certain amount of money for each person in the hospital who has a certain diagnosis, for each day the person is in the hospital. This gaming of payment methodologies is supposed to encourage hospitals to be precise and efficient, to track every expense (unit billing), to use limited resources wisely (diagnosis-related case rates) and to get people in and out of the hospital quickly (day rates). No one knows how effective this miasma of payment methodologies actually is. What we do know is that the marketplace approach to hospital reimbursement creates its own accounting nightmare. It also provides hospitals and insurers hundreds of opportunities to game the system, playing intricate, complicated games of cat and mouse, three-card Monte and high-stakes chicken, games that employ lots of accountants and thousands of clerks, but that may not contribute much to the efficiency or effectiveness of hospital services.

State funding the hospital system

Clearly, the way to protect hospitals and other institutions in a high-deductible environment is to state fund the hospital system, so that the operating costs of hospitals are paid by taxpayer dollars, and the health insurance companies become responsible only for utilization costs derived from the part of hospital spending that cannot be considered fixed overhead. Fixed overhead costs are those costs related to keeping the hospital open: the costs of basic nursing and medical staff, the housekeeping staff and the plant-management expense. There can be no secure system of care without a hospital services infrastructure, so those costs should be spread over all citizens through the state's taxation policy, and so we fund basic hospital care the same way we fund police and roads and schools. The cost of staying in the hospital – utilization of food, of linens, of extra medical and nursing care beyond the basic staffing needed for safe operating, as well as the cost of medications and surgical supplies – those items and costs should be charged to individuals and funded by their high-deductible major medical plans. This methodology gives insurance companies an interest in overseeing utilization and making sure it is appropriate, a useful role for them to play as a check and balance in an otherwise publicly funded environment which might be a set-up for bloating costs. And this methodology helps contain the cost of care covered by insurance, so that high-deductible health insurance remains affordable by all.

Of course, the state needs a way to determine how many hospitals and hospital services it needs to support, and at the same time insure that the tax dollars it spends on basic hospital services are spent wisely and effectively. State health departments, perhaps recast as state health authorities, are the natural organization to measure and estimate need, using measurement and analytical tools developed during the managed-care era. Those health departments are also the ideal organizations to measure and compare hospital performance. With guidance from the federal government, it will not be difficult to measure and benchmark hospital costs and relative efficiencies, so that state governments can look critically at their own spending and return on hospital investment.

Such a state-supervised hospital system, however, does not preclude the operation of a private-hospital system which receives no state funding. In fact, a private-hospital system, run entirely on marketplace principles and operating on private funds alone, provides a valuable check and balance on the state-funded system. The demand for private services provides an indicator of the capacity and quality of the state-funded system. Increasing demand for private services is an indicator that the state-funded and supervised system needs to expand capacity for a new services, or pay close attention to the quality of the service being delivered in the state-funded system. It also indicates that private hospitals have developed new services unavailable under the state system, which may (or may not) also be developed under the state-funded system, as budget allows and consensus supports.

But the major risk of including the state in the funding and supervision of the hospital system is that the state will underfund the hospital system in the face of other needs and other priorities. How many states used tobacco lawsuit settlement funds for roads or schools instead of for health services? Too often, state-level budget allocation is a function of personalities and politics, instead of a clear assessment of the burden of disease and the resources that are needed to fight disease in the hospital environment. Perhaps the best approach to budget risk, particularly in smaller states, which have greater risk from budget wars, is to make the state hospital authority independent of state government, but with its own taxing authority. An elected or legislatively appointed semi-autonomous hospital authority, analogous to a turnpike authority, a port authority, or a water treatment authority, gives a state the ability to raise funds for the operation of its hospitals. It also guarantees the hospital authority the independence to insure that hospital funds are spent fairly with good geographical distribution of hospital facilities, and provides the hospital authority insulation from the exigencies of other state budget needs and crises.

FUNDING A REGIONAL AND NATIONAL HOSPITAL AND MEDICAL SCHOOL SYSTEM

The risk of getting a rare disease is compounded by the chaos of marketplace medicine. In addition to the pain and disability from the disease process, the ill person has many worries to face: treatment, when it is available, is often not available near home. Sometimes treatment is speculative, is in the realm of what we hope will work, but cannot show will work. And then both treatment and supportive care are often scandalously expensive, expensive enough to bankrupt families and even small communities. Even so, some treatments postpone death and prolong suffering, while others may be completely curative, and there is no way for an educated layperson (or even a practicing physician) to tell the difference. Not a good situation, if you are a person with a rare or expensive to treat disease, and all you have is your life.

On the other hand, the public policy impact of expensive treatment is real, and we as a society seem to have almost no ability to look relative costs in the face, and make appropriate choices. Like the sexually active teenager who tells herself that good girls do not do "it" and so will not use contraception, because to use contraception is to admit to herself she is going to do "it" and thus will not be a good girl, the American public seems unable to admit to itself that everyone dies of something, that death is sometimes not defeat, and that we need to make choices about what we can afford. Does it make sense to buy everyone with cancer bone-marrow transplants at $500,000 a pop? Liver transplants? Kidney dialysis at $100,000 a year? Does it make sense that college costs $50,000 a year and now many bright kids cannot afford to go? That we are not spending anything on public housing, so there are more homeless people than ever before?

Limiting what we pay for

The first critical notion of publicly funding a regional and national hospital and medical school system out of tax dollars, which is what we will argue for here, is to tie that funding to a mechanism by which we agree to limit what we pay for publicly. This way, we are not in the situation of trying to buy everything for everybody, a situation which will bankrupt a public system in a hurry. To make the healthcare system work, we will have to choose to make some treatments available only to those who can afford them. One can imagine a world in which it will be possible to buy insurance against the need for treatments that are experimental, or just too egregiously expensive for the public domain, a super high deductible insurance. But it will be more effective, and more fair, if we make explicit the notion that not everyone gets everything; instead everyone has equal access to what works. (Elsewhere in this book, we have argued for age limits on publicly funded treatments, aimed at giving everyone an equal share of community resources.)

The justice-as-fairness argument can be attacked on humanitarian grounds, but we believe the central organizing principle of democratic society is the argument to fairness, and so are committed to using age discriminators as more fair than any other mechanism of achieving fair resource allocation. Similarly, we argue for effectiveness discriminators to decide about costly experimental – and often last-ditch – treatments. If there is no evidence that a treatment works for a disease or condition, or even incredibly scrimpy evidence, publicly funded hospitals should not provide that treatment, and community-rated insurances shouldn't pay for them. The small child with a terrible cancer is always going to wring our hearts and our souls, but what of the healthy African American kid from the South Bronx, who we are condemning to death by violence because we are not spending anything on his education or on making his community safe? It hurts to say no, but there are times we will have to learn to say no, even if it takes committees of experts, and new laws to shield the people on those committees, and the doctors and nurses and hospitals, from liability for doing what we need them to do. This is not to say there is not room for fundraising and for appeals by individuals who want expensive treatments, nor is it to say there will not be some unfairness around who gets expensive experimental treatments (here, the rich are favored in the pursuit of what probably does not work). But the unfairness involved in giving expensive experimental treatments that probably do not work to a few desperately ill people who can afford them and not to a few desperately ill people who cannot afford them pales beside the unfairness of not giving decent housing, education, and communities to millions of young people while we give futile treatments to a very few people who are unlikely to live full or functional lives.

Oversight and accountability

The second critical notion of a publicly funded regional and national hospital system is oversight and accountability, of using standards developed to measure the efficiency and effectiveness of hospitals in one place to test and track the efficiency and accountability of all publicly funded hospitals. The role of federally funded, national health institutes like NIH and CDC should be more than research and disease control. We need a national hospital standards bureau, that sets standards for all parts of the medical-services delivery infrastructure. It would focus first on regional hospitals and medical schools, but extend to state health departments, community hospitals and community health centers, and then measure the performance of all the elements of the system, contrasting, comparing, understanding, and suggesting opportunities for improvement, so all Americans have equal access to medical services of equal quality.

Keeping private-sector hospitals

The third critical part of publicly funding regional and national hospital and medical school systems is not publicly funded at all. It is the existence of private-sector hospitals, which must be allowed to exist and compete, but without public funding of any sort. The existence of private profit-making competing institutions is a check and balance on the performance of public systems. However, this will only be the case if no public funds, no Medicare and no Medicaid, flow to the private institutions, so they do not cherry pick cases, and create profit by skimming off what is easy and inexpensive but charging as if those services are difficult and expensive.

The U.S. Health Authority would also be responsible for research and development and for control of infectious disease, as it is today with the National Institutes of Health and the Centers for Disease Control of the U.S. Public Health Service. But they would have research and development tied directly to the base of regional hospitals, area community hospitals, and population-based primary-care centers would change the character of research and development, and allow it to focus on improving individuals' ability to function in relationship and what works in communities, instead of just what works in the lab. NIH and its sister organizations devote billions of research dollars to the arcane and expensive, instead of what is practical and what communities need. Linking NIH to the U.S. Health Authority as its research and development arm would allow it to grow an applications component, where we could develop applications strategies for new technologies that help individuals to function in community. This would insure developed new technologies have an application and that we have a process for getting those new technologies available and applied equally to everyone who needs them. That is a far cry from the NIH of today, which funds the development of new technologies, many of which have no real application, or, if they have an application, lack a mechanism for delivery to the people in communities who need them most.

Can the healthcare system build community instead of help take it apart? We believe it can, and we believe a healthcare system that builds community, as described here, though unlike anything the United States has ever seen, will be local, personal, rational, and just, at the same time as it is secure, technologically sophisticated, and supportive of personal choice. We *can* do it. We just have to see it, and want it enough.

which doctors?

Desiree worked in my office for five years. She was a smart, connected Cape Verdean woman, with sepia skin, laughing eyes, and a weird sense of humor. She had a huge family – 30 brothers and sisters when you count the half sibs, the children of her father with women who are not her mother, and of her mother with men who were not her father – and she took care of them all. The Cape Verdean community in Rhode Island is an energetic, hard-working, boisterous but happy group. Brown-skinned people descended from Portuguese and Portuguese Creole-speaking people who originally lived on islands off the coast of Africa, the Cape Verdeans in the United States are clustered in a few communities of the East Coast: Pawtucket and Central Falls, Rhode Island and Fall River and New Bedford, Massachusetts. Most Cape Verdeans are descended from people who immigrated to the United States in the 1960s 1970s and 1980s, and they in general followed friends and families who were attracted to the Portuguese-speaking communities of Southeastern New England, communities that formed from immigrant Portuguese whalers and fishermen in the late 1700s and early 1800s.

Desiree was born on the small island of Brava, and came to the United States when she was 10. Raised in this broad, loosely organized, loving community (the Brava-descended, Cape Verdean population of Pawtucket and Central Falls, Rhode Island was, by 2000, larger than the population of Brava itself), Desiree had a high school education and two children by the time she was 20. But she was ambitious and hard-working, and managed to train as a medical assistant. She started working two jobs, for a community health center, and nights and weekends in the student health services at Brown. She was actively involved with the lives of her two sons, planning their birthday parties – to which she invited about a thousand people – and attending their school plays. I never figured out when she slept.

There was no better medical assistant and, eventually, no better clinical director. Desiree knew all of our patients, and they all knew and loved her. She remembered their families, their medications, their worries. She was a magnet for the Cape Verdean community, who followed her *en masse* to the practice, and left *en masse* when she left, and who called her at 3 am with problems or sicknesses. She was a quick student, and instantly mastered the panoply of screening recommendations and immunization schedules primary-care doctors have to keep track of, and somehow knew which patient was missing what, and ingeniously implemented this knowledge to connect people with their missing data. She managed to keep everyone, and their files, up to date (to find the people who were missing things, then bring them in and help those people stay up to date).

I thought she should go to medical school. I could not imagine a better primary-care doctor. I could not imagine a better situation, a primary-care doctor of a community, in her community, bringing health services and people together.

But Desiree will never go to medical school. She's in her early thirties now, and working for a pediatrician colleague; she eventually burned out carrying all the weight we asked her to carry. She dreamed of going to nursing school – and we offered to send her – but she could not figure out how to create the time. Perhaps she will manage to attend nursing school – we are in the midst of a nursing shortage, and there are all sorts of incentives available for minority women to go. But I doubt, given the constraints of married life, a third child, family and community responsibilities, and the entropy of trying to survive in a more complicated world, that she will make it. I hope she gets there.

But she cannot go to medical school. That door is closed. The roadblocks are insurmountable.

THE ROADBLOCKS TO MEDICAL-SCHOOL ENTRY
Preparation: bachelor's degree

What are the roadblocks? First is the roadblock of preparation. In order to go to medical school, Desiree would have to obtain a bachelor's degree, and complete specific course work. The costs, in time and money, are over-whelming. Who would support her family while she studied? Who would organize her children's birthday parties? Even if she could do the relevant, required course work, which itself takes three or four years at night school, the need to complete a bachelor's degree consumes 10 to 20 years, if you complete one course at a time, assuming you can continue to study in the summers. And that is not including the financial cost, at $3,000 to $4,000 a course, something like $9,000 to $16,000 a year, or about a third of Desiree's income.

The filter

Even more than cost and time, the filter is the major roadblock. The filter is the weeding-out process, the hidden way we have of selecting who will go to medical school. This is done by selecting for attributes that have nothing to do with the ability to practice medicine, and everything to do with weeding out those who have expansive minds and souls, those who think about and are moved by the relationship between people, and the way the world is organized, and how all the moving parts work together. Pre-medical studies, so called – chemistry, organic chemistry, calculus, physics, biology, and biochemistry – are a set of college courses that together are intensely boring, require no imagination, inspire no or little hope, and are only peripherally related at best to the knowledge base, skill set, and personality traits needed for the intelligent and compassionate practice of medicine. Two of these courses, organic chemistry and calculus, are completely irrelevant to the practice of medicine, but do require an incredible tolerance for boredom, an ability to memorize voluminous amounts of uninteresting, unimportant detail, and a willingness to follow orders blindly, regardless of how silly the order given. Organic chemistry itself is the major filter (there is a beauty to calculus, if you work at finding it), discouraging the imaginative and the idealistic, and selecting for the dull and the prosaic. Would it be possible for Desiree to get through Organic? Anything is possible, given enough time, resources, and determination. But even if someone like Desiree had the time and the resources, given the constraints of working every day, and needing to be emotionally available to her kids and spouse, only one Desiree in a thousand, or one in a million, would ever make it though.

Money

But of course, even if Desiree could make it through organic chemistry, she would still have the roadblock of money. It costs an incredible amount of money to make it through college and medical school, something like $40,000 a year for eight years, before you earn a penny – and that's without room and board. At this writing, the average medical school debt is $150,000, but that's looking backward, at the college and medical school costs of eight years ago, and those costs climb every year. One can only assume that the average medical school debt of students beginning college today will be $300,000 by the time they finish. $300,000! Before they earn a penny!

Is that intimidating to people like Desiree? It's intimidating to me, someone who has been in practice for 20 years! But it is worse than intimidating. Despite the availability of some scholarship money, the cost of medical school turns away hundreds and thousands who do not have the stomach for that kind of debt, or the self-confidence of lions and superstars. And it biases the choices of those who make it through. If you are an idealistic, relationship-focused, community-oriented medical student, and you have $300,000 of debt and you are 27 or 28 and you haven't bought a car or a house yet, and you can choose between making $100,000 as a primary-care doctor, and $400,000–500,000 as a radiologist, an ophthalmologist, or a dermatologist, what do the economists say you choose? Any wonder why we have lots of dermatologists and radiologists, and few new primary-care physicians.

Location

Desiree has one other roadblock, though that roadblock is worse because of the state in which she lives. Still, the roadblock of location affects many people like Desiree, people with young families. Rhode Island has no publicly funded medical school; Brown University School of Medicine, just six miles from Desiree's home, accepts mostly students right out of high school for an eight-year combined undergraduate liberal arts and then medical education. It aims to attract students with the best national credentials, and attracts many students from around the country. But it accepts few students from Rhode Island, and fewer students like Desiree, whose focus was never academics. If Desiree was able to get through organic chemistry, and if she was somehow able to afford medical school, she still would not be able to go, because she would have to leave the state, and her support system, to do so. Imagine Desiree moving her spouse and three young children 500 miles away, without the network of aunts, uncles, and cousins who she takes care of, and who takes care of her?

Now even if the unimaginable were able to happen, and Desiree, mustering superhuman strength, won the lottery (winning a $1 million lottery pays out about $35,000 a year for 20 years, so that's what it would take to make this happen) and was able to get through organic chemistry, afford medical school, move and somehow survive four premedical years, four years of medical school, and at least three years of residency, what do you think the chances are that she would come home and practice primary care in her own community? Incredibly small. Most physicians stay close to where they go to medical school and are trained, and all the financial and cultural incentives after medical training push people away from primary care, and into specialty training. Even if Desiree lived in another state, one with a publicly funded, primary-care oriented medical school, the chances are she would have to move to go to medical school, and that move would probably break her sense of connection to her family, community and the place she calls home.

No continuity between community and medical training

Can some individuals transcend all the barriers, break through all the roadblocks, and return to their own communities to practice primary care, to build relationship and community? It is *possible*, and rare individuals can do it. But the entropy in the system is very strongly opposed to this pattern, and the medical training system functions as if by design to break the continuity between community and medical training. Rare individuals can do it. But not enough young people can ever survive a distorting, alienating training system to build a healthcare system that is community and relationship-based, as well as personal, rational and just.

A COMPLEX NETWORK OF CROSS-REFERENTIAL SYSTEMS

Consider another person. Richard Stein M.D., 52, grew up in Highland Park, Illinois, the son of two real estate brokers. He went to the University of Chicago Laboratory School, the University of Wisconsin at Ann Arbor as an undergraduate, and Dartmouth Medical School. After a year in a radiology residency, he switched to anesthesia, and took subspecialty training in pediatric anesthesiology. He is the best pediatric anesthesiologist in New England, an elegant and precise practitioner, and a great teacher. Though not terribly interested in research, he publishes one or two papers a year in respected subspecialty journals. He works six to seven hours a day (starting at 6 am), is on call for emergencies one night in six and one weekend in six, takes six weeks of vacation a year. He married at 28, and his wife, who is a respected pediatrician, works four half days a week. They have one child, born when Richard was at the end of his training, when he was 32. Richard earns about $325,000 a year. His daughter has just finished her third year of college. His wife is retiring, and Richard plans to retire in three years, at 55, for a life of golf and travel.

The fix is in. You get to go to medical school if you are 20 and middle class, and can or will put off family until you are 30, and have an incredible tolerance for boredom. The system trains and rewards specialists. Even if we could get to a social consensus about fixing the healthcare system, we would still have to contend with our medical education and health workforce, which is tilted hard in another direction. The medical education and health workforce is tilted so hard it is difficult to know who is leading whom, or what is leading what. Is the medical education and health workforce just feeding bodies into a distorted medical-services supply sector of the economy? Or does the medical-services sector of the economy look the way it does because of the shape and hegemony of the medical education system, and its resulting specialty-dominated health workforce?

This medical-education and health-workforce system is unlikely to change, because it is built on a complex network of cross-referential systems, one built on the next, each with a powerful constituency that believes itself to be defending the public's health (though none have any mandate to do this from anyone other than themselves). Consider one tiny historical mistake: family physicians, general internists, pediatricians, public health physicians and emergency-room physicians do very similar work, and address a very similar knowledge base. It would make sense to train all primary-care physicians together, and allow individuals the ability to tailor their practices to their own personal styles and to their communities' needs. But each "specialty" (which none of them is; they are all generalists) has its own certifying board, which is in turn certified by a self-appointed superboard, the American Board of Medical Specialties; its own residency programs, which each must be certified by a self-appointed superboard, the Accreditation Council on Graduate Medical Education; its own specialty organization, which must be a member of the American Medical Association, their super-organization; in order to be a doctor you must train at a medical school, which has to be certified by the American Association of Medical Colleges (and gives a test for premedical students, the Medical College Admission Test, which helps decide who gets into medical school); to take a licensing examination called The United States Medical Licensing Examination (USMLE™), sponsored by the Federation of State Medical Boards (FSMB) of the United States, Inc.; and to apply for, pay for and be licensed by the Medical Board of individual states, and maintain that licensure. In addition physicians must, in general, maintain admitting privileges at a hospital, which has to be certified by the Joint Commission on Accreditation of Healthcare Organizations, which is a collaboration between the AMA, the American Hospital Association, the American Dental Association, and the American Society of Internal Medicine-Society of Internal Medicine, the American College of Surgeons (the last two are, not surprisingly, medical specialty organizations which are, remember, members of the AMA and have associated certifying boards and residency training boards, themselves certified by the American Board of Medical Specialties and the Accreditation Council on Graduate Medical Education, respectively), as well as have contracts with a number of health insurance plans and HMOs, which themselves must be belong to the America's Health Insurance Plans and be certified by the National Council on Quality Assurance, each of which must independently verify each physician's credentials, often on a yearly basis. To admit to a hospital or have contracts with health insurance plans or HMOs physicians must graduate medical school and take a licensing exam, get a state license, do a residency and take specialty exams, maintain their license and board certification by continuing to study, provide documentation of that study and, often, to sit recertification exams every six to 10 years.

Are you short of breath yet?

Now making sure physicians are adequately prepared, are telling the truth about their certification and training, and continue to read, study and learn is a good thing. But it is worth noting that there are many interlocked boards and councils. Each has its own tax-exempt status as a private non-profit, its own budget and funding source, and its own employees and board members, few of whom have ever been elected by anyone, and few of whom have a real public mandate, other than that carved out by themselves as a niche in what sometimes appears to be an impenetrable system of interconnected niches, boards, relationships, and examinations, products, trademarks, certifications, recertifications and credentials. (It is also worth noting that the cost of maintaining this system, spread out over all these non-profits which each pays their employees well and has a business plan, runs to several thousand dollars per physician per year, costs which are passed on to, and shouldered by the public at the end of the day. One wonders if we would do it better, or worse, if we let government, which is democratically elected, and does have a public mandate and a social contract, run the whole training, certification, and validation system. It is tempting to think we could shave a few acronyms, and run a more transparent system more responsive to public need and public policy, but there is no evidence that supports such a choice.)

And it is worth reflecting on the biases that such an interlocked system produces, and on how those biases influence the character and direction of the medical services sector of the economy today. The whole process of testing and certification puts enormous power in the hands of the testers and certifiers, who influence what is taught by the questions they ask; and whose questions are inevitably influenced simply by what we can and do measure. The process is also influenced by the form of the testing itself. How can we assess relationship skills? How can we access personal integrity, or community organization? Once, these qualities were assumed, as critical in every citizen of a functioning democracy. But in the postmodern, post-9/11 world of consumer capitalism, can integrity, relationship ability, and community focus be assumed in anyone?

The problems and biases inherent in the medical education world of 2007 aside, think of the difficulty of moving, or changing, this whole interconnected system.

ANOTHER PATH

All other things being equal, U.S. health services training fails in four inter-related areas: diversity, career laddering, affordability, and community focus. These failures build on one another to create a workforce that is elitist, self-involved, self-referential and self-serving, and that workforce effectively undermines any community focus that the healthcare system might have left.

There is another way to approach health-workforce training, which I will describe in a moment. But here's a disclaimer before I start. The time you spend reading this chapter from here on in is likely to be wasted time, because the medical education system as we know it is not likely to change. Each of the cross-referential systems within it has a powerful constituency, and each is very likely to defend itself and the dysfunctional system we have built along with it.

The workforce we need

Let's turn medical education on its head, and consider the health workforce we need. We need a workforce that is community oriented, that is diverse as America's communities are diverse, that is able to build and maintain relationships with individuals but is also able to work as part of a team of people who are asked to deliver a complicated range of services in a complicated world. We need a workforce that is altruistic and socially conscious but attends to the need to conserve a scarce resource, one that can match resource to need, one that addresses the needs of populations of people as it attends to the needs of individuals, and one with skills and abilities across a range of narrow and exacting technologies.

Say there was no medical education system. Let's think out what features might get us the workforce we need.
▶ broadly trained;
▶ selected by exhibited relationship abilities;
▶ no financial constraints to selection – just the best people;
▶ cares for people as we train them – so we get whole people on the other end;
▶ selects for the best and brightest;
▶ teamwork abilities.

Note that the present education training system can argue only that it selects for the best and brightest, but that is an assertion I would argue with. Would a bright person sign up for a course of study that requires you to work 16 to 18-hour days for seven to 10 years in a profession that, if you practice it with integrity, keeps you from ever seeing your family, taking vacations, or traveling? Would a bright person consider working in a job with endless overwhelming responsibility, with working conditions dictated by a host of faceless bureaucrats who make money figuring out ways to make your job difficult? By this logic, the best and brightest go to business school or law school, become consultants or money managers, or should they become doctors, become radiologists or dermatologists.

This, sadly, is what the best and brightest usually do.

The medical education system we need

Let's see if we can think out a training system that selects for the attributes and abilities we just delineated.

A just medical education system would have no barriers to entry. Imagine this: if you wanted to become a doctor, you enter the system as a hospital or nursing home housekeeper, dietary, orderly or transport worker, or as a filing clerk or receptionist in a medical office. If, after six months or a year, you prove that you are responsible and capable, you move to working as an assistant to a radiology technician, a group home worker, to a physical therapist, to a laboratory technologist, to a food inspector in a department of public health, to a vital statistics clerk or morgue attendant at the medical examiner's office in the same department, or to an operating room technician – or working as a milieu therapist in an Alzheimer's unit or a mental hospital. If you show aptitude and ability, you are allowed progressively more responsibility. As you are allowed more responsibility you are allowed to take instruction in mathematics and science: calculus, computer science, cell biology, chemistry, anatomy, sociology, epidemiology, psychology, physics, and physiology. The science studied would be relevant to the area in which you are working: physics if you are working as a radiology or radiation oncology technician, chemistry and cell biology if you are working as a laboratory technician's assistant, anatomy if you are working as a physical therapy assistant, or physiology if you are working as an operating room or intensive care unit technician. After perhaps 18 months in one area and after showing proficiency in a prescribed course of study, you move to another area, developing experience, knowledge, and ability as you move from one area of study to another. But you would be providing service as well, developing relationships, learning teamwork skills, earning an income, and walking the walk and talking the talk of every part of the medical services marketplace.

After six or seven years of experience, education and testing, you then might be ready to start functioning as a doctor in training instead of a technologist in training and practice. As a doctor in training, you would work, as third- and fourth-year medical students, interns and residents do now, in specific parts of the medical services delivery system, in hospitals, essentially apprenticed to more senior physicians, helping them care for the ill, or in offices, providing access for people who need it in an unscheduled way, but with slowly increasing levels of complex decision making, benefiting from the experience, relationships, and intellectual skills of more experienced physicians. Like the technologists in training, you would be paid a living wage during this period, perhaps at salary levels more commensurate with your training, experience, responsibility, and knowledge. Like technologists in training, your progressive experience and responsibility would be accompanied by both classroom instruction, much like that which now happens at hospitals or in good primary-care practices, and analysis or your own work and performance. After three years of in-hospital and three years of primary-care training, you would be allowed to practice primary care; first, for two years in an underserved area of the country or world, and then, for three years back in your own community, or in a new community, if you choose to remain serving the underserved, or in a new place, if you choose to go there.

After five years of primary-care practice, you would be allowed to take specialty training, if that is the path you choose, or, to remain in practice in your own community, maturing with that community, and seeing your children grow up where you live and work with the people in a place who grow stronger because you are there. If you choose to become expert in a more focused area of knowledge, you would bring to that expertise a wealth of experience in the breadth and depth of the healthcare system, as well as great relationship and teamwork skills, developed in years of practice.

The disadvantage of such a training system is time. To train people in this way doubles both the time required before people are ready to practice as physicians at all, and doubles the already lengthy period required before people are ready to practice as specialists. (The flipside conclusion one draws from thinking out our current system is that its major – and perhaps only – advantage is that it trains people for specialty medicine quickly, and screens out those who might want to change things as they are.) Instead of four years of medical school and three to six years of specialty training, we are talking about seven years of preparatory training, three years of inpatient training, three years of primary-care training, five years of primary-care practice, and then two to six years of specialty training. That's 18 to 20 years to make a neurosurgeon, instead of the 10 to 11 years we now require.

But think of the advantages, which, in a country whose primary values are democracy and justice, are overwhelming. Anyone can start, and anyone can progress. Everyone earns an income as they move through the system, so there is no financial barrier to entry. You can stop and rest at any point along the way, and still have both the training and skills to earn a living. A system like this allows people to remain in their own community while they both learn and earn. By spreading out the training, we can eliminate the 18 to 36-hour days common to medical trainees, and end up with people whose training did not leave them angry and exhausted. Such a system breeds team players – people who have walked the walk and talked the talk of everyone they work with, and whose work they direct. And it gives us many people in the system to pay attention to the quality of their own performance and experience, since they are on a career ladder, and they have to be invested in the performance of the whole system, which will support their growth and future.

We need Desiree to go to medical school if we are to have a healthcare system that meets people where they are, that is going to be effective in reducing the burden of disease in all America's communities, that allows people to function in relationship, and that builds the communities we need to maintain health as it builds health itself.

We need 100,000 Desirees, and we need 15,000 population-based health centers for the Dr. Desirees of the future to work in. Train the doctors, and build the health centers, rebuild our communities, and rebuild our lives and then we will have a healthcare system for the United States, and a better, stronger, and healthier United States, which might then just be the dream we all dream together, and the ticket to a better, stronger, safer, saner, and more just world.

references

Foreword

1 Krugman, Paul. "The Waiting Game", *New York Times*, July 16, 2007.
2 International Covenant on Economic, Social and Cultural Rights, G.A. res. 2200A (XXI), 21 U.N.GAOR Supp. (No. 16) at 49, U.N. Doc. A/6316 (1966), 993 U.N.T.S. 3, *entered into force* January 3, 1976.
3 Alexis de Tocqueville. *Tocqueville: Democracy in America*, Library of America, 2004.
4 Murray, C.J.L., Kulkarni, S.C., Michaud, C., Tomijima, N., Bulzacchelli, M.T., et al. "Eight Americas: Investigating Mortality Disparities across Races, Counties, and Race-Counties in the United States." PLoS Med 3(9): e260 doi:10.1371/journal. pmed.0030260, September 12, 2006.
5 http://www.pasasa.org/pasasa/research/ottawa%20charter.pdf accessed July 6, 2007.
6 http://www.unhchr.ch/udhr/lang/eng.htm accessed July 6, 2007.

Introduction

1 L. A. Green, G. E. Fryer, S. M. Dovey, R. L. Phillips, "The contemporary ecology of U.S. medical care confirms the importance of primary care," *Am Fam Physician* 64 (2001): 928.

Chapter 1

1 *CIA World Factbook* (March 2005); UNICEF, *Official Summary: The State of the World's Children 2002* (New York: Oxford University Press 2002); OECD, World Bank, *World Development Indicators 2002* (CD-ROM, Washington, DC 2002).
2 R. C. Kessler, K. A. McGonagle, S. Zhao, et al., "Lifetime and 12-month prevalence of DSM-III-R psychiatric disorders in the United States: Results from the National Comorbidity Survey," *Archives of General Psychiatry* 51 (1994): 8–19.
3 http://www.surgeongeneral.gov/library/mentalhealth/chapter2/sec2_1.html
4 http://www.drugabusestatistics.samhsa.gov/nhsda/2k3nsduh/2k3Results. htm#1.1.

5 OECD, *OECD Health Data 2004* (2004).
6 http://www.ama-assn.org/sci-pubs/amnews/pick_00/gvsa0828.htm
7 Institute of Medicine, *Unequal Treatment: Confronting Racial and Ethnic Disparities in Health Care* (2003): 35.
8 Dennis P. Andrulis and Betsy Carrier, *Managed Care in the Inner City* (1999): 12.
9 Institute of Medicine, *Unequal Treatment*: 35.
10 Ibid., 83.
11 Ibid., 8.
12 Physicians for Human Rights, *The Right to Equal Treatment: An Action Plan to End Racial and Ethnic Disparities in Clinical Diagnosis and Treatment in the United States, 2003.* http://www.phrusa.org/research/domestic/race/race_report/other.html. June 27, 2005.
13 Gerald, F. Anderson, *Multinational Comparisons of Health Care: Expenditures, Coverage and Outcomes* (The Commonwealth Fund, October 1998).

Chapter 2

1 Population Reference Bureau, "How many people have ever lived on earth?," (November 1995), available at: http://www.prb.org/Template.cfm?Section=PRB &template=/Content/ContentGroups/ PTarticle/Oct-Dec02/How_Many_People_ Have_Ever_Lived_on_Earth_.htm
2 J. Gross, "In effort to pare Medicare rolls, long-term care is the focus," *New York Times* (June 27, 2005): 1.
3 D. R. Hoover, S. Crystal, R. Kumar, et al., "Medical expenditures during the last year of life: findings from the 1992–1996. Medicare current beneficiary survey," *Health Serv Res* 37(6) (2002):1625–42.
4 The Center for Medicare & Medicaid Services.
5 Since we believe that the terms *health care* and *healthcare* have slipped their moorings from the true meaning of health, we will use these terms advisedly. In general, when referring to the collective enterprise of medicine and bioscience we will use the terms *medical services* or *medical services industry*. We think that these terms much more accurately describe the nature of these activities and that perpetuating the misuse of *healthcare* supports a significant category error.

Chapter 3

1 Ichiro Kawachi, "Long live community," *The American Prospect*, available at http://www.prospect.org/print/V8/35/kawachi-i.html
2 Note that these *findings* are typical of a primary-care diagnostic workup. Primary-care physicians deal for the most part with conscious people. The nature of their responsibility entails understanding the biological and social status of the patient as a whole person. Subspecialists, whose area of interest is not the person but an organ system or element of the person, normally limit findings to a narrower range.
3 Daniel Callahan, *What Kind of Life* (1990).
4 Daniel Callahan, *False Hopes* (1998): 82.

Chapter 4

1 http://www.kff.org/rxdrugs/loader.cfm?url=/commonspot/security/getfile.cfm&PageID=13796
2 Robert D. Putnam, *Bowling Alone* (2000): 327–335.
3 J. M. Keynes, *The General Theory of Employment, Interest, and Money* (1936).
4 There is no good, concrete measure of the multiplier effect that compares actual business and actual industries in given communities and nations. Though the concept is potent, the lack of a well-standardized measure opens the idea of a multiplier effect to use by anyone who has an economic argument to make. As such, it is frequently misused by every business or industry trying to appeal to government for tax breaks and incentives.

Chapter 5

1 M. Fine, "Sacred space or marketplace. The Kern case and the meaning of medicine as a profession," *Med Health RI* 86 (2003): 40–44.
2 Public health physicians do advocate for the health of the public as a whole. Here we use the term physician to mean the professionals who care for individuals. Public health physicians are trained as physicians, to be sure, but practice their profession as expert advisors to government, and less as professionals employed by individuals, obligated to provide self-interested advocacy.
3 Leiyu Shi and Douglas Singh, *Delivering Health Care in America, A System Approach* (2001).
4 L. Shi, B. Starfield, B. Kennedy et al., "Income inequality, primary care, and health indicators," *Journal of Family Practice* 48(4) (April 1999): 275–284.
5 Leiyu Shi, personal communication.
6 M. McGinnis, P. Williams-Russo, J. R. Knickman, "The case for more active policy attention to health promotion," *Health Affairs* 21(2) (March–April 2002): 78–92.

Chapter 6

1 P. C. Gøtzsche and M. Nielsen, "Screening for breast cancer with mammography," *The Cochrane Database of Systematic Reviews* 4 (2006).

Chapter 7

1 James Burke and Robert Ornstein, *The Axemaker's Gift* (1995): 38.
2 Burke and Ornstein, 258.
3 J. B. Bury, *The Idea of Progress* (1932).
4 Burke and Ornstein, 258.
5 It is estimated that the world population reached six billion at the end of the 20th century, a remarkable expansion. While historical records are inexact, it is believed that at the beginning of the 20th century, the world population was approximately 1.6 billion, which means that global population nearly quadrupled in just 100 years. Most of this expansion in population occurred in the 50 years following World War II. (Source: http://www.enviroliteracy.org/subcategory.php/30.html)
6 Burke and Ornstein, xvi.
7 Ibid., 37.
8 Ibid.

9 William Julius Wilson, *The Truly Disadvantaged* (1987): 58.

10 C. B. Macpherson, *The Political Theory of Possessive Individualism* (1962): 275.

11 Philip Cushman, *Constructing the Self, Constructing America* (1995).

12 Cushman, 38.

13 H. Dobyns, *Native American Historical Demography* (1976).

14 In 1776, one-fifth of the inhabitants of the American colonies lived in bondage. Most of the growth of slavery had taken place since 1680. In 1680, Africans accounted for just five percent of the population in Maryland and Virginia. But in 1760, enslaved Africans comprised nearly 40 percent of Virginia's population. By 1776, the number of slaves in the colonies had reached 500,000. Slavery in 18th-century America was not confined to the South. Slaves could be found in each of the 13 colonies, and were especially numerous in New Jersey and in New York's Hudson River Valley. http://www.gliah.uh.edu/database/article_display.cfm?HHID=265

15 http://factfinder.census.gov/servlet/GCTTable?_bm=y&-geo_id=01000US&-_box_head_nbr=GCT-P1&-ds_name=DEC_2000_SF1_U&-_lang=en&-format=US-1&-_sse=on

16 Robert D. Putnam, *Bowling Alone* (2000): 206–207.

17 http://factfinder.census.gov/servlet/GCTTable?_bm=y&-geo_id=01000US&-_box_head_nbr=GCT-P13&-ds_name=DEC_2000_SF3_U&-_lang=en&-redoLog=false&-format=US-9&-mt_name=DEC_2000_SF1_U_GCTP1_US1&-_sse=on

18 M. Fine, "Governor Lucius F.C. Garvin, MD – Rhode Island's Champion Dreamer," *Medicine and Health RI* 84(3) (2001): 83–86.

19 Wilson, *The Truly Disadvantaged*.

20 Kevin Fitzpatrick and Mark LaGory, *Unhealthy Places* (2000).

21 Dennis Andrulis and Betsy Carrier, *Managed Care in the Inner City* (1999).

Chapter 8

1 Jared Diamond, *Guns, Germs, and Steel* (1997): 205.

2 Abraham Flexner, "Medical Education in the United States and Canada. A report to the Carnegie Foundation For The Advancement of Teaching", Carnegie Foundation Bulletin Number Four (1910).

3 Rosemary Stevens, *American Medicine and the Public Interest* (1971).

4 Paul Starr, *The Social Transformation of American Medicine* (1982): 340–347.

5 http://www.nih.gov/od/museum/exhibits/history/index.html

6 In at least one case, the process was reversed: vitamin D, a treatment for rickets, and warfarin, an anticoagulant discovered at the University of Wisconsin, were both licensed to private companies for economic exploitation, with the profits plowed back into research at the University of Wisconsin by the licensing foundation, the Wisconsin Alumni Research Foundation, after which warfarin was named.

7 A. S. Relman, "The new medical-industrial complex," *N Engl J Med* 303 (1980): 963–970.

8 Starr, *The Social Transformation of American Medicine*, 194–195.

9 http://www.healthypeople.gov/About/goals.htm

Chapter 9

1 http://kclibrary. nhmccd.edu/decade10.html
2 Abraham Flexner, "Medical Education in the United States and Canada. A report to the Carnegie Foundation For The Advancement of Teaching", Carnegie Foundation Bulletin Number Four (1910).
3 Paul Starr, *The Social Transformation of American Medicine* (1982): 118.
4 Rosemary Stevens, *American Medicine and The Public Interest* (1971).
5 The term doctor, which means "teacher" and implies a professorial role and appointment would clearly be inappropriate as a title for most turn-of-the-century practitioners. Its *gravitas* and built-in respectability, however, made it the tag preferred by the emerging profession and the one that has come to be most commonly used. No such honorific applies to members of the legal profession, aside from judges, while "Reverend," "Father" and other respectful titles designate some members of the clergy – the third profession. "Professor" or "doctor" are also often used as respectful titles for university instructors.
6 David Rothman, *Strangers at the Bedside* (1991): 118.
7 The vision persists even today, although as medicine becomes more transparently a matter of business, many more skeptics have emerged to peek behind the wizard's curtain.
8 Consider the culture message of *that* construction: The inability of America's small-town frontier be to kind and caring, committed to the common good or self-sustaining – a subtle, distressing observation for the late 1980s and early nineties, one which revealed a very deep anxiety about the future of small-town American life.
9 Leon Speroff, *Clinical Gynecologic Endocrinology and Infertility* (1999).
10 The Hormone Foundation, *The Evolution of Estrogen*, http://www.hormone.org/publications/estrogen_timeline/et7.html. (February 13, 2003).
11 Susan M. Love *Dr. Susan Love's Menopause and Hormone Book* (2003): 30–32.

Chapter 10

1 Robert D. Putnam, *Bowling Alone* (2000): 326.
2 Haggerty, RJ. Community Pediatrics. *N Engl J Med* 1968: 278; pp. 15–21
3 Committee on Community Health Services. The pediatrician's role in community pediatrics. *Pediatrics* Vol. 115 No. 4 April 2005, pp. 1092–1094
4 Cull WL, Yudkowsky BK, Shipman SA, and. Pan RJ. Pediatric Training and Job Market Trends: Results from the American Academy of Pediatrics Third-Year Resident Survey, 1997–2002. *Pediatrics* Vol. 112 No. 4 October 2003, pp. 787–792.
5 Garibaldi RA, Popkave C, and Bylsma,W. Career plans for trainees in internal medicine residency programs. *Acad Med.* 2005 May;80(5):507–12.
6 Life as a property right is an inherently absurd notion, because property rights cannot be defended until they are infringed on, and once life is infringed on, its "owner" is erased and cannot defend it. The idea comes from, and is buried deeply inside, our jurisprudence, which is built entirely on property rights, and represents a simple category mistake, in that our understanding of the genesis and meaning of life is in the spiritual or religious domain, and not an issue to be decided by the courts! It is interesting to see how powerful the notion that life

as property has become, coming out of judicial market fundamentalism, and spreading to characterize our culture. How different the outcome might have been if we had a jurisprudence of the common good, instead of a jurisprudence of property rights! See Michael Tigar and Madeleine Levy, *Law and the Rise of Capitalism* (1977): 327.

7 Crawford Brough MacPherson, *The Political Theory of Possessive Individualism* (1962).

8 Philip Cushman, *Constructing the Self, Constructing America* (1995).

Chapter 11

1 Paul Starr, *The Social Transformation of American Medicine* (1982).

Chapter 12

1 *Pocket Economist*: http://www.economist.com/research/

2 http://hspm.sph.sc.edu/Courses/Econ/Classes/nhe00/

3 IntraLase.com

4 http://www.hrsonline.org/swPressFiles/press97931961.asp

5 It is also worth noting that people whose lives might be saved are usually older, male and white. That's because the find of heart disease occurs most commonly in people over 60, and because any expensive invasive cardiac procedure is performed more commonly in white people than people of color, even when matched for clinical condition and insurance status. See *The Right to Equal Treatment*, Physicians for Human Rights (2003): http://www.phrusa.org/research/domestic/race/race_report/other.html; *Unequal Treatment*, Institute of Medicine, Board on Health Sciences Policy, National Academies Press, 2003; and P. W. Groeneveld, P. A. Heidenrich and A. M. Garber, "Trends in implantable cardioverter-defibrillator racial disparity: the importance of geography," *J Amer Coll Cardiol* 45 (2005): 72–78.

6 A. J. Moss, W. Zareba, W. Jackson Hall et al., for the Multicenter Automatic Defibrillator Implantation Trial II Investigators, "Prophylactic implantation of a defibrillator in patients with myocardial infarction and reduced ejection fraction," *N Engl J Med.* 346 (2002): 877–883.

7 http://www.phrma.org/publications/policy/2003-11-07.865.pdf

8 Many cardiologists, many primary-care physicians, and most of the pharmaceutical industry will argue that spending on statins now will save more money on hospital and treatment costs for people who might have benefited from statins and who develop heart disease in 5, 10 or 20 years. It's a specious argument, one that is impossible to make with precision. First, it is not possible to know what technologies we will be using to care for people with heart disease, or what those technologies will cost, in 5, 10 or 20 years. Second, there has never been a double-blind clinical trial that compares medical-services costs in people receiving statins with those not receiving statins, even in current dollars and with current technologies. Because statins do not appear to produce a benefit in total mortality (but only in heart disease related mortality) and because we do not know what other things people who take statins die of and what the medical services they consume cost, it is not possible to claim a cost benefit, either to individuals or to society. Finally, because we *never* consider the cost offset, the meaning of

the money we spend on statins that we therefore do not spend on other social programs, we have no way to evaluate the true cost and benefit of statins to our culture, and to the culture's health.

9 Richard Godfrey, Executive Director, Rhode Island Housing and Mortgage Corporation, personal communication.

10 http://www.nationalhomeless.org/numbers.html

11 If we wanted to make this argument from the perspective of longevity alone, spending on housing should probably take precedence over spending on statins and many other things. Homelessness carries a mortality rate of two to three times the average American mortality, and there are about 3.5 million Americans who are homeless at any one time in the course of a year. We could probably have an equal to or greater impact on longevity by housing all American than we can by lowering the cholesterol of everyone with elevated cholesterol, although, as in the case of statins, no one has ever done a study showing that housing homeless people lowers their total mortality. Of course, homeless people usually do not vote, and heart disease kills many people who are white and male, which may help explain why we devote resources to statins, however questionable the benefit.

12 http://www.collegeboard.com/highered/res/hel/hel.html#grads

13 Berry Wendell, *Sex, Economy, Freedom & Community* (1994): 119–120.

14 It is clear that societal messaging is very powerful by itself. Medicare does not, as of this writing, pay for pharmaceuticals. But one often hears stories of elderly people who buy their medicine when they cannot afford food, even though it is very clear that cholesterol-lowering medicine is useless to the malnourished.

Chapter 13

1 Daniel Callahan, *False Hopes* (1998): 22.

2 David Crystal, *The Cambridge Encyclopedia of the English Language* (1996): 22.

3 Many Americans use *gesundheit* as an alternative to "God bless you" in reacting to another's sneeze – perhaps more aptly, in that "God bless you" in this context arose in the Dark Ages from the fear that a portion of the soul was expelled during a sneeze and thus at risk of capture by an ever-vigilant imp or demon.

4 http://www.bartleby.com/61/58/H0105800.html

5 *The Compact Edition of the Oxford English Dictionary* (Oxford: Oxford University Press 1971): 1273.

6 E. J. Jewell and A. Abate (eds), *The New Oxford American Dictionary* (Oxford: Oxford University Press 2001): 784.

7 Preamble to the Constitution of the World Health Organization as adopted by the International Health Conference, New York, 19–22 June, 1946; signed on July 22, 1946 by the representatives of 61 States (Official Records of the World Health Organization, no. 2, p. 100) and entered into force on April 7, 1948.

8 http://www.bartleby.com/61/59/H0105900.html

Chapter 14

1 James Burke and Robert Ornstein, *The Axemaker's Gift* (1995).

Chapter 15

1 Rene Dubos, *Mirage of Health* (1959): 27.

2 Ivan Illich, *Medical Nemesis* (1976): 273.

3 Ibid., 128.

4 Ibid.

5 Daniel Callahan, *What Kind of Life* (1990): 39

6 Daniel Callahan, *Setting Limits* (1987): 211–212.

7 J. McKnight, "Two Tools for Well-being," in M. Minkler (ed), *Community Organizing and Community Building for Health* (1999): 24.

Chapter 16

1 http://www.uic.edu/classes/osci/osci590/14_2%20The%20Roseto%20Effect.htm

2 Stewart Wolf and John G. Bruhn, *The Power of Clan* (1998).

3 These differences began to disappear in the 1970s and 1980s, when the second and third generation Roseteans, the beneficiaries of the fathers' and mothers' hard work and values, began to attend college and became more upwardly mobile economically.

4 Lisa Berkman and Ichiro Kawachi, *Social Epidemiology* (2000): 186.

5 John McKnight, *The Careless Society* (1995): 68–69.

6 I. Kawachi, B. P. Kennedy, K. Lochner and D. Prothrow-Stith, "Social capital, income inequality, and mortality," *Am J Public Health* (1997): 1491–1498.

7 L. Shi, B. Starfield, B. Kennedy and I. Kawachi, "Income inequality, primary care, and health indicators," *J Fam Pract*, 48(4) (April 1999): 275–84.

8 E.L. Idler and Y. Benyamini, "Self-rated health and mortality: a review of twenty-seven community studies," *J Health Social Behav*, 38 (1977): 21–37.

9 I. Kawachi, B. P. Kennedy and R. Glass, "Social capital and self-related health: a contextual analysis," *Am J Public Health*, 89 (1999): 1187–1193.

10 A. Deaton, "Policy implications of the gradient of health and wealth," *Health Affairs* 21(2) (2002): 13–30.

11 There is much argument about the character of the relationship between income and longevity, however. Distilled, it appears that a certain level of economic achievement is need to improve longevity across a society, a level which marks the difference between the developing and developed world: inside societies, there is some evidence that the relationship between income is straightline, and some evidence that it is curved, that increases in wealth do not produce much increase in longevity after a certain point. See Richard G. Wilkinson, *Unhealthy Societies* (1996), Chapters 3, 4 and 5.

12 Wilkinson, *Unhealthy Societies*: 25.

13 There is probably justification, from the perspective of fairness, for asking society to maintain a minimum level of income for all its members, because there appears to be a threshold level of income which is associated with longer life spans, and giving everyone in society an equal chance at what appears to be the natural human life span would appear to be a social good.

14 Many conservatives would argue that, from an ethical perspective, providing any guaranteed income floor to adults rewards shiftlessness and unfairly penalizes the successful. From a macroeconomic perspective, some conservatives may accept the notion that creating a more cost-effective medical system might necessarily entail subsidizing access for the poor – as distasteful as that might be from the standpoint of values. But the argument that providing equal access to the health

services that produce equal happiness and equal life chances is much stronger than the argument that society needs to provide a minimum level of income for all. This is because, from the perspective of fairness, services that promote equal happiness and equal life chances cannot easily be said to promote sloth in some and unfairly penalize the successful, since life and economic function are a necessary condition for economic function and competitiveness.

15 Stephen Knack and Paul J. Zak, "Building Trust: Public Policy, Interpersonal Trust, and Economic Development" (March 2002). http://ssrn.com/abstract=304640

16 Wilkinson, *Unhealthy Societies*.

17 Ichiro Kawachi, "Income Inequality and Health," in Lisa Berkman and Ichiro Kawachi(eds), *Income Inequality and Health* (2000): 76–94.

18 R. J. Waldman, "Income distribution and infant mortality," *Quarterly Journal of Economics* 107 (1992): 1283–1302.

19 Note here the connection, weak but always present, of health and social justice. Social interconnectedness is a necessary condition for health. Social justice is a necessary condition for social interconnectedness, which is where the income inequality, trust, and social capital literature always takes us. Talk about an individual's health often takes us to population health, which often takes us to health inequalities, which often takes us to social justice. Talking about social justice often takes us to inequalities in population health which often takes us to individual stories about people whose health suffered as a result of social injustice. So social justice and health often – and perhaps always – *reflect* on one another. Again, social justice and health are not the same thing by any means, but talking and thinking about one concept often leads us to talking and thinking about the other. We will expand on this relationship in the next chapter.

20 Ichiro Kawachi, "Income Inequality and Health", 76–94.

21 It is worth noting here the difference between social capital and what we mean when we talk about the health of families, the health of communities, the health of populations, and the health of society as a whole. Social capital is a set of *measures* of the extent of social interconnectedness in a place, and also the notion of accumulated value of the social interconnectedness of a place. The health of families, communities, populations, nations, and of society as a whole is always metaphoric, always a broadening of our notion of the health of individuals, because the definition of families, communities, populations, nations, and of society is fluid, with the size, shape, and constitution of family, community, population, nation, and society constantly changing over time, where the designation, or definition, if you will, of a person is fixed. By analogy then, we take the health of a family, community, population, nation, and society to be the ability of the family, community, population, nation, and society to protect and facilitate the relationships that occur between its members over time, and, again, by analogy, we also understand the health of one of these groups to be the condition of the family, community, population, nation, and society vis-à-vis those relationships, at any point in time. The utility of the notion of "ability to function in relationships" in understanding how we use the term analogically is evidence that this definition is closest to what we mean by health.

Chapter 17

1 John Rawls, *A Theory of Justice* (1971): 3.

2 In this way, there is an interesting analogy between the Rawlsian concept of justice and the notion of health we develop here: justice is the functional umbrella for society; health is the functional umbrella for individuals. This analogy is part of the matrix of relationships and reflections that tie justice and health together.

3 John Rawls, *Political Liberalism* (1993): 272. Note here the emphasis on ability of persons to reason is what is paramount, and the similarity between the ability to reason (and thus function in society), and the ability to function in relationship – our definition of health.

4 Norman Daniels, Bruce Kennedy and Ichiro Kawachi, *Is Inequality Bad For Our Health?* (2000): 88.

5 Rawls, *Political Liberalism*, 21, 244–245.

6 Ibid., 184.

7 Norman Daniels, *Just Health Care* (1985): 11.

8 Ibid., 56–57. Note that though Daniels does not explicitly consider the meaning of health, confining himself to the just distribution of healthcare resources, he does refer here to the need to *maintain normal species functioning*, another description which approaches the definition of health we have developed in this book.

9 Daniels does not distinguish clearly between the social need for health as such, the individual desire for longevity as a consumer good, the effectiveness of high-cost technologies, or the social meaning of an individual whose function has declined to the point that he or she cannot ever be expected to have a normal opportunity range, as he looks at the fair distribution of medical services spending. Even so, his analysis supports the analysis offered here: that fairness and justice are critical parts of the healthcare equation, especially in so far as health is a necessary condition for participation in the social contract.

Chapter 18

1 M. Fine, "Sacred space or market place: the Kern Case and the meaning of medicine as a profession," *Med Health RI* 86(2) (2003): 40–44.

2 Managed care tried to rearrange those incentives, and reward doctors and hospitals for protecting society's resources. But that attempt almost created a social counter-revolution, as people fought back against managed care, and vigorously resisted managed care's attempt to balance the desire of individuals for life and choice against the need for society to distribute resources fairly. Because we very quickly moved to a for-profit managed-care environment, people correctly perceived that the restriction of resources for individuals would yield profit for some, a situation filled with conflicts of interest. Clearly, the social contract that requires un-self-interested advocacy of doctors and hospitals is very deeply held, though rarely explicit.

3 http://www.fdncenter.org/pnd/newsmakers/nwsmkr.jhtml?id=15100011

Chapter 20

1 M. Moon, L. Nichols and S. Wall, "Medical Savings Accounts: A Policy Analysis," Urban Institute (1996): http://www.urban.org/template.cfm?Template=/TaggedContent/ViewPublication.cfm&PublicationID=6135&NavMenuID=95; accessed May 3, 2005.

bibliography

Andrulis, Dennis P. and Betsy Carrier. *Managed Care in the Inner City: The Uncertain Promise for Providers, Plans, and Communities.* San Francisco: Jossey-Bass Inc. Publishers, 1999.

Angell, Marcia. *The Truth About The Drug Companies: How They Deceive Us and What to Do About It.* New York: Random House Inc., 2004.

Arras, John D. and Bonnie Steinbock. *Ethical Issues in Modern Medicine, 4th edition.* Mayfield Publishing Co., 1995.

Barrett, William and Henry D. Aiken. *Philosophy in the 20th Century: An Anthology.* Random House, 1962.

Beatley, Timothy and Kristy Manning. *The Ecology of Place: Planning for Environment, Economy, and Community.* Washington, DC: Island Press, 1997.

Berkman, Lisa F. and Ichiro Kawachi. *Social Epidemiology.* New York: Oxford University Press, 2000.

Berkman, Lisa and Ichiro Kawachi eds. *Income Inequality and Health.* Oxford: Oxford University Press, 2000.

Bernstein, Richard J. *The New Constellation: The Ethical-Political Horizons of Modernity/Postmodernity.* Cambridge: MIT Press, 1998.

Berry, Wendell. *Sex, Economy, Freedom & Community.* New York: Pantheon Books, 1995.

Burke, James and Robert Ornstein. *The Axemaker's Gift: Technology's Capture and Control of Our Minds and Culture.* Tarcher/Putnam, 1995.

Bury, J.B. *The Idea of Progress: An Inquiry into Its Origin and Growth.* New York: Macmillan, 1932.

Callahan, Daniel. *False Hopes: Overcoming the Obstacles to a Sustainable, Affordable Medicine.* New Brunswick: Rutgers University Press, 1998.

——— *Setting Limits: Medical Goals in an Aging Society with "A Response to my critics".* Washington, DC: Georgetown University Press, 1995.

——— *What Kind of Life: The Limits of Medical Progress.* Washington, DC: Georgetown University Press, 1990.

Canada, Geoffrey. *Fist Stick Knife Gun.* Boston: Beacon Press, 1987, 1995.

Chesney, Kellow. *The Anti-Society: An Account of the Victorian Underworld.* Gambit, 1970.

Cockerham, William C. *Medical Sociology.* Prentice Hall, 1995.

Cohen, Mark Nathan. *Health & The Rise of Civilization.* Yale University Press, 1989.

Colton, Theodore. *Statistics in Medicine.* Boston: Little, Brown and Company, 1974.

Coney, Sandra. *The Menopause Industry: How the Medical Establishment Exploits Women.* Alameda, CA: Hunter House Inc., 1994.

Conrad, Peter and Joseph W. Schneider. *Deviance and Medicalization.* St. Louis: The C.V. Mosby Company, 1980.

Crystal, David. *The Cambridge Encyclopedia of the English Language.* Cambridge, 1996.

Currer, Caroline and Stacey Meg. *Concepts of Health, Illness and Disease: A Comparative Perspective.* Bergen Publishers Limited, 1986.

Cushman, Philip. *Constructing The Self, Constructing America: A Cultural History of Psychotherapy.* Cambridge, MA: Perseus Publishing, 1995.

Daniels, Norman. *Just Health Care.* New York: Cambridge University Press, 1985.

Daniels, Norman, Bruce Kennedy and Ichiro Kawachi. *Is Inequality Bad For Our Health.* Boston: Beacon Press, 2000.

Daniels, Norman and James E. Sabin. *Setting Limits Fairly: Can We Learn to Share Medical Resources?* New York: Oxford University Press, 2002.

Deaton, A. "Policy implications of the gradient of health and wealth." *Health Affairs* 21(2) (2002):13-30.

Diamond, Jared. *Guns, Germs, and Steel: The Fates of Human Societies.* New York: W.W. Norton & Company, 1997.

Dobyns, H. *Native American Historical Demography.* Bloomington, Indiana: University of Indiana Press, 1976.

Douthwaite, Richard. *The Growth Illusion: How Economic Growth Has Enriched The Few, Impoverished the Many, and Endangered the Planet.* British Columbia, Canada: New Society Publishers, 1999.

Downing, Raymond. *As They See It: The Development of the African Aids Discourse.* London: Adonis & Abbey Publishers Ltd, 2005.

Dubos, Rene, *Mirage of Health: Utopias, Progress and Biological Change.* New Brunswick: Rutgers University Press, 1959, 1996.

——— *The Art of Medicine (Self-healing a Personal History, The Faith That Heals, Creative and Adaptation.* ISHK Taperbacks (audio cassette set), 1985.

Dubos, Rene, Maya Pines and the editors of Time Life Books. *Health and Disease, Revised Edition.* Time Life Books, 1980.

Elinson, Jack. "The End of Medicine and the End of Medical Sociology?" *Journal of Health and Social Behavior,* 26 (December 1985): 268–275.

Fine, M. "Governor Lucius F.C. Garvin, MD – Rhode Island's Champion Dreamer." *Medicine and Health RI* 84(3) (2001): 83-86.

Fine, M. "Sacred space or marketplace: The Kern case and the meaning of medicine as a profession." *Med Health RI* 86(2) (2003): 40–44.

Fitzpatrick, Kevin and Mark LaGory. *Unhealthy Places: The Ecology of Risk in the Urban Landscape.* New York: Routledge, 2000.

Flexner, Abraham. "Medical Education in the United States and Canada. A Report to the Carnegie Foundation For The Advancement of Teaching." New York: Carnegie Foundation Bulletin Number Four, 1910.

Fuchs, Victor R. *Who Shall Live? Health, Economics, and Social Choice.* New York: Basic Books Inc., 1974.

Gordon, Benjamin Lee. *Medieval and Renaissance Medicine.* Philosophical Library, 1959.

——— *The Romance of Medicine: The Story of the Evolution of Medicine from Occult Practices and Primitive Times.* F.A. Davis, 1949.

Gøtzsche. P. C. and M. Nielsen. "Screening for breast cancer with mammography." *The Cochrane Database of Systematic Reviews* 4 (2006).

Govern, Frank. *U.S. Health Policy and Problem Definition: A Policy Process Adrift.* Philadelphia: Xlibris Corp, 2000.

Groeneveld, P. W., P. A. Heidenrich and A. M. Garber, "Trends in implantable cardioverter-defibrillator racial disparity: the importance of geography." *J Amer Coll Cardiol* 45 (2005): 72–78.

Gross, J. "In effort to pare Medicare rolls, long-term care is the focus." *New York Times.* June 27, 2005: 1.

Harvey, David. *The Condition of Postmodernity.* Cambridge, MA: Blackwell, 1990.

Hollister, Robert M., Bernard M. Kramer and Seymore S. Bellin. *Neighborhood Health Centers.* DC. Lexington, MA: Health and Company, 1974.

House, James S., Nicole Lurie and Catherine G. McLaughlin. *The Social Determinants of Health: A Special Supplement to Health Services Research.* 38(6), Part II. Blackwell Publishing, Inc, 2003.

Idler, E.L. and Y. Benyamini. "Self-rated health and mortality: a review of twenty-seven community studies." *J Health Social Behav*, 38 (1977): 21–37.

Illich, Ivan. *Medical Nemesis: The Expropriation of Health.* New York: Pantheon, 1976.

Institute of Medicine. *Unequal Treatment: Confronting Racial and Ethnic Disparities in Health Care.* Washington, DC: National Academies Press, 2003.

Kawachi, Ichiro and Lisa F. Berkman, *Neighborhoods and Health.* New York: Oxford University Press, 2003.

Kawachi, Ichiro and Bruce P. Kennedy. *The Health of Nations: Why Inequality is Harmful to Your Health.* New York: The New Press, 2002.

Kawachi I., B.P. Kennedy and R. Glass. "Social capital and self-related health: a contextual analysis." *Am J Public Health*, 89 (1999): 1187–1193.

Kawachi I., B.P. Kennedy, K. Lochner and D. Prothrow-Stith. "Social capital, income inequality, and mortality." *Am J Public Health* (1997): 1491–1498.

Kearns, Robin A. and Wilbert M. Gesler, eds. *Putting Health into Place: Landscape, Identity, & Well-Being.* Syracuse, New York: Syracuse University Press, 1998.

Keynes, J.M. *The General Theory of Employment, Interest, and Money.* London: MacMillan, 1936.

Kinsella, W.P. *Shoeless Joe.* New York: Ballantine Books, 1982.

Kleinke, J.D. *Oxymorons; The Myth of a U.S. Health Care System.* San Francisco, CA: Jossey-Bass, 2001.

Korten, David C. *The Post-Corporate World: Life After Capitalism.* San Francisco, CA and West Hartford, CT. Berrett-Koehler and Kumarian Press, 1999.

Kotelchuck, David. *Prognosis Negative: Crisis in The Health Care System.* New York: Vintage Books, 1976.

Kretzmann, John P. and John L. McKnight. *Building Communities from the Inside Out: A Path Toward Finding and Mobilizing a Community's Assets.* ACTA Publications, 1993.

Kropotkin, Peter. *Mutual Aid: A Factor of Evolution.* Boston: Porter Sargent Publishers Inc., 1914.

Kukathas, Chandran and Philip Pettit. *Rawls: A Theory of Justice and its Critics.* Stanford California: Stanford University Press, 1990.

Lasch, Christopher. *The Culture of Narcissism: American Life in An Age of Diminishing Expectations.* New York: W.W. Norton & Company, 1979.

Le Fanu M.D., James. *The Rise and Fall of Modern Medicine.* Carroll & Graf Publishers, 1999.

Levitan, Sar A. *The Great Society's Poor Law: A New Approach to Poverty.* Baltimore: The John Hopkins Press, 1969.

Loudon, Irvine, ed. *Western Medicine: An Illustrated History.* Oxford University Press, 1997, 2003.

Love, Susan M. *Menopause & Hormone Book.* New York: Three Rivers Press, 1997.

Ludmerer, Kenneth M. *Time to Heal: American Medical Education from the Turn of the Century to the Era of Managed Care.* Oxford University and Press, 1999.

Lyon, David. *Postmodernity.* University of Minnesota Press, 1994.

Macpherson, Crawford Brough. *The Political Theory of Possessive Individualism: Hobbes to Locke.* Oxford: Oxford University Press, 1962.

Manchester, William. *A World Lit Only By Fire.* Little Brown/Back Bay Books, 1993.

Marmot, Michael and Richard G. Wilkinson. *Social Determinants of Health.* Oxford: Oxford University Press, 1999.

Marshall, P.J. *The Oxford History of the British Empire: The Eighteenth Century.* Oxford University Press, 1998.

Mason, Mark, *Health and the Rise of Civilization.* New Haven: Yale University Press, 1989.

McGinnis, M. P. Williams-Russo and J. R. Knickman. "The case for more active policy attention to health promotion." *Health Affairs* 21(2) (March–April 2002): 78–92.

McKeown, Thomas. *The Role of Medicine: Dream, Mirage, or Nemesis.* Princeton: Princeton University Press, 1979.

McKnight, John. *The Careless Society: Community and its Counterfeits.* New York: Basic Books, 1995.

McLuhan, Marshall. *The Gutenberg Galaxy: The Making of Typographic Man.* University of Toronto Press, 1965.

Minkler, Meredith, ed. *Community Organizing & Community Building for Health.* New Jersey: Rutgers University Press, 1999.

Moe, Richard and Carter Wilkie. *Changing Places: Rebuilding Community in the Age of Sprawl.* New York: Henry Hold and Company, 1997

Morris, David B. *Illness and Culture in The Postmodern Age.* Los Angeles, CA: University of California Press, 1998.

Moss, A. J., W. Zareba, W. Jackson Hall et al., for the Multicenter Automatic Defibrillator Implantation Trial II Investigators. "Prophylactic implantation of a defibrillator in patients with myocardial infarction and reduced ejection fraction." *N Engl J Med.* 346 (2002): 877–883.

National Civic League. *The Civic Index, Measuring Your Community's Civic Health.* National Civic League, 1999.

O'Brien, Lawrence J. *Bad Medicine: How The American Medical Establishment is Running Our Healthcare System.* Amherst, NY: Prometheus Books, 1999.

Orme, Nicholas. *Medieval Children.* New Haven: Yale University Press, 2001.

Pledge, H. T., *Science Since 1500: A Short History of Mathematics, Physics, Chemistry, and Biology.* Harper Torchbooks, 1959.

Porter, Roy. *The Greatest Benefit to Mankind: A Medical History of Humanity,* W.W. Norton, 1997.

Porter, Roy, ed. *Cambridge Illustrated History of Medicine.* Cambridge University of Press, 1996.

Putnam, Robert D. *Bowling Alone: The Collapse and Revival of American Community.* New York: Simon & Schuster, 2000.

Rawls, John. *A Theory of Justice.* Cambridge, MA: The Belknap Press, 1971.

――― *Political Liberalism, expanded edition.* New York: Columbia University Press, 1993, 2005.

――― *The Law of Peoples.* Cambridge, MA: Harvard University Press, 1999.

Reader, John. *Africa: A Biography of the Continent.* New York: Alfred A. Knopf, 1998.

Relman, A. S. "The new medical-industrial complex." *N Engl J Med* 303 (1980): 963–970.

Rhyne, Robert, Richard Bogue, Gary Kukulka and Hugh Fulmer. *Community-Oriented Primary Care: Health Care for the 21st Century.* Washington DC: American Public Health Association, 1998.

Rivera, Felix G. and John L. Erlich. *Community in a Diverse Society.* Boston, MA: Allyn and Bacon, 1992.

Robbins, Richard H. *Global Problems and the Culture of Capitalism.* Boston: Allyn and Bacon, 2002.

Rothman, David J. *Strangers at the Bedside: A History of How Law and Bioethics Transformed Medical Decision Making.* United States: Basic Books, 1991.

Schor, Juliet B. *The Overworked American: The Unexpected Decline of Leisure.* New York: Basic Books, 1992.

Shi, Leiyu and Douglas Singh. *Delivering Health Care in America: A System Approach.* Gaithersburg, MD: Aspen Publishers, 2001.

Shi, L., B. Starfield, B. Kennedy et al. "Income inequality, primary care, and health indicators." *Journal of Family Practice* 48(4) (April 1999): 275–284.

Sontag, Susan. *Illness as Metaphor.* Farrar, Straus and Giroux, 1978.

Speroff, Leon. *Clinical Gynecologic Endocrinology and Infertility.* 6th ed. Baltimore, MD: Williams and Wilkins, 1999.

Starfield, Barbara. *Primary Care: Balancing Health Needs, Services and Technology.* New York: Oxford University Press, 1998.

Starr, Paul. *The Social Transformation of American Medicine.* United States: Basic Books, 1982.

Stevens, Rosemary. *American Medicine and the Public Interest: A History of Specialization.* Berkeley: University of California Press, 1971, 1997.

——— *In Sickness and in Wealth: American Hospitals in the Twentieth Century.* United States: Basic Books, 1989.

Stewart Jr, Charles T. *Healthy, Wealthy, or Wise: Issues in American Health Care Policy.* Armonk, NY: M.E. Sharpe, 1995.

Tigar, Michael E. and Madeleine R. Levy. *Law & the Rise of Capitalism.* New York: Monthly Review Press, 1977.

Totman, Richard. *Social Causes of Illness.* New York: Pantheon Books, 1979.

Waldman, R. J. "Income distribution and infant mortality." *Quarterly Journal of Economics* 107 (1992):1283–1302.

Wendell, Berry. *Sex, Economy, Freedom & Community.* New York: Pantheon Books, 1994.

Whorf, Benjamin Lee. *Language, Thought & Reality.* Cambridge, MA: MIT Press. 1956, 1972.

Wilkinson, Richard G. *Unhealthy Societies: The Afflictions of Inequality.* New York: Routledge, 1996.

Wilson, William Julius. *The Truly Disadvantaged: The Inner City, the Underclass, and Public Policy.* Chicago: University of Chicago Press, 1987.

Wolf, Stewart and John G. Bruhn. *The Power of Clan: The Influence of Human Relationships on Heart Disease.* New Brunswick: Transaction Publishers, 1998.

Milton Keynes UK
Ingram Content Group UK Ltd.
UKHW020026071024
449327UK00032B/2950

9 780367 446192